Cammie Up!

Cammie Up!

Memoir of a Recon Marine in Vietnam, 1967–1968

STEVEN A. JOHNSON

Foreword by Ray W. Stubbe

McFarland & Company, Inc., Publishers
Jefferson, North Carolina, and London

LIBRARY OF CONGRESS CATALOGUING-IN-PUBLICATION DATA

Johnson, Steven A., 1946–
    Cammie up! : memoir of a recon Marine in Vietnam, 1967–
1968 / Steven A. Johnson ; foreword by Ray W. Stubbe.
        p.   cm.
    Includes bibliographical references and index.

    ISBN 978-0-7864-6600-9
    softcover : acid free paper ∞

    1. Johnson, Steven A., 1946–   2. Vietnam War, 1961–1975 —
Personal narratives, American.   3. Vietnam War, 1961–1975 —
Reconnaissance operations, American.   4. United States. Marine
Corps. Reconnaissance Battalion, 3rd — History.   I. Title.
DS559.5.J644   2012
959.704'345092 — dc23
[B]   2011041727

BRITISH LIBRARY CATALOGUING DATA ARE AVAILABLE

Front cover: In the air after the ambush, looking out the rear of the
CH-46, from left Rudd, Tuthill, Cooke, Johnson, Sargent, Doc
Rosser (photograph by L/Cpl Standiford); 3rd Reconnaissance
Battalion logo

Manufactured in the United States of America

*McFarland & Company, Inc., Publishers
   Box 611, Jefferson, North Carolina 28640
   www.mcfarlandpub.com*

To all those who did not come home,
to those who did, but never left Vietnam,
and to those who left Vietnam but have died since,
long before their time.
SEMPER FIDELIS

Table of Contents

Foreword
by Ray W. Stubbe

This book places the reader into the life situation of a Marine in a reconnaissance unit in Vietnam. The Vietnam War eludes a single, simple story or image. It is complex, involving widely divergent geography, type of unit and work, and time frame when one was there, not to mention the political, strategic, and ethical dimensions. We can only have individual stories that, like threads in a tapestry, together form an image of the reality of a war so controversial, it will probably be discussed and debated for many decades. In a sense, Mr. Johnson's book reminds one of an orthodox icon, not a picture as such, but a window through which we peer into and are drawn into another reality.

Steve Johnson's story authentically and realistically provides one of the important strands of that tapestry. Plentiful details involving tactics, geography, equipment, and individual personalities, far from distracting, helpfully guide an understanding of what it meant to be a young Marine suddenly living in a strange place, a strange time, and in unexpected, strange events. His descriptions of local plant and animal life, his use of real persons (I personally knew many of those he mentions) with all their quirks and strengths, his recall of dramatic actions and, more important, the emotional reactions of how he felt and what it meant, bring his story into sharp relief. Those who were there will say, "Yes, this is what it was really like!"

His is a story of life in a place of death, of resilience and courage in the face of sheer terror. The reader of this remarkable book, even one who was at the same place at the same time but involved in a different focus, will learn much that is new and will appreciate yet another facet of the total Vietnam experience. In this book we find ourselves preparing for and engaged in Marine reconnaissance patrols. We find ourselves in places like Khe Sanh; we learn the human significance of living with exotic plant and animal life, monsoon rains, and enemy contact.

The well written, first-hand account not only provides a good read for those who were there and those who seek to understand what happened, but contributes a lasting and valuable resource for the future.

Ray W. Stubbe, Lieutenant Commander, U.S. Navy (Ret.), is a coauthor of Valley of Decision, Inside Force Recon, Battalion of Kings, *and numerous other books on Vietnam, and is the founder of Khe Sanh Veterans, Inc. He was a chaplain at Khe Sanh, Vietnam, July 1967–March 1968.*

Preface

In 1998, I took a two-week tour to Vietnam with a group of former and active duty Marines. The former Marines and I had all served at one time or another in the I Corps Tactical Zone that notably includes Da Nang, Phu Bai, Hue, Quang Tri, Dong Ha, Con Thien, and Khe Sanh. I kept a brief journal of that trip and when I got home, I typed it all up and that resulted in about 30 pages worth for the family archives.

I ran off a few copies on my printer and distributed them to family members and friends who I thought might be interested. Several years went by, and every now and then, someone would hint that now I needed to write up a "memoir" of my experience in Vietnam the first time around in 1967–68. Having at least a tiny clue of how difficult that would be, I resisted for a long time. Finally, my friends harassed me into starting to put some thoughts (or memories) on paper. Four years later, my memory banks were empty. I could not remember another name, another funny thing that happened, or another way to say how hot, humid, cold, muddy, fetid, exhausting, terrifying, disgusting or beautiful Vietnam was. I could not remember another death.

I joked at the time that this story of mine would never be seen on a bookstore shelf. I just didn't plan to send it to a publisher because I could not see how anyone who did not know me personally would be at all interested in it. I suppose I ultimately sent it to McFarland so I could say to myself, "There, I did it, now leave it alone." Nevertheless, here we are.

If I have erred on some detail or time frame to any great degree, I ask forgiveness. If three people witness a barn fire, you will get three different descriptions of the same fire. I have written this account to the best of my recollection aided wherever possible by supporting documentation.

I must give tremendous credit to a longtime military friend of mine for harassing me into completing this and for doing a much-appreciated amount of editing. I first met 2nd Lieutenant John K. Vintar, CD, Canadian Army, when I was in the Marine Corps reserve in about 1985. We were heading off to Fort Wainwright, Alaska, in February of that year for our two weeks of annual duty. John was loaned to my unit, India Company, 3/25, USMCR, as an exchange officer from the Royal Regiment of Canada based in Toronto. He was designated as my platoon commander and I was to see that nothing happened to him. The rule was that John was to be ultimately returned to Canada in undamaged condition — at least, physically. We went on to have several adventures and have stayed in contact for many years.

John began his editing chores just before he made major, while stationed in Edmonton, Alberta, as a logistics officer. He has done tours of United Nations duty in Bosnia and Sudan. In the original draft I had several parts that were both literary genius and terribly clever. Of course, that was just my opinion. Armed with a bachelor of arts (English) from St. Francis Xavier and a master of arts (medieval literature) from the University of Wales, John not only pointed out that they didn't fit or weren't needed, but he also made me look into my head and see things from outside my own viewpoint. I tend to be rather linear but John made me think about emotion and feelings (in a manly way, of course). In short, the Major made me shine my brass. Marines would understand. John is currently a Canadian Army exchange officer to the U.S. Army National Guard in Washington, D.C.

Several long ago Recon Marines contributed photos and memory joggers: L/Cpl Wayne Standiford, Cpl. Kevin Macaulay, Lt. Jeff Fisher, Lt. Nels Youngstrom, Lt. Al Pfeltz, Sgt. Bob Mullaney, L/Cpl. Clark Christie and Maj. Chuck Riel, CH-46 pilot. Thanks, Marines.

Reverend Ray Stubbe was my muse and, among others, instrumental in motivating me to finish this project when I felt that it would never end. His basic advice was, "You'll be sorry if you don't." Based on his own extensive research and personal knowledge of Khe Sanh, Ray was my fact checker on early versions of the manuscript.

I would never have been able to get back in contact with many of my former comrades without the tireless help of a recruit platoon-mate of mine, SgtMaj. Jim Butler, USMC (ret), and his band of "Baker Street Irregulars," Cpl. George Reilly, SSgt. Stan Lawson, Sgt. Chris Sloman, and Col. Wayne V. Morris, USMC (ret).

Finally, I would be remiss in not mentioning the occasional help I got from the *Unofficial Unabridged Dictionary for Marines* at OldCorps.org/USMC/dictionary.html. compiled by Glenn B. and Beverly D. Knight, both Marine veterans.

Introduction

"To see the elephant" is a saying from the Gold Rush era that seems to have fallen out of use in these enlightened and cynical days. Those traveling west would bring back for their city slicker friends wild tales of incredible sights, strange and wonderful destinations, and bizarre exotic animals. And, when you had finally gone west and "seen the elephant" for yourself, it meant you too had made that journey and experienced for yourself the wonders of a world or an event so fantastic and incredible that you were just sure the folks at home wouldn't believe you.

To "see the elephant" was also a slang term used by Civil War soldiers meaning to be in a battle or to see the world. The premise was that you could not describe an elephant to anyone who had not also seen one (or been there, done that, etc.).

My original title for this book was "Path of the Elephant." Upon completing the manuscript, however, I felt that *Cammie Up!* was more indicative of the recon mission and the means of accomplishing it. What follows is an account of my tour in Vietnam in 1967 to 1968. I have written much of it from memories of over 40 years ago and I have often wished I had paid more attention then because I probably have a few geographical or command structure points that aren't precise. Friends of mine who are sharper than me have helped me with some of the technical or historical facts that I refer to. The fog of time is sometimes merciful in blurring or erasing disturbing things, but it's also a nuisance when one is trying desperately to remember something or someone that is important.

A lot of accounts from the battlefield contain filthy language. Marines aren't choirboys ... at least, not anymore. However, unless it has a direct bearing on the situation, I have chosen to civilize the dialogue. Nevertheless, there is a word that some people, in this day of the mindless pursuit of political correctness, might find offensive. The word is *gook*.

One legend has it that when the British occupied India, there were allied Indian troops who were barracked at least on the same base, if not the same buildings, as the British troops. The Indians had their own junior officers but they were subordinate and therefore inferior to the British officer class. Mess facilities for the officers were segregated, as it simply wouldn't do to have dark skinned lieutenants rubbing elbows in the mess with Royal Military Academy trained captains. Therefore, the Indian officers had their own mess, which was identified by a sign above the entrance saying Gentlemen of Other Colors, or GOOC. The acronym became associated with any indigenous (non–British) person and eventually was used as a derogatory term for any foreign (non-white) enemy.

It is nothing more than human nature to try to denigrate your opponent in order to make him less powerful. It is done in sports, business, or any competition including war. It's as much a sociological thing as it is military.

To the allies in World War I, the enemy was the Hun, Boche, Heinie, or Fritz. In World War II, they were Krauts or Jerrys, or Japs, Nips, and Slant Eyes. Don't forget the Fascist Italian Eyties and Dagos. Korea brought with it Luke the Gook and Link the Chink. Vietnam narrowed it back down to Gook but you occasionally heard Slope, Fender head, Gooner, or Dink. The hostilities in the Middle East have resulted in Camel Jockey and Towel or Rag Head.

I'm sure our enemies had equally unflattering names for us but I don't know what they might have been. I will use the term gook interchangeably with NVA or VC. Vietnamese civilians were not nearly as often referred to as gooks but the little shops they set up outside our bases were commonly called "gook shops." Well, you couldn't call them Montgomery Ward, could you? Locals were generally called Viets, or in the case of the hill people, 'Yards.[1]

A couple of years ago while shooting the breeze with a group of people, most of whom I knew well, I used the term gook in relating a story. A barely 20-year-old college student sitting there immediately took umbrage with me. I pointed out to her that she was much too young and far too removed from that situation to pass judgment on me or anyone else. I then asked her how she would refer to someone who had just attempted to rape her. Would she call him a gentleman, or would she call him several profane names and wish him a horrible and imminent death? I don't think she liked that analogy but she shut up.

All of the names mentioned herein belong to real people. The use of an obvious pseudonym is meant to shield those individuals from embarrassment even if they don't deserve it.

Anyway, that's how it is. Don't get wrapped around the axle over it.

For a place so focused on death, we were never more alive.

PART ONE

IN WHICH I MAKE PREPARATIONS TO SEE THE ELEPHANT

1. Transition

The patrol was to the northwest of Khe Sanh and we had moved out of the thickest growth into an area where we could at least see the sky from time to time. I was considering taking a break when my Tail End Charlie passed the word up that he thought he could hear noises behind us. That's bad! He said it sounded like somebody was breaking through the bush making no effort to be quiet. We were not on or near a trail so that could only mean that we had apparently been seen at some time and were being followed.

I whispered to the point man to look for a place to take cover, quick. There was a natural lump on the ground just ahead of us so we moved around behind it and tried to be very small. We were down in the undergrowth and spaced out on line facing back the way we had come. We could now plainly hear movement coming our way through the bush about 50 meters away. Then one sound really got my attention. I looked at my radioman and he mouthed the word that I was thinking. "Chopping!"

They were actually beating the bush looking for us! This was damn scary! If they were being that aggressive in looking for us, there must be a bunch of them. Solutions to the situation raced through my head. Fix bayonets? That's crazy! Give the area they were approaching from a full magazine from everybody and then run? No! My training and experience said to freeze and depend on our camouflage and discipline. A quick thought came to mind. Maybe they were from the area of last night's Arclight and had chanced to see us that morning and assumed we had called it in on them. The gooks knew what Recon looked like and they knew what we were out there to do. The other guys were looking at me. I hoped my face didn't look as scared as I felt. I started to whisper to the radioman but my mouth was so dry nothing came out.

After a few seconds, I worked up enough spit to carefully call in a brief SALUTE report so that somebody at least knew we were in a potential jam. I called it in myself because I didn't want to waste any time or make any extra noise having the radioman do it while I was sitting right beside him. The anticipation was palpable. Just as the noises got to where I expected to be able to see someone, they stopped. For probably three minutes, there was silence. Then it started up again but they were now moving to the north, 90 degrees away from us. We all started breathing again! We never did actually see any of the enemy troops that were looking for us.

We stayed there for about fifteen minutes to make sure they were moving on and not trying to encircle us. Rifles were put back on safety and grenade pins were re-bent so they wouldn't fall out. We moved out cautiously to try to see where they had gone but lost track of them in the thick bush. I didn't really feel like bumping into the rear end of a large NVA unit anyway.

It was in early March of 1967 that two things coincided. The first was the last weeks of my two-year tour as a member of the Marine Detachment on the USS *Albany* CG-10, a U.S. Navy heavy cruiser. It had been converted from a gun cruiser to carry three different types of missile as well as two 5-inch gun mounts as its armament. The second was the entry of the *Albany* into the Charlestown (Boston) Navy Yard for what would be about an 18-month overhaul. Because of the length of time the ship would be in the yards, nearly all of the ship's crew, including the Marines, was being either transferred to other duty stations or moving on to transient posts pending discharge because their enlistment was nearly up.

I had enlisted in the Marines a little over two years earlier in my home-town of Jamestown, NY, expecting to go into the infantry or some other area of combat arms because that's what I figured Marines do. After all, hadn't I seen all the John Wayne movies? After high school, my chances of going to college were just about zero. My grades had been good enough to graduate (I was in the top 90 percent of my class) but, for the most part, I was bored silly and found it very hard to concentrate. Being the oldest of seven kids pretty much ruled out the financial end of furthering my education, too. Even though in 1964 it was considered something of an achievement to be a high school grad, it still wasn't likely to garner anything much better than a laborer or a drone doing piecework in a factory. This was also before the fast food joints began popping up like weeds. I think the nearest McDonald's might have been in Buffalo, 75 miles away.

Before I enlisted, I knew that ours was a military family. Grandpa Johnson was in the Army's 346th Infantry Regiment in France in 1918, and dad was a World War II Navy submariner (USS *Bluefish*). Two uncles were also in World War II. One was Navy (USS *Bon Homme Richard*), and the other was an Army Air Corps B-29 pilot. A third uncle was in the mid 1950s Army National Guard. During the Cold War, two brothers would become Marines and another brother and a sister would join the Navy. Now I was going to my war and John Wayne was holding a place in line for me.

The military draft was in full effect and there was no question in my mind that as soon as I turned 18, I would get a letter from Uncle that started with, "Dear ____, greetings from your friends and neighbors on the local draft board." In fact, I did get my draft notice while I was in boot camp. Like an idiot, I showed it to my drill instructor and he thought it was so amusing that he permitted me to demonstrate my expertise in the art of many, many pushups.

Going into the service had always held an attraction to me and since it looked like I was probably going anyway, I wanted to have my own choice in the matter. I had eliminated the Army, Navy, and Air Force for various reasons, mostly because it seemed to me that you were just a tiny part of a faceless mob. The Marines, however, based on the John Wayne movies I had seen, were all high stepping, low crawling, fire breathing, butt kicking, and ruggedly handsome specimens of red-blooded American patriotism. I had never excelled at much of anything. I liked playing baseball but I couldn't even make Little League. I liked playing football too, and I tried out, and made, my junior high and senior high school football teams. I guess they needed tackling dummies because in neither case did I play a single minute of a regular game. It probably had as much to do with my Ichabod Crane physique as much as anything; arms, legs, knees and elbows sticking out in various directions. I decided I had nothing to lose by trying to make the toughest varsity team on the planet ... so, choice made.

At the age of 17, I held up my right paw and (with parental signatures on several forms), recited the oath of enlistment, signed up with Uncle Sam's Misguided Children, and in October of 1964, traveled to beautiful, sunny Parris Island.

To my surprise, as I was nearing graduation from boot camp, my senior drill instructor, Sergeant Arthur Cowan, *strongly suggested* (meaning ordered) that I put in for Sea Duty. I had never heard of Sea Duty and therefore didn't know that it was a very choice duty assignment, indeed. For as much hell he and the other two D.I.'s (drill instructors) had put us through for thirteen weeks you will find that, almost to a man, Marine recruits trust their D.I.'s with their lives. For some of them (but me not included in this case) the drill instructor was the only father figure they had ever had. It's almost a dog-like loyalty. I took Sgt. Cowan's *suggestion* and applied for Sea Duty.

Upon graduation, I received orders to report to Marine Barracks, Portsmouth Virginia Navy Yard, for Sea School. This would follow my infantry training with the Infantry Training Regiment (ITR) at Camp Geiger, North Carolina, and a short period of "boot leave" at home.

Sea Duty is the oldest post of the Corps. It's what Marines were invented for. That is, to operate at sea as naval infantry. Marines were the ship captain's personal guard, and they served as gun crews when engaging enemy ships at a distance. When the ships closed to grappling range, some were sharpshooters high in the rigging and others led the boarding party onto the other ship. Marine Detachments were known as Marine Guards in the late 18th and early 19th centuries and rated one drummer, one fifer, twenty to forty privates, a couple of corporals, a sergeant, one lieutenant, and one captain. By the turn of the 20th century MarDets had long since shed the fifer and drummer but were still made up of from 40 to 70 enlisted of all ranks, one lieutenant and one captain. They were also, if the need arose, the nucleus of the ship's landing party, which was augmented by all sailors not needed to operate the ship.

Sea School was about three weeks long, and was mostly a crash course on duties and responsibilities of the Marine Detachment (mostly security related), and rendering honors to dignitaries while in foreign ports. A lot of time was spent on keeping uniforms in perfect order, spit shining shoes, shining brass, etc. We were issued two tailored sets of dress blues, and we went through several days at the Portsmouth Navy Yard damage control school. There, we practiced fighting shipboard fires of various kinds, and making temporary repairs to stop flooding from hull breaches caused by naval gunfire, torpedo hits, or even icebergs.

Being on a Navy base, there were, of course, lots of squids around. Your common sailor was an everyday sight but we rarely saw Navy chief petty officers. These were the "old salts" of the Navy and just like Marine staff NCOs, they commanded respect. Unfortunately, to us brand new Little Green Amphibious Monsters, the chief's uniform was nearly identical to the Navy officer's uniform. The only major difference was that the chief's hat had a single brass anchor on the front and the officers had brass crossed anchors and other elaborate trimmings on theirs. The old military saying is, "When in doubt, salute!" So we did. Most of them took it good-naturedly but a few were downright offended. "You don't salute me, I work for a living!" or, "Don't salute me, my parents were married!" were common responses and usually delivered at a very high decibel level. Until we got it figured out, a lot of chiefs got a lot of salutes from a lot of confused junior Leathernecks.

However, now that my two years of traveling the high seas and a lot of spit and polish duty was over, it was time to become a "real Marine." We were instructed to let our detachment first sergeant, 1st Sgt Arundale, know where we would prefer to be stationed next. It's called a "wish list" and you could make three choices, none of which were even vaguely liable to be fulfilled, because Marines serve at the discretion of the Corps. I indicated that I wanted to be sent to WestPac. That's military for Western Pacific ... in other words, Vietnam.

Shortly thereafter, our detachment commanding officer, Captain Ed

Congratulations.
Jack L. Wohler

Top: Marine Detachment USS *Albany*, January 1967. The author is 2nd row 5th from right, Huggard is 2nd row 3rd from right, Darcus is 2nd row far right, 1st Sgt Arundale is 1st row center left and Capt. Butchart is 1st row center (U.S. Navy photograph, PH3 Richard Clarke, USS *Albany*). *Bottom:* Johnson is promoted to Corporal of Marines by ship's Captain Wohler (left) onboard the *Albany* (U.S. Navy Photograph PH3 Richard Clarke USS *Albany*).

Butchart, collared me and asked me if I was sure of my choice because, in this case, my wishes were almost guaranteed to be realized. Remember that this was early 1967 and the war in Vietnam was approaching a very hot point. Oddly enough, having been overseas in an easterly direction for the majority of the previous two years, we were very out of touch with world events. In fact, by my recollection, we rarely heard about Vietnam.

I told the captain that I was pretty sure, even though in my mind I didn't really know what I was headed for. Little did I know that Captain Butchart and some other members of the Mardet would also be ordered to Vietnam at about the same time that I was there.

We were in Charlestown for about a month while new assignments were made and orders were cut. Our regular duties included standing guard over very tight access to the ship's missile launching spaces. The missiles had been offloaded at the Yorktown Naval Base a couple of weeks earlier so we had little to do. We wandered around the base or went by train into Boston to an area known as the Combat Zone. It was all bars, pawnshops and movie houses. I and a few buddies usually went to the movies, then to a restaurant for some non–Navy chow and then back to the ship. I think we may have gone on a couple of area tours as well. Cpl. John Huggard was from Hicksville, NY, on Long island. One weekend, he went home and came back with his car. Now we had wheels! I think the carburetor needed a little work because that car idled at 30 miles per hour. Around the base, John rarely used the gas pedal.

Somewhere around the end of March, I threw my sea bag on my shoulder and saluted my way off the *Albany* for the last time. I had two or three weeks of leave coming so I spent that time at home just goofing around and looking up the handful of high school friends that weren't in college or the military. There weren't many left.

My leave ended and I was ready to head west. I was actually kind of anxious to get going anyway. I had five days of travel time allowed to get to Camp Pendleton, California, and the way the Greyhound routes were set up, I had to catch the bus in Mayville, the Chautauqua County seat about 25 miles from Jamestown, at about 11 o'clock at night. Dad drove me to the bus stop and when the bus pulled up, he shook my hand and said, "I was a Navy submariner but I know enough to tell you to keep your powder dry." I guess then it hit me that I was now really on the way to see the elephant because I choked a little. I didn't start blubbering, though, because, first, I was wearing the uniform of a Corporal of Marines, and second, I knew that this was the start of a seriously big adventure.

I don't remember a lot about the three-day bus ride across the country because half of it was at night and the rest was boring. I do remember seeing the brand new arch as we went through St. Louis and a lot of sand crossing

Arizona and New Mexico. We stopped briefly at Albuquerque and I only remember that it was hot and dusty and there were Indians lying around passed out on all the outdoor benches at the Greyhound terminal.

I didn't go directly to Camp Pendleton because I had to change buses in Los Angeles. After about a two-hour drive south, the bus dropped me off at the front gate at Pendleton and I was then transported to wherever it was that new personnel report in. I stood in front of a desk wondering where I would be assigned while a sergeant perused my orders and Service Record Book. The sergeant looked up at me and said, "You're a corporal and you're not married. You're going to Recon."

This was quite a surprise. I flashed back to Camp Geiger where I went through basic infantry training at ITR after boot camp and recalled that there was a Recon unit barracked right across the street from us. Recon Marines are sometimes referred to as "Snake Eaters" or "Super Grunts." These guys were all certifiably insane. They had shaved heads, muscles all over the place, and would frequently be away from the area for days. When they returned, usually in the wee hours, they would jump off their trucks screaming and yelling, tear into the barracks where there would be about an hour of relative calm, and then come screaming back out, with faces freshly painted green and black, to jump back on the trucks and roar away. Even though they were "fellow Marines," we were terrified of them and believed every grisly rumor we heard.

Whenever we saw them in their human form, they all sported parachute and scuba qualification badges. About all we really knew about them was that they were an all-volunteer unit, mainly due to the jump and scuba prerequisites. Oh, and they ate puppies alive.

I really didn't think I wanted Recon; I just wanted to be a Mud Marine. Manfully managing not to burst into tears, I mentioned to the sergeant that I thought Recon was a strictly volunteer unit. He explained to me that there were two Recons. One was called Force Recon (insane, eating puppies, etc.) and the other was called Battalion Recon. The difference, I would learn, was that Force frequently operated farther into enemy territory and sometimes in smaller units than Battalion did. Since they usually operated in more remote or difficult to reach areas, they had to have parachute or underwater insertion capability. However, taking away the requirement for jump and scuba, any physically and mentally (shut up!) qualified Marine could be ordered to Battalion Recon. Otherwise, the missions were nearly identical and in fact, Battalion Recon was often as far away from friendlies as Force.

2. Reconnaissance School

Now that you are confused, I'll explain the basic difference between regular infantry structure at the company level and its mission as opposed to Recon. An infantry rifle company consisted of about 200 Marines made up of three to five platoons of about 40 Marines each and each platoon has three squads of twelve to fourteen men.

Besides their basic weapons, they have 60mm mortar teams, machine gun teams, and various attachments such as artillery FOs (forward observers) and Marine pilots assigned to the infantry as FACs (forward air controllers). These last two were experts in their field and could call upon those supporting assets when needed.

When the tactical situation dictates, they may have a platoon of three to five tanks attached. It was also common to have a section of combat engineers, 81mm mortar teams and other heavy weapons sent from battalion or regimental assets. A very formidable force, to be sure. When they went on operations or patrols, they went looking for a fight. There was very little stealth involved.

Recon companies, on the other hand, were only about 85 men. Recon squads, also known as teams, consisted of anywhere from six to nine Marines. The mission was to be inserted by whatever means, usually helicopter but sometimes trucks or on foot, deep into the enemy controlled territory. We were generally five to eight miles from any friendly position and sometimes as far out as ten to twelve miles. Unless something unpleasant happened, our normal duration of patrol was five days. We spoke only in whispers to each other and on the radio. Hand signals were used extensively. We were stealth personified. We did not wear helmets or flak jackets like the grunts did because of the bulk it would add to our load and ability to move quietly. We wore green and black camouflage paint on all exposed flesh. Yes, even the black guys. A sweaty black face will reflect light almost as well as a white one.

The grunts followed trails because they were the paths of least resistance and usually led to the enemy. We *rarely* followed trails for the same reason.

Our job was to observe any enemy activity without being detected, and radio the information back to the base. Although we frequently called artillery or air support on enemy units or facilities, we avoided face-to-face contact if at all possible. Our job was to "Sneak and Peek, Snoop and Poop, Creep and Peep."

Weapons were M-16 rifles, M-79 grenade launcher, M-26 hand grenades, C-4 explosive, Claymore mines, det cord, and LAAW rockets. I'll get into the rest of our equipment later.

The sergeant handed me my new orders and I was directed to a truck outside which took me to Camp Horno. This is a small enclave back in the hills of Camp Pendleton and was the home of Recon School. There was a barracks building, several classrooms and offices, and the requisite parade deck with an obstacle course running along one side. There was also a small PX, and I seem to recall a four-lane bowling alley. Way too much fun.

The landscape was like the rest of Camp Pendleton ... rolling hills of mesquite, sand, gravel, rocks, occasional trees, and lizards. At that time of year, the climate could range from very hot and dry to very cold and wet. Sometimes on the same day.

I had a couple of days to myself until a full class was assembled. Some of the other students were volunteers but most had been *voluntold* and were from all manner of military occupational specialties. I was pleasantly surprised to see a total lack of boot camp attitude from the instructors. In fact, every instructor was a Recon Marine who had already done at least one tour in Vietnam, so they knew exactly whereof they spoke.

Many military schools are months if not years behind the real world. It often takes so long to formulate a curriculum, build a training facility, and put it into the system that tactics and policies change in the meantime. Then when you get to where you're going to use what you learned, you have to re-learn everything. That takes time and on the battlefield, it can cost lives. That was not the case in Recon School. The course of study was constantly updated as new instructors rotated from Vietnam to the school.

The training syllabus consisted mainly of learning new patrol tactics. Every Marine is a basic infantry rifleman. The training at Camp Geiger right after boot camp is specifically for that purpose. That way, no matter what your specialty was, if the tactical situation makes it necessary, all Marines, including officers, can pick up a rifle and function as infantry. However, the tactics of a rifle squad are much different from those of a Recon squad. By the way, Recon squads are more often referred to as teams and so it shall be from this point forward.

Ideally, an infantry rifle squad consists of three four-man fire teams, each led by a corporal. One man in each fire team is designated to carry an automatic weapon. There is also one grenadier armed with an M-79 grenade launcher, and the whole squad is lead by a sergeant. The squad leader can use the flexibility of having three maneuvering elements (the three fire teams); or, at his discretion, the three fire teams can operate independently under the fire team leader's supervision. The grenadier is the squad leader's mini-artillery to supplement the firepower of the squad.

A Recon team is not generally broken into fire teams. However, there is usually an informal structure that half of the team, if necessary, operates as a fire team under the sergeant team leader and the other half is under the control of the assistant patrol leader (APL) who is usually a corporal. Due to the small size of Recon teams, though, it is rare, but not unheard of, that the team would split into two elements.

Where a rifle squad acts as three small elements within a larger one (the platoon), the Recon team acts as a single, but larger, fire team unto itself. Clear?

Other classes had to do with camouflage technique, communications, and calling in artillery or air support, and moving as silently as possible through heavy vegetation. Recon teams never chop their way through the bush as in Tarzan movies. It's very noisy and it tells the bad guys exactly where you are, or where you have been, or where you are going. A bad thing. However, probably the most important skill to learn was land navigation. Being able to quickly and accurately read a map could mean life or death. Some people just never quite master it, but to me, the contour lines on the map became almost three-dimensional. Being able to locate yourself, or another point on the ground accurately, can save your life.

When I was on Sea Duty, I took a Marine Corps Institute course on land navigation and found it to be right up my alley. The Recon School course only added to my navigating ability because it was out there on the ground rather than just on paper.

Each Recon School class consisted of all ranks from private to staff sergeant so we all took the same courses. With Recon teams being so small and usually some distance from help, everybody was cross-trained in everyone else's skills. Some were more proficient at some things than others were, but in the end, it evened out. The only potential team members that we didn't have with us at the school were the Navy corpsmen, or medics. Their official rating is hospital corpsman, hence HM3 (Hospital corpsman 3rd class, equivalent to a corporal) and so on. Medic is an army term and I use it here for clarification only. It won't happen again.

All corpsmen assigned to the Fleet Marine Force go through a rigorous field medical course before they are assigned to a Marine unit. In Recon, as in other units, the corpsmen, or "Docs," are concerned only with medical matters. Anything else they learn related to Recon is picked up by osmosis. However, there have been rare occasions where corpsmen actually led patrols because they were good at it. Some corpsmen I served with were better Marines than some Marines.

I don't recall anyone not making it through the school. We were all young and in good shape. Once we got into the course, it was self-motivating and we began to realize how challenging and essential our role was to become. One of Recon's mottos is "The Eyes and Ears of the Division." Another is, "Where the Infantry Goes, We've Already Been." At the same time, it dawned on us that our mission was not without a distinct element of danger.

The training was thorough, tough, and enlightening, but like any situation where a group of guys were together for any length of time, there were moments where we fooled around too ... almost always at someone else's expense.

Marine Corps Reserve units from all over the West Coast periodically came to Camp Pendleton for more advanced field training. These people were Marines in that they had gone to boot camp (most all of them at Marine Corps Recruit Depot San Diego), but they were therefore just slightly inferior to the real Marines who were hammered into shape at Parris Island. They were often referred to as Hollywood Marines. It is rumored among Parris Island Marines that Hollywood Marines are issued sunglasses in boot camp. There are no female Hollywood Marines since all female Marines go through boot camp in the 4th Recruit Training Battalion (formerly WM Battalion) at MCRD Parris Island, SC. Ergo, female Marines are therefore Real Marines but Hollywood Marines were trained in San Diego. See the difference?

By the end of our second week as fledgling Reconners, we thought we were the epitome of stealth and sneakery. One Saturday night, knowing that a reserve company was camped about a mile down the road from Camp Horno, several of us went on a mission. Not having access at that time to the sticks of camouflage paint that we would soon be using, somebody pilfered some carbon paper from the school office. All exposed hide being blackened, we set out to infiltrate the enemy camp. Several rather dastardly plans were propounded but ultimately ruled out as being a bit excessive. By the time we arrived in the vicinity of the reserves, we had decided just to do a little sabotage and then make our escape. We would be as the wind in the night.

It was sometime after midnight when we made our move. The reserve unit had been seen that day practicing some pretty physical maneuvers in the hills around Camp Horno, so they were snuggled in their shelter halves fast asleep. Adding to the fun were two or three sentries walking their posts around the bivouac site so we had to elude them while we practiced our dark arts.

In reality, about all we managed to do was tie lengths of cord from one support pole on the shelter halves to the next in line ... a total of maybe seven or eight. When we all arrived back at our predesignated rally point outside their camp area, somebody tossed a cherry bomb into the middle of the camp. The reserves came rolling out of their tents, and as they ran around in confusion, they tripped over the cords collapsing a number of the tents onto their occupants. Giggling maniacally, we ran like dogs back to Horno.

Have you ever tried to scrub carbon paper stuff off your face? It isn't carbon, it's ink.

On Monday morning, the whole class received a rather listless lecture on why we, or whoever did it, should not harass the reserves. They are our fellow Marines, comrades in arms, etc., and may be sharing a foxhole with us someday. Blah, blah, blah.

In addition to the occasional reserve unit training in the Camp Horno area, we also saw platoons of recently graduated Hollywood Marines from MCRD San Diego, who were there for their ITR training. One night as we prepared to do some night patrolling, we were told that we were to go down a specific road and turn left onto a specific trail and then head off to our designated patrol areas. Each team was sent off at about 10 minute intervals and my team was the last to leave.

The ITR trainees were set up in an ambush site that was only a few hundred yards from our starting point. By the time the third team left, it became obvious from the firing that we were all being sent into a night ambush for the benefit of the trainees. I guess the instructors thought we were not only deaf but had no deductive reasoning ability. I decided that I didn't want to just lie down, roll over, and be used as a training aid, so I told my team that we were going to do things a little different.

Looking at my map, I figured that the ambushers were between the trail we were to follow and a ridgeline that ran parallel to the trail. They would have their backs to the ridgeline. When it came our turn, we started down the road but just short of the left turn to the trail, I directed the point man to turn left and climb the ridgeline. We went up the ridge until I figured we were above and behind the trainees. I spread the team out a bit and waited. The ITR instructors were getting impatient. They knew there was one team left to blunder into their clever little ambush and it was getting late. I heard a couple of people, probably instructors, hollering to each other about "Where are they? When are they coming?" and so on. I said "Fire!" and the eight of us opened up with a 20 round magazine each from our rifles. There was almost no return fire because this wasn't (*gasp*) part of the plan! They were practicing to be ambushers, not ambushees. Again, we ran like dogs while our erstwhile attackers screamed naughty things at us. They were steamed!

When we got back in the next day, my team was summoned to the school director's office. Again, we received a very brief, halfhearted lecture about sticking to the training schedule and these new Marines were still our colleagues, sharing foxholes, etc. The captain dismissed us and as I turned to go he said, "That was good initiative, Corporal Johnson." A high compliment, indeed.

We continued to practice our patrolling skills. Camp Pendleton is a very large base and we ran patrols far enough away to be transported by helicopter. This was the first time I had been up in a chopper and I was really looking forward to it. The choppers we used were CH-34s. The 34 was a leftover from the Korean War and looked much like a giant grasshopper. The pilots sat up high and forward while the crew chief and any passengers or cargo were ensconced behind and below in the cargo bay. There was one big sliding door on the right side of the fuselage for entry and exit. I don't know how much weight a 34 can pick up but its human capacity, in addition to the crew, was about eight fully loaded Marines. Lift capability, however, depended greatly on the elevation of the terrain. The higher it was, the thinner the air, the less it could lift. At a later point in this opus, I will relate how that factor was nearly the cause of the very premature demise of several of us.

On this particular patrol, my team was choppered out into the hills some miles from Camp Horno. Our basic mission was to cover the area back to Horno without being seen by instructors, who would be out and about on foot or jeep. We were also to take note of anything we felt was worth reporting, and radio it back to base using specific formulas, brevity codes, and shackle codes. More about those later, too. Camouflage, noise and light discipline were to be observed at all times. In other words, we were putting into practice all of the techniques and tactics we had been taught.

> Dear Dad,
> In the last week of school we went out to an area that is known as the Stone Age. This is really wild country and we had to stay there for 4 days ... and patrol the area the same as we would in Vietnam. To make it more realistic, there were aggressors out there too, and we had to treat them exactly as if they were the enemy. The whole 4 days it was cold and rainy and the only thing we had for protection was a field jacket and a poncho.[1]

As the last afternoon of the patrol wore on, the temperature, which was in the low 60s, began dropping. Then the sky began to darken and it became obvious that it was going to get stormy. Then the wind really kicked up. We had stopped for a short break under a scrawny tree in an otherwise fairly open area. Much of Pendleton used to be ranch property. The movie and TV actor Leo Carrillo, who played Pancho on the old *Cisco Kid* TV show, is said to have donated hundreds of acres to the Marine Corps from his property, which bordered the base. That was back in the 50s. Just at dusk, a message came over the radio to all patrols (there were several out on this exercise) to go admin — go administrative — as opposed to tactical. In other words, forget the training schedule and listen up for further word. We were to build a fire, set up shelters, or whatever, because a very nasty storm was due soon. This was for safety reasons. We all agreed that it was more likely that the instructors didn't fancy staying out in that mess watching for us.

At any rate, we built a fire but the only shelter we had was that tree. Remember the shelter halves the reserves stayed in? Well, for several reasons, Recon does not carry them in the field. They are bulky, and do not blend in to the natural foliage well because they have straight lines, and if you are in one, it is difficult to see or hear what's going on around you.

As it grew later and darker and colder, we managed to get quite a bonfire going. Seated around the fire, it was cozy enough until it started to rain. Then

The author at Recon School, Camp Horno, the morning after the storm.

it started to *rain*! We were all supposed to have ponchos with us but for reasons known only to them, a few did not have them. Between the increasing wind and rain, the fire eventually went out despite our efforts to keep it going. Now it was getting miserable. We spread some of the ponchos on the now sodden ground and placed the rest of them over our side-by-side bodies. Sort of a giant poncho sandwich.

We were still getting soaked right through our field jackets and then some idiot said, "At least it's not snowing." Somebody else told him to shut up. Too late. But it didn't snow ... it *hailed*. Marble sized pellets began whacking onto our ponchos and some of them really stung. All we could do was lie there and take it. Eight frozen, soaked, Devil Dogs[2] who, only the week before, had taken on a whole company of sleeping reservists and emerged triumphant. Those same reservists who were now at their various civilian homes tucked into their warm, dry little beds.

During the night the base radioed that at first light, we should make our way back to Horno. We stayed awake all night telling really stupid jokes and running back and forth to try to get warm. Believe it or not, one guy actually fell asleep and was snoring like a lumber mill. As soon as the sun poked its nose over the horizon, we packed up and left. Humble Camp Horno never looked so good.

Recon School was not set up for SCUBA training and qualifications, but since water was a means of entry into enemy territory, we were expected to be at home in the water. We were Little Green Amphibious Monsters, after all. We spent a day at the pool on Mainside and worked on swimming techniques that allowed us to move fairly quietly through the water. The stroke we used the most was the sidestroke and if done correctly made no noise and hardly a ripple.

Then one of the instructors decided we needed to go through a confidence builder. I don't know why because no one yet had demonstrated a lack of confidence. Anyway, the plan was to climb the stairs to the top level of a 10-meter diving platform at this pool. We were then to leap off; using any technique we cared to, and hit the water. Dropping thirty-something feet into the water was not my idea of being Swift, Silent, or even Deadly except to us.

A number of the group climbed up and jumped right off without hesitation. The rest of us formed a reluctant line and waited our turn. One particular Marine, upon reaching the platform, seemed to hesitate for a bit. I was beginning to think he was not going to jump. Then he slowly approached the lip of the platform, placed his hands on the edge between his feet and carefully pulled up into a perfect handstand. We were now all aware that we were witnessing the performance of someone with talent! After pausing briefly in the handstand position, he slowly rotated forward and executed some kind of double back dingus with a half throttle kluge followed by an inverted frou-frou. He hit the water with barely a splash and emerged to thunderous applause and shouts of, "OORAHH!" Apparently he had done this once or twice before.

When I got up there, I was amazed at how far down it was. Maybe it was because the sun reflecting off the water magnified the ... oh, what the hell! I jumped, folded into a cannonball, and hit the water with a smack. That wasn't so bad after all. When I popped to the surface and was in the process of congratulating myself for still being alive, I was missed by about an inch by the idiot who jumped after I did. When we got to the side of the pool, he apologized and said he forgot to wait until I was out of the way because he just wanted to get it over with.

Late one night in the barracks at Camp Horno, probably around 2:00 A.M., I was awakened by howling. My first thought was that it could be a wolf, but was more likely a coyote. It sounded like it was coming from some distance away outside one end of the squad bay. The howling went on intermittently for about a half an hour. The squad bay was very quiet and after a while, I thought I could hear some muted talking. I wanted to go back to sleep so I got out of my rack and strolled down to the far end to see what was going on. As I got closer to the end of the squad bay, the howling got louder as well as the talking. Arriving at the last set of bunk beds, I deduced the source of both noises. I had never heard of Wolfman Jack, a rock DJ who was famous in Southern California for his late-night radio show that was broadcast from near Tijuana. He frequently played a sound effect of a wolf howling and he talked a lot. One of the guys had fallen asleep with his radio playing softly and that's what sounded like a distant howl fest.

3. California to Okinawa

Sundays were not usually training days and I was getting bored with the minimal attractions of Camp Horno. I went to the bus station and took a little trip to Anaheim and from there, another bus to Disneyland. I had a pretty good time and don't remember much of it but I did see a celebrity. Maybe I should say that I saw a person you would recognize as a celebrity if you ever opened a book in school.

I noticed a crowd of people in three-piece suits clustered around a replica antique car driven by a uniformed Disney tour guide. In the car beside her I saw a man I recognized as His Imperial Majesty Haile Sellasie I, Conquering Lion of the Tribe of Judah, King of Kings of Ethiopia and Elect of God. (Honest, boys and girls, that's his official title.) He looked like a cadaver and didn't even appear to know where he was. I took a couple of pictures with my trusty Kodak Instamatic. He was deposed several years later. Probably because he looked like he didn't know where he was.

> Dear Dad,
> Well I finished Recon School and I came in second out of 85 other students. The way they determined how the standings were was that about the next to last day of training they interviewed the 4 top students according to test marks. We only took two [written] tests and I got a 96 & 98 on them. Anyway, at the interview they asked us questions and according to our answers they picked the best of the four.
> Well, I didn't really expect to get it because the other three were PFC's and the reward for honor student is a meritorious promotion and I figured that they would promote one of the PFC's before me because I was already a corporal and besides that I only had 3 months in grade. Actually I wasn't disappointed when I found I came in second.
> To tell the truth, I don't think I'd want to go to Vietnam as a sergeant because they would almost surely make me a patrol leader right away and I didn't want that much responsibility until I got a little experience.
> Steve[1]

After completing the school, we were moved to the staging barracks at Mainside, the "downtown" or administrative center of Marine bases, after

Haile Sellasie at Disneyland, April 1967.

which we would be bused to Marine Air Corps Station (MCAS), El Toro, California, for further transport west to the exotic Orient. I wound up spending several days there. Were my finely honed skills to be blunted by lolling around eating pogey bait?

Well, I had not much to do and nowhere in particular to go so one Saturday I decided to take the base bus to the small town of Oceanside, located at the southern tip of Camp Pendleton and right on the coast. I had not been there before but I figured there had to be a theater where I could watch some ten-year-old movies.

Arriving in beautiful downtown Oceanside at about 11:00 A.M., it didn't take long to find the movie theater. It took even less time to see the sign that said it didn't open until 4:00 P.M. Great. Walking down the sidewalk, I couldn't help but notice that there were a great many empty storefronts. It dawned on me that with Camp Pendleton being the home of the 1st Marine Division, which was completely deployed to Vietnam, there was a definite shortage of potential customers in the area. Twenty-five thousand customers, in fact.[2] Of the businesses still functioning, there were lots of bars (not open yet), and lots of tattoo parlors. The latter were open for business. I had thought from time to time about getting a tattoo. I just never worked up the nerve to do it. However, here I was, in Oceanside, standing outside a tattoo joint with nothing else to do. What the heck, and why not?

Now I did have something to do. The front windows of all the tattoo joints were covered with hundreds of designs one might select to disfigure oneself with. I spent probably an hour strolling up and down the street trying to decide which one I wanted. I was finally torn between the Marine Corps emblem, or a bulldog, the official mascot of the Marine Corps, with a World War I helmet on its head. Remember the Devil Dogs? However, it was at that moment that I saw *the sign*. The sign said you had to be 21 to get a tattoo. Everything suddenly came together. I had to be 21 to get a tattoo (I was 20), I had to be 21 to buy a beer in California, and I had to be 21 to vote.

At no time have I ever questioned what I consider my duty as an American citizen, not even that day in Oceanside. However, I could not help but think what a bass-ackward system it was that allows me to join the Marines at the age of 17, and go through the training that prepares me for no other purpose than to destroy my county's enemies by the most vicious means. But I am prohibited from tattoos, beer, and helping to select my commander in chief.

This all flashed through my mind in one enlightening second. My whole day was ruined, so I turned to head toward the bus stop. As I walked slowly along I thought this revelation must have really bothered me because I felt a little disoriented and it almost seemed like the sidewalk in front of me was undulating up and down just slightly. The feeling passed in a few seconds and then I realized I had just witnessed a very minor earthquake! This was turning out to be a day of firsts. There didn't seem to be any panic among the few in the streets. In fact, no one else appeared to even notice. As I sat on a bench at the bus stop waiting for the bus back to Pendleton, I began to feel a small sense of relief. I hadn't really wanted a tattoo, I didn't especially like beer, and the movies, as I said, were about ten years old. And voting? I wasn't much into politics anyway. However, I did survive being crushed to death in an official earthquake. Cool!

Our graduating class of newly minted Recon Marines had already received our orders for WestPac, so a day or so later we packed our sea bags and got on buses and headed south to MCAS El Toro. Upon arrival, we were shown to the transient barracks and told that we would be flying out early the next morning. The barracks we occupied were for temporary housing only and were not terribly well maintained.

The building was on a peculiar little hump on the otherwise flat terrain.[3] About 4 o'clock the next morning, we were rousted out of bed, marched to the mess hall for breakfast, and then bused to the airstrip. Like thousands of our World War II and Korean War predecessors who had headed across the Pacific Ocean, I expected to make the crossing to Vietnam on Navy troop ships ... a decidedly uncomfortable way to spend 20 days. My previous maritime home on the *Albany* was luxurious by comparison.

I therefore figured that since we were now at an airfield, we'd fly over on Marine cargo planes. Cargo planes are much more uncomfortable than troop ships but you only have to endure about 12 hours of it. However, I was pleasantly surprised to see a regular commercial airliner waiting for us with real seats and real stewardesses. We were joined by a number of other Marines, all headed for Vietnam, some of them for a second or even third time. We settled in and took off.

The flight was uneventful but it was a charge for me. I had never been on a big jet before. We landed in Hawaii — Honolulu, I presume — for refueling. We were allowed off the plane but we could not leave the terminal. The airliner was a Boeing 707 and looked like all the other planes in the airport. All, that is, except the new Braniff planes. They were decked out in the most garish colors and each one was different. The stewardesses were something else, too, wearing very "mod" uniforms featuring miniskirts and white knee-high "go-go boots." Braniff was the airline the army used. It figured that the Marines would not get treated that well.

> Dear Dad,
> When I got here on Okinawa, I found out they'd changed my orders from 3rd Marine Division to 9th Marine Amphibious Brigade, or 9th MAB for short.
> We left El Toro on Sunday and got here on Tuesday. We completely lost Monday when we crossed the International Date Line....
> We flew by Continental Airlines in a Boeing 707 jet. It took 5½ hours to reach Honolulu, Hawaii where we refueled.... The trip from Hawaii to Okinawa was 9½ hours and the weather was a little rough. We flew 600 mph at 31,000 feet and we were way above the clouds.
> I was amazed when I walked into the mess hall here at Camp Schwab. There were Okinawan women working there instead of [Marine] mess cooks. There are more Okinawans working here driving trucks and buses and other types of work than there are Marines....
> Well I guess that's it for now. The next place I write from will probably be Da Nang.
> Steve[4]

The next leg of the flight would take us to the big Marine air base at Da Nang. I was sitting on the aisle and two other guys from Recon School were in the other two seats beside me. The one in the window seat suddenly turned to us and said, "I'm not coming back. I'm going to die over there." It surprised me for just a second that he would say such a thing. Then I recalled that every John Wayne movie has some idiot that says the same thing, and sure enough, they are tragically killed just as the last battle is won. I thought it was a little phony but assured him he'd be fine. To the best of my knowledge, he made it through without a scratch.

"Oh, stewardess, another bourbon and branch water, please."

PART TWO

IN WHICH I ENTER
THE ELEPHANT'S REALM

4. In Country: Phu Bai

We began our descent to Da Nang through a bright but hazy sky. All around me, the others were craning their necks trying to see what lay below. I expected to see a lot of greenery but all I could see was varying shades of drab brown. Brown vegetation, brown buildings, brown shacks, bare brown earth and several brown runways.

We thumped down on the airstrip and eventually rolled up to the terminal, such as it was, a large but low plywood building with a tin roof. Imagine a barn with no hayloft. The upper third of each wall was screened and absolutely everything had a thick layer of dust on it. Marines were lounging about on the ground outside the terminal and as we came to a stop in a swirl of blowing dirt and dust, they stood up and began forming into a line. Each had a ditty bag and every face was as brown as everything else was. Part of that was the dirt that was blowing around but it was mostly a deep tropical tan. Even from inside the plane, the sun's glare was blinding. It was only April but it was full summer here.

The plane's engines stopped, the ventilation system shut down, the stewardess opened the exit door, and hell blew in to slap us in the face. The wave of heat almost took my breath away. I was stunned by the unexpected blast of hot, thick air.

As we filed down the stairs to the ground, someone directed the first man into the terminal and we all formed up behind him. Now I knew why all those other guys were waiting. They were going to board the plane we had just gotten off to go home. They had completed their tours. I noticed that more than a few were limping and several had casts or dressings on arms, heads, and elsewhere. Crutches and canes were also evident. As we went into the terminal, we heard a few "You'll be so-o-o-ory's," but for the most part, they were all rather solemn for people who were getting on the Freedom Bird. Maybe it hadn't quite sunk in yet that they'd made it.

Inside, I went to one of several check-in counters and showed a bored corporal my orders.

Dear Dad,

When we left Okinawa I had orders that said I was going to 2nd battalion, 3rd Marine regiment ... 2/3 is a regular infantry unit commonly known as grunts. Well I wanted to go to a Recon unit. When we turned in our orders at Da Nang I told them I had a Recon MOS [military occupational specialty] and had been thru the training and didn't want the infantry. Well I was in luck because it seems there's a shortage of Recon people so I was reassigned to the 3rd Marine Recon battalion which is in the 3rd Division.[1]

After getting organized, I was told to go outside and wait by a sign that said 3d Recon Battalion and a truck would be along soon. First, though, I had to go retrieve my sea bag that by now had been heaved off the airplane along with a couple hundred other identical green sea bags. In my sea bag was everything I owned. My dress blues, dress greens, khakis, tropicals, footwear, skivvies, socks, towels, raincoat, overcoat, shave kit, and extra utility uniforms. You'd be amazed how much you can stuff into a sea bag.

By this time, I was sweating profusely. All the troops I had seen who were either waiting to go home or were otherwise employed in running the airfield were wearing the Vietnam issue jungle utilities. Stateside utilities were thick cotton and we usually starched them heavily in order to have a sharp crease pressed into them even though the creases disappeared about 30 minutes after putting them on.

Jungle utilities were lightweight poplin and were never starched. They dried quickly when wet and were rip resistant. The shirt was worn outside the trousers allowing at least minimal circulation. The jungle boots were unique, too. Instead of the heavy, hard to dry, black leather boots we were normally issued, these had leather lowers but a canvas upper. They were lighter, dried quicker and even had drain vents in the instep to quickly let out water. Unlike the standard issue LPCs — leather personnel carriers — which had smooth soles, the jungle boots had a rubber lug sole that gave them decent traction even in mud.

I found the sign for Recon and sat on my sea bag. Having a few moments to myself, I was taking notice of other things ... like the smell. Vietnam smelled dirty. I couldn't quite put my finger on it but there it was. Notable, too, was a heavy stench that I had never smelled before but it smelled like something burning. I'll tell you about that smell in due time.

There was also a frequent blast of sickening jet fuel exhaust that seemed to ride on the shimmering gusts of heat. Da Nang was the home of one or more Marine Air Groups (MAGs) and there were jets and helicopters taking off, landing, or taxiing everywhere. Even inside the terminal, the noise was terrific. Add to that the diesel exhaust fumes of dozens of jeeps and 2½-ton trucks busily running to and fro.

I couldn't see very far due to the numbers of plywood, screen, and tin roof buildings. Almost all of them had a red sign with yellow numbers or letters on them identifying their function. From the air, I could see the base had been laid out in straight lines, but I had also noticed that outside that area was probably a couple of square miles of haphazardly placed shacks and a few larger buildings. That was the city of Da Nang. When someone said Da Nang, though, they were speaking of the base. It was a large, bustling place and I was fervently hoping that my destination was a bit more serene.

It wasn't long before a truck rolled to a dusty stop in front of me. "Third Recon?" asked the PFC driver. I said "Yup" and jumped in the back. Apparently, no one else was going to 3rd Recon.

The 1st Marine Division was headquartered in Chu Lai, about 55 miles south of Da Nang. Therefore, 1st Recon Battalion also had its headquarters there. The four companies that composed the battalion were OpConned out to subordinate infantry regiments but the Recon Battalion headquarters itself remained with the division headquarters (HQ). The 3d Marine Division was headquartered here in Da Nang, so 3rd Recon's Battalion HQ was here too, and its companies were similarly OpConned out to the division's infantry regiments. Since I did not know which company I would be assigned to, I still had to go to the Recon Battalion HQ to find out.

The short ride to the Recon area was dirty and hot in the back of that six-by. We called the 2½-ton trucks six-bys because they had six wheels with six-wheel drive, hence six-by-six. Sometimes they were called Deuce-and-a-half's and they could go almost anywhere. I felt like I was being broiled alive in the open truck bed. Although there were bench seats on each side of the bed, the floor was covered with a couple layers of sand bags. I was to learn that this was a debatable means of helping to prevent injury to personnel in the back if the truck hit a land mine. It was called "hardening" a vehicle. There were a surprisingly large number of Vietnamese civilians on the base. Almost everyone wore the round, cone shaped reed hats typical of most of Asia.

Arriving at Recon Battalion HQ, the driver said to leave my sea bag in the truck because I probably would be going elsewhere after being assigned to a company. I took my orders inside the office, which was a copy of all the other buildings I could see. Although it was what is officially called a "Southeast Asia Hut," they were universally called "hooches" by the troops. They were about 18 feet by 36 feet with a door at each end, and the lower halves of the walls were plywood while the upper half was screened. There were tarps rolled up under the eaves and they were let down at night to keep the light from showing out, or during the monsoon season to keep the rain from getting in. The ubiquitous tin roof topped each hooch.

Top: Recon Battalion HQ at Phu Bai (courtesy 1st Lt. Fisher). *Bottom:* First Lieutenants Al Pfeltz (left) and Jeff Fisher at Bravo Company office hooch in Phu Bai (courtesy 1st Lt. Fisher).

I handed my orders to a Remington Raider and waited to report to the battalion commander. After a bit, a major came out of another office area and introduced himself as the battalion XO; I popped to attention and was about to say the required words when reporting to a new unit; "Sir, Corporal Johnson reporting as ordered," but he quickly stopped me and said that the commanding officer was away that day and besides, they didn't stand on a lot of ceremony here.

He welcomed me to the battalion and then asked the office pogue which company needed a corporal. After scratching around on his desk and peering through very thick glasses at numerous scraps of paper that only pogues can read, he announced that Bravo Company needed someone of my caliber. "Bravo it is," said the major, "They're in Phu Bai." I did a smart Sea Duty about-face, left the pogue a copy of my orders and went back out to the truck to tell the driver that we needed to go to Phu Bai to where Bravo Company was.

Phu Bai was about twelve miles north of Da Nang. This time I exercised my lofty rank and climbed up into the cab with the driver. I asked if he minded if I rode up front and he said, "No problem." I guess I should have thought of that before.

It took about 45 minutes to travel the twelve miles. Route 1 was, in reality, barely two lanes wide and may have been marginally paved at one time. Everything that needed to move up or down the coast from bicycles to tanks moved on Route 1. The trip was otherwise uneventful and we eventually rumbled up to the gates of the base at Phu Bai. There were sandbagged machine gun emplacements on either side of the gate and rows of barbed wire and rolls of concertina wire stretching off in either direction. After asking the MP where Bravo Recon was, we drove by several areas where other units were housed. I didn't see as many hooches here as I did in Da Nang. It appeared that most everybody lived in squad-sized tents.

What I could see of the base was limited but it seemed to consist of the aforementioned tents, a few larger, more substantial buildings, and sand. White sand like you'd find on a beach. There were a few scrubby little bushes but not a tree, or blade of grass ... just sand.

These olive drab canvas tents are actually quite roomy at 32 by 16 feet and will accommodate a dozen or more people with their cots and other equipment. The sides of the tents were about five and a half feet high so at the center, they were probably ten feet tall. There was plenty of room to move around. The floor, rather than dirt or sand, was covered with wooden pallets. This served mainly to keep people up off the rivulets of mud that flowed through the tents during the monsoon. The pallets were scrounged from the ammo dumps and supply points. Ordinance and other supplies were banded onto the pallets for shipment and once they had arrived and were unloaded at their destination, the pallets were used as is, or taken apart and used for a myriad of other purposes. Making rustic furniture was a popular use.

Dear Dad,
    Greetings from Phu Bai. We left Okinawa on the morning of the 2nd and got to Da Nang about noon on the same day....
    I was assigned to Bravo Company, 2nd platoon. This platoon has the highest number of kills in the battalion so it looks like I wound up in a hard charging outfit. Here, we are about a quarter of a mile from the Viet Cong. At night the artillery batteries nearby shell suspected areas in the mountains. Sometimes you can see the tracer rounds as they move toward the hills. Last night I heard machine gun fire from somewhere out there.[2]

I went through the reporting in process again with the company commander, Captain Jerry Hudson. Somebody showed me to a tent that was occupied by a team that was on patrol. They would be back tomorrow but there were a couple of extra cots that looked unused, so I picked one and got settled in. It was late in the day so I was told to get checked in the next day and draw my 782 gear and rifle. Checking in means you have to trudge around to all the support units such as medical, supply, armory, and so forth so they know who you are, where you live, and issue out various items as necessary.

I was getting the hungries by now so I asked where the mess hall was and I was directed to a large tent a couple hundred yards away with other tents angling off from it. The sides of all the tents were rolled up to allow some ventilation, but there was one major drawback. With the tent flaps rolled up the sand and grit was free to enhance your slab of Spam. Well, birds swallow gravel to help digestion, don't they?

It was a typical field mess with cauldrons of things steaming over industrial strength burners. The tents that went off to the sides had a number of picnic type tables for one's dining enjoyment. If the ambiance of the mess tent was not to your liking, you were free to take your tray back to your tent. This mess tent served several hundred Marines at each meal and was one of many scattered around the base. Other than it being my first chow in a combat zone, the meal was not memorable.

I spent the remainder of the daylight wandering around the immediate area and meeting a few people. Bravo Company was within 100 yards of other unit areas but removed enough so that it was relatively quiet. Nobody had weapons or helmets so I assumed it was a fairly safe area. I found the six-holer, or head, the piss tube, the Lister bag, the water buffalo, and other essentials.

The next morning I made the rounds checking in and when I got to supply I was issued one pair of jungle boots, three sets of jungle utilities, a helmet, flak jacket, and pack. The standard issue USMC pack was the haversack, which was designed in 1941. It was very small and didn't hold much more than a pair of boots and a change of skivvies and socks. It was OK for a one or two day, short-range patrol. Recon needed a pack that you could live out of for at least five days to a week so we used what were called NATO packs. Some called them ARVN (Army of the Republic of Vietnam) packs. They were the size of a large rucksack and had external pockets for canteens or whatever. I was also issued a rifle belt with four magazine pouches, canteens, canteen pouches, a canteen cup, Ka-bar knife, and a set of belt suspenders. The combat load of water, grenades and ammunition attached to the belt can reach 25 pounds so the suspenders are a necessity.

I wasn't through, yet. I also got a compass, field jacket, poncho, poncho liner, sleeping bag (never used in the field but in the hooches it made a nice mattress on the cot), leather gloves, cammie sticks, bug juice, 1st aid pack, gas mask, etc. There was so much I had to take two pair of utility trousers, tie the cuffs off, stuff them full, fill the pack, wear the helmet and flak jacket and stagger back to my tent. Our flak jackets, by the way, were not like the army type. Theirs were made of layers of Kevlar and although thick, they were a bit lighter and more flexible. Ours were constructed of overlapping plates of reinforced fiberglass inside a canvas vest. They were stiff, heavy, and very bulky. They even clanked when you ran. In fact, they resembled nothing so much as the lorica segmentata body armor worn by the Roman legions of the 1st to 3rd centuries A.D.

I checked in at the Battalion Aid Station (BAS). This is basically a hospital (think of M*A*S*H) where daily ailments are looked after as well as combat injuries until the patient is stable enough to be transported to the Naval Hospital in Da Nang or a hospital ship offshore. At the BAS, I was rewarded with several shots in both arms and elsewhere. "Thank you very much, Sir! Can I have another?"

At the armory, I was issued fifteen 20-round magazines, a bayonet with scabbard, and my very own 5.56mm Colt M-16 automatic rifle. Oddly enough, this was the first M-16 I had ever handled. In my two years plus in the Marines I had trained with an M-14 in boot camp, an M-1 Garand in ITR, an M-1 on Sea Duty, back to an M-14 in Recon School and now here I was holding a short, black, plastic and magnesium alloy Mattie Mattel rifle. It was often referred to as a Mattie Mattel due to its scary similarity to a popular toy gun at that time. The rifle was so new to the inventory that many Marines were still carrying the highly reliable but heavier and longer M-14. There was not even a formalized manual of arms for the M-16 yet.

I schlepped back to my tent with my new toys and sat there pondering on what I was going to do with everything I had been issued as well as the full sea bag I had brought with me. At that moment, I heard several approaching voices. They all sounded in high spirits, and as I got up to look outside, in came a group of the dirtiest, smelliest, nasty looking bunch of pirates I had ever seen. It was the returning team fresh off their patrol. For one second we stared at each other and then they all started introducing themselves at the same time. There were few real names and ranks. They called each other by nicknames, mostly of the not-to-be-repeated in genteel company variety. One in particular had the most peculiar high and broad forehead. He looked like the old-time boxer Carmine Basilio (who, incidentally, was a Marine). Then someone explained that they had been attacked by a swarm of NVA wasps and he had gotten several stings to the forehead causing painful swelling. The others were not stung and found it all very amusing. I would run into some of those bees later. Basilio (can't remember his real name) went off to the BAS, and the patrol leader and APL headed for the S-2 shop. There are four levels of support units in a company, battalion, or regiment. S-1 is the administrative section. S-2 is the intelligence section. S-3 is the operations and training section and S-4 is the logistics and supply section. At division level, these are identified as G-1, etc.

Except for the bees, their patrol had been uneventful. After showering and squaring away their gear, turning in ordnance, and just winding down, a couple of them turned to helping me get organized. The first thing I had to do was sort out what I needed from what I didn't. That meant that 90 percent of the stuff in my original sea bag was unnecessary, but what to do with it? It turned out that there was a staging area set aside for that purpose. It was one of many Butler buildings built by the Navy Seabees or Marine combat engineers. Butler buildings are a pre-fab, steel arch and sheet metal covered building about the size of a small barn built on a cement pad. They are used for workspace or storage and several can be built in one day.

The company had a slops chest so somebody dug out a spare sea bag that I could use for storing the unnecessaries. Slops chest is a naval term for a locker box with castoff but still serviceable uniform or equipment items. If you are loaned something from the slops chest you are expected to eventually return it in good order or replace it in kind. After sorting things out I made sure my name and serial number were on a tag firmly secured to the sea bag and, since it was some distance to the Butler building, one of the guys helped me carry it over there, not to be seen again for thirteen months. Everybody in the team was friendly and helpful but, except for Basilio, I can't remember a specific face or name. For some reason they just didn't seem to register until a few weeks later. Then it was as if I'd known them for years.

In my original sea bag, I now placed anything that I would not be wearing that day. It was my closet and dresser all in one. I noticed that some of the guys had a small piece of furniture about the size of a nightstand. These had been built either by the owner or, in many cases, they were bought from little shops the local Vietnamese put up a little way outside the main entrance to the base. In either case, they were made from old wooden pallets or large caliber ammo boxes. These nightstands didn't hold much but it was a handy place for toiletries, writing materials, and other small personal items. They were never locked.

They also helped me assemble my web gear so things were easier to get to. Positioning of equipment is very important because when things get dicey you don't have time to look around and wonder where you put that spare grenade or whatever. Everything had to be accessible and in the same place all the time. We even practiced removing an "empty" magazine from the rifle and replacing it with a full one without looking down to see where your hands needed to be.

In reality, during a firefight, empty magazines were not placed back into the ammo pouch. Far too time consuming. The mags were dropped to the ground and then when there were a few seconds to spare, they were stuffed into your shirt. They couldn't fall out the bottom because the rifle belt prevented that. Not putting empty mags back in the pouch also prevented you from wasting time pulling an empty magazine out when what you really, really wanted right then was a full one. At the first opportunity, we would then refill them from boxed ammo in our packs, but only one Marine at a time. It could be fatal to have several people absorbed in digging ammo out of their pack and refilling magazines while there was still the remotest chance of hostilities recommencing.

I also had to learn how to field strip and operate my M-16. An M-16 was simple because it broke down into three basic parts. This was very unlike my previous experience with the M-1 and M-14, both of which broke down into 8 to 10 parts.

They are phasing in the new M16 rifle which is the same as the AR15 [semi-automatic civilian version of the M-16]. It fires a .223 caliber bullet which is usually referred to as 5.56mm. Every rifle has a selector on it to fire semi-auto or full auto. It has a recoil just a little heavier than a .22 rifle. I think one of the twins [author's younger brothers] could shoot it and hardly feel it.

We are not allowed to have or spend american [sic] money here. Instead we convert it to MPC. Military Payment Certificate. They have all paper money instead of coins. If you don't want it in MPC you can change it to Piastras which is the Vietnamese money. They are worth about 1 piastra to 1 cent or just a fraction less.

I am enclosing 2 bills. One is 50 piastras or 50¢ and the other is 20 piastras or 20¢. On the bill you'll see Hai Mu'o'i Dông and Nam Mu'o'i Dông. The Mu'o'i is ten Hai is two and Nam is five. 2 tens is 20 piastras and 5 tens is 50. Dông is the Vietnamese word for piastra. I am trying to learn some Vietnamese. So far all

I can say is, "Tôi Thuo'C Thuy-Quân Luc-Chiên My," which is pronounced Toy Tuoc Tuy-Qwun Luc-Chien My. It means "I am with the U.S. Marines."... So long (Chao Ba)

Steve

P.S. I don't know how many letters you've sent but I haven't gotten any yet so [if] you had any questions or anything, I haven't answered them because I haven't gotten them yet.[3]

Then one fine day, it came to pass that I found out what that horrible stink was that I had noticed while sitting on my sea bag in Da Nang. Once a week, a small detail of two or three snuffies was selected and whose job it was to "burn the shitters." Under each of the six seats in the head was a cutoff 55-gallon drum waste receptacle. These drums were dragged out and five were dumped into one along with a generous slosh of kerosene. The five empties were placed back under the seats and a little sign saying "Secured" was placed on the lid of the sixth seat. A little gasoline was then poured into the mixture and ignited by a tossed burning match. The resultant fire produced thick black smoke and an overpowering smell. A stick was kept at hand to stir up the mess and make sure everything was burned away. It was a dirty but necessary job. Once everything was burned, the empty drum was put back under seat six. As distasteful as this job was, it was very effective in helping to control vermin and odor. Except, that is, for the stink that the burning itself caused.

One morning, I went out to the Lister bag to get some water in my canteen cup for shaving. As I was decanting the heavily chlorinated elixir, I heard a voice say, "That better not be for shaving!" I turned and observed a corporal standing a couple of tents away whom I recognized as the supply NCO. He always had a

Military Payment Certificates —$1 and 10 cents.

rather superior air about him because everyone knows that the supply people keep the rest of us mortals from stumbling around in utter confusion and quite possibly doing ourselves a mischief. That's not to even mention the fact that every item in supply is personally bought and paid for by the supply personnel and it is only through their enormous generosity that the necessities of life were doled out free of charge to us.

Technically the Lister bag water was for drinking only. All other aquatic needs were to be met by a trip to the water buffalo. Why there was a difference I'll never know. It was all the same water. However, it was my habit to brush my teeth first, and then shave using the same water. When most people brush their teeth they use water to rinse their mouth, right? I felt that constituted internal consumption. Besides, I didn't like his attitude. I said, "It isn't," to his comment and walked back into the tent casually sipping the water. Then I brushed my teeth and shaved. Corporal Lister and I were to converse again.

The next few days were mainly a matter of simply adjusting to an environment that was totally new to me. For the time being, I was assigned to the team in whose tent I resided and I was told that soon I would go on patrols as an observer. In other words, even though I was a corporal and would normally be an APL, as an observer I was last in the chain of command behind the most junior man in the team. If everybody else became incapacitated, I would, God forbid, be in charge. Yes, I was a proud graduate of Recon School but all that meant was that even though I had a glimmer, I was otherwise totally without experience. After a break-in period as an observer, I would then become an APL. I would learn from the team leader everything (hopefully) I would need to know to become a patrol leader, accomplish the mission, and keep the Marines in my charge as safe from harm as possible.

I had only given occasional thought to that which most human beings would rather not think about and that would be the act of deliberately killing someone. Up until now, we had "killed" bayonet course dummies, targets on the rifle range, each other (hand to hand combat training), and, in our imaginations, waves of maniacal enemy forces who were stupid enough to charge into our rifle sights. Now, however, there was the distinct probability that my actions would result in either the direct or the indirect cause of the demise of others. I tried to mentally create the moment that I would point a weapon, pull the trigger, and watch a man fall. Strangely, in my mind, I could create this "movie" but it was always silent. I couldn't come up with the sounds associated with battle. Having seen countless war movies one would think that would be easy but for some reason, a Hollywood sound track did not fit.

Being in the military, the topic of conversation naturally often turns to warfare. Someone will eventually ask the question, "Do you think you could kill someone?" The required manly answer was always something like, "Hell yeah! Then I'd rip off his head and puke down his neck and then I'd really get mad!" Easy to say, and we were convinced we could do it without missing a beat. Now, however, as a spanking new member of a Marine Corps combat unit, I was standing side by side with men who had killed. They didn't look any different from anyone else. They didn't appear to be guilt ridden about anything they had done but they also did not brag and crow about it. Usually, the only time that specific topic came up was within the context of making a tactical point. "This is what happened, and this is what we had to do." Of course every now and then (daily), a few guys would start spinning Sea Stories about all kinds of courageous derring-do and feats of strength beyond human capability. I was to find out that this was one way of blowing off steam after a particularly difficult patrol. In fact, most of these stories were pure fiction. Everybody knew it and nobody cared.

One afternoon I was helping to load boxes onto a six-by when a couple of the guys yelled greetings to a lone figure walking toward us. It was explained to me that it was 1st Lieutenant Albert Pfeltz, who had been on leave. He had already completed a full thirteen-month tour in Vietnam but had extended for an additional six months. Lt. Pfeltz was held in high esteem among Bravo Marines. He was a hard-charging but evenhanded officer and he definitely believed in leading from the front.

Lt. Pfeltz came over to us and was greeted with slaps on the back and salutes all around. I was introduced to him and was impressed with his easy-going manner. Everyone was still, "Yes Sir," and "No Sir," but it was obvious that he didn't hold himself off from the enlisted swine. He was a combat Marine just like the rest of us (or, as I hoped, I would be).

Each Recon platoon was commanded by a lieutenant, along with a platoon sergeant who normally held the rank of staff sergeant. If there was a shortage of staff NCOs, that billet could be filled by a senior sergeant or even with the sergeant squad leader of the first squad doing double duty. Recon patrols are led by sergeants and sometimes corporals but rarely by officers unless they consisted of two or more teams, but that was a rare event. However, the company commander wanted each of his platoon commanders to go on an occasional patrol, figuring, I suppose, that if they were going to lead Recon Marines, they ought to know what their men are doing. If he went along on a one-team patrol, the officer was not necessarily in command of the team. That responsibility was still on the shoulders of the sergeant team leader. However, Lt. Pfeltz liked going on patrols.

Dear Dad,
Yesterday I got back from my first patrol. The patrol leader [Lt. Pfeltz] is breaking me in as an assistant patrol leader. We went about 5000 meters from the base camp

and although that doesn't sound very far, it's a long ways when there's only 10 of us.

The first night we spent out there I couldn't sleep at all. There are all kinds of weird sounding birds that hoot and yell all night long. Because so much of that jungle is rotten and dead there are twigs and branches falling out of the trees all the time. I kept hearing things all night long. We were out there 4½ days and on the 3rd day out we were taking a break ... and we heard firing about 400 meters away. In the same area was a company of grunts ... who were working on a road that ran along one edge of our patrol zone. Anyway, one of their patrols ran into some gooks (V.C.) and they got into a firefight. We moved a little closer to the noise and came into a semi-clearing. We could see about 35–40 feet in front and on the sides and spread out on a skirmish line. The plan was to wait there until something happened. We didn't have to wait long. We heard the grunts start to mortar the gooks and then it was quiet for a few minutes. Then we heard the gooks start to fire. They have .30 caliber carbines and russian AK-47s which is a sort of sub-machine gun. The grunts were returning fire and we could tell they were using M-16s because that .223 cal. round makes a loud pop when it goes off. The firing got louder and was coming right for us. Apparently the grunts were giving them a running fire fight. We could hear yelling from the gooks and when they got about 200 meters away the firing stopped. We radioed the grunts and asked if they needed any help and they said no thanks but we'd better clear out because they were going to call in artillery on the gooks and we might get caught in it. We hi tailed it out of the area (much to my relief) and shortly after we heard artillery coming in over us....

The rest of the patrol was pretty quiet. You wouldn't believe how thick the jungle is here. Most of the time our visibility is less than 10 feet and that includes up. We went for 3 days without seeing the sun. Its well over 100° in the day and it cools off to about 80° at night. There are leeches all over the place. You can't feel them on you until they get full of blood and then you notice a squishy lump under your clothes. 8 inch centipedes and scorpions are a problem too....

Could you get me a pair of golf gloves (leather) or something similar to protect my hands and still leave me a free trigger finger. Every bush and vine over here has prickers on it. Some are 3–4 inches long.... I am enclosing 200 dollars from my travel pay and you can take any cost out of that or send me a bill. That's all for now.

Steve[4]

5. Learning My Trade

I think I was on about my third patrol out of Phu Bai as an observer and this time I was in the secondary point position. That's right behind the point man. I was there because I was nowhere near bush-wise enough to walk point but I would be able to observe how the point man did his job. In a small unit, it's vital that everyone knows everyone else's position. Our corpsmen were encouraged to give us as much field medical knowledge as we could absorb. In the rear, they had access to moulage kits to make the 1st aid drills quite realistic. These rubber prosthetic devices could simulate any number of injuries from a compound fracture to disembowelment. They even pumped blood colored water and were very effective.

Walking point is a lot more than just being the first one in line. One might think that the point would be the first one to get shot. That's not necessarily so. Any well-managed ambush will have predetermined targets, radioman (antenna sticking up in the air), officer (carrying only a pistol or binoculars, visible rank insignia, someone obviously giving orders) medical personnel (if they're foolish enough to wear armbands or other identifier), troops carrying machine guns, etc. The point man has to be the eyes of the patrol. The patrol leader tells him generally which way to go and then the point man picks his route based on vegetation and terrain appreciation. He needs to pick a route that offers as much natural concealment as possible while at the same time allowing for the fact that some of the men are carrying larger and more awkward loads than others. Also, moving through dense bush is noisy and must be avoided if possible but that's a tactical decision for the patrol leader.

Terrain appreciation is the art of using the contours of the land you are crossing to your advantage. Sometimes the easy way is not the best way. Rather than going straight up a hill, you traverse back and forth. This lengthens the route somewhat but reduces the incline considerably. If you move along the spine of a ridge where the ground under your feet is relatively flat, you can be silhouetted, so you move parallel to it but just below the crest. This is known as the military crest of a hill. Walking crossways to a steep slope is hard on the ankles but it's safer.

The point also has to be aware of signs or sounds ahead that indicate the fact that, recently or in the past, humans had been there: freshly broken vegetation, obviously a footprint or cigarette butt, or a disruption to the forest floor such as drag marks, or, in denser bush, vegetation that has been pushed in one direction indicating the passage of people. An area that appeared to have been moved through but had a layer of dust or other natural litter on top would indicate that it has been a while since it was used. Although we normally avoided trails like the plague because they were made and used by the enemy and we didn't really want to bump into them, sometimes we had to use them.

The point man had to have the tactical knowledge to be able to determine if we were entering a possible ambush site. The presence of an enemy ambush was detectable if the point was very, very alert. Careless movement or noise, smells, absence of animal noises, or sometimes it just didn't look right to an experienced eye could be a give-away. Not everyone is cut out to walk the point and a sharp point man can keep people alive. Point men most often volunteered for the job because they felt they had the smarts and "bush time" to do the job. Most patrol leaders had, at one time, been point men themselves and it didn't take long for a prospective point to prove to the patrol leader that he had the potential, or not. Having civilian experience as a hunter was not necessarily an attribute. Deer and woodchucks don't shoot back.

Being the point man in a Recon team was a place of pride and sometimes, on a very difficult march, the point had to be ordered to relinquish his spot to the secondary point ... at least for a while. The secondary point and the Tail End Charlie had to be equally alert and observant. Their wariness and bush sense were often lifesavers. I walked secondary point on a number of my early patrols and learned from very sharp Marines. Sometimes, as patrol leader, I would temporarily take the point because I was looking for a very specific landmark or terrain feature for navigational purposes. I think, if I hadn't been selected as a patrol leader, I would have wanted to be the point. When you're the first one out there, your senses just bristle with awareness.

This particular patrol was in especially dense bush. It was thick enough so that we were making noise (at least a lot more than was desirable) and getting almost nowhere. We came across a trail that did not appear on the map. Major trails that had existed for, probably, generations were on our maps but many of them were under the canopy and could not be seen from the air. Finding them randomly was common. The patrol leader decided we would cautiously follow it for a while so we could plot some of it for the S-2 people. Yes, we were following a trail and, yes, in this case it was our job. Plotting previously unknown trails was definitely Recon business. This one was dirt and fairly well worn-in, indicating frequent use.

The point was really pussyfooting now. His pace was slow and his steps were very deliberate. I noticed that he never looked down. He minded his footing with peripheral vision. He was looking up ahead and constantly scanning from side to side. I found myself doing the same thing and noticed that I seemed to be seeing more detail that way. Every twenty feet or so he stopped and listened intently as he looked around. The heavily canopied jungle turned the litter on the jungle floor into rotting compost and the air was full of the odor of decaying vegetation. Foreign smells, like cooking or unwashed bodies, could be detected from time to time, but our own stench sometimes blotted that sense out. The rest of the team was totally silent and spaced at about eight foot intervals. In cover that is more open, we were usually 20 to 30 feet apart.

The air was stagnant, oppressive, and so quiet under that overgrowth that the silence was palpable. I do remember hearing dripping noises from the moisture that formed on the leaves far above. It was almost eerie that nine heavily loaded Marines could move without making a sound. It was now abundantly clear why the pre-patrol inspection included a thorough check for noisy, unsecured gear.

The point was sometimes armed with a Winchester Model '97 shotgun. These are often called trench guns and were patented in 1897. The truth is that the Model '97 was a sturdy, well made weapon and the 12-gauge double-ought buckshot it fired could plow through the bush with authority. The Model '97 wasn't especially heavy but it was a full-length shotgun. More like what a game bird hunter might use. The only thing I didn't like about them was that when you used the pump action to chamber a new round the action opened on the top of the receiver and slid back right over your right hand. If you were holding the weapon even slightly awkwardly, you could easily slice off a chunk of skin between your thumb and index finger! When the point man chose to carry the '97, he did not carry an M-16. Two weapons of similar bulk plus all the ammo for both would have been a real load. Originally intended for use in the trenches of early 20th century battlefields, it was equally suited for close up jungle warfare. The point man usually moved with his weapon's safety off. The rest of the team moved with their trigger finger on the trigger and their thumb on the safety lever in the safe position. Moving through the kind of terrain and bush that we did could often produce a stumble and we had enough to worry about besides an accidental discharge, let alone someone getting shot in the back.

The bush was close on either side and came together about 25 feet overhead making a green, leafy tunnel about five feet wide. Some sunlight filtered down so it wasn't dark ... more like dusk. The light was so diffused that there was no one source and no real shadows ... just gloom. Over the point's shoulder, and about thirty feet ahead, I could see the trail make an abrupt right turn and disappear.

Just as we stepped off again, and without a sound, an NVA soldier appeared around the turn coming toward us. His rifle was resting on his shoulder and he was holding it casually by the barrel. He saw us immediately and his cry of surprise was instantly followed by the roar of the point's shotgun. Perforated by the buckshot, the front of his shirt erupted as the NVA was bowled backward into the bush. Contrary to Hollywood, great gouts of blood do not fountain forth. (The bleeding comes seconds later as the heart continues to pump until it stops ... dead.)

I was momentarily stunned at how fast that happened. The point turned and ran straight at me. "Move!" he shouted. We executed the immediate action drill for a point-to-point contact and I can't say I did my part gracefully but we accomplished the purpose. I turned and flew down the trail after the rest of the team. We were not out there to get into pitched battles. Our survival depended on getting the hell away before unwelcome help arrived.

Immediate action drills are something like football plays that the team executes in certain situations. If we are ambushed from the right or left, if there is point-to-point contact, or if we are being followed, there is an immediate action drill to cover the situation. The key word is *immediate*. If an immediate action drill becomes necessary, it usually means there will be a fight, and soon! There is zero time to formulate and call out a plan when there are just seconds to react. Everyone on the team must know instinctively what to do and not wait to be told. To get to that point, immediate action drills are practiced in the company street on a daily basis between patrols.

Immediate action drills also included what to do if we got into a firefight. Our most effective was the drill we used to break contact. The NVA knew that grunts wear helmets and flak jackets and ran around in relatively large numbers. They also knew that Recon wore floppy bush hats and camouflage and were seldom in units of more than ten Marines. Therefore, if they saw one Recon Marine, they instantly knew whether their own unit outnumbered ours and would try to maneuver around the team and cut them off. Due to their relatively small size, Recon teams got surrounded (usually unsuccessfully) often enough so that we changed our official motto of "Swift, Silent, and Deadly" to the unofficial "Swift, Silent, and Surrounded."

As I mentioned previously, each of us carried a gas grenade. It was designated CS gas and was like a strong version of tear gas. CS causes choking, drainage of all tear ducts and mucous membranes, and a burning sensation to the skin. It can even cause vomiting in heavy doses. We would try to determine where the least amount of fire was coming from and then toss a couple of CS. The gooks rarely carried gas masks and the ones they had were very ineffective Russian masks. If we threw CS, they had virtually no defense against it. We carried very good gas masks and after giving the gas a few moments to spread out, we'd throw a couple of fragmentation grenades into the same area. That wounded or chased off any gooks lingering in the gassed area. As soon as the last frag went off, we high tailed it right through the gas.

Especially under the humid and airless canopy, the gas would hang in the air for some time, which discouraged pursuit. The Tail End Charlie would also drop another CS every 50 meters or so. The teams who needed to use this means of breaking contact were rarely chased for very long.

We did not drop gas or frags this time because we bugged out so fast after contact and then got off the trail that, pursuit, if any, would have been ineffective. We didn't know if he was a lone courier or the point man for a battalion. Either way, we got out of there fast!

We were extracted, as planned, the next day so it was all very fresh in my mind when we got back to the base. I kept remembering that seconds-long event in a series of mental snapshots. This contact happened so fast and so violently that I guess my brain had a little trouble digesting it. There was the dim, silent trail; the NVA materialized in front of us; he was blasted down; we were running. Four quick images.

Back at Phu Bai, cleaning up my gear, and released from the other tensions of being on patrol, the incredible realness of what happened caught up with me. That guy must have realized that he was already dead a millisecond before his chest was torn apart by double-ought buckshot.

I had seen someone die right in front of me! If he had been more alert, he could have killed me!

Just a few hours before, we left a man lying dead in the jungle. At least, because he was lying on the trail, he would eventually be found. He would be mourned but almost certainly not returned to his family. An unmarked grave near the trail would be his version of Arlington National Cemetery.

Sitting on my cot, I became totally absorbed by the mental images ... the rapidity and consequence of it all. I fought a rising feeling of nausea but I lost and vomited into the sand at my feet. I scraped sand over the mess with my boot. Then I surprised myself by experiencing a feeling of vast relief, I guess because I was now safe and alive. One of the guys walked past me and gave me a biff on the shoulder. Nothing was said nor needed to be. I kept seeing that NVA at the instant the buckshot hit him. In my mind, I could not see the point man in front of me anymore. It was just the NVA and me. Over the next few days, I made a point with myself not to dwell on it. In time, I rarely thought about it anymore.

Years later, when that memory did pop into my head, I really thought that it was me who had shot that guy, but it was still just snippets of mental images. Then I completely forgot about it until very recently when a friend I had told that story to reminded me of it. At first, I had trouble recalling it, but then it slowly came back. It was still out of focus, though, and for the first time I began to question my memory. Over the following two weeks or so, I tried to recall the smells, sounds, and sights and even lost a little sleep over it. Bits began to drop into place and, though still not crystal clear, it now makes sense to me. I am not haunted by it. I merely remember.

6. Khe Sanh

The word was going around that Bravo would be pulling up stakes and heading to a new home. Unknown to most of us, for a few weeks, a serious battle had been taking place north of us in a little spot named Khe Sanh. These battles were for possession of two major hill masses strategically located west of a remote airstrip and tiny base. The hills, numbered for their elevation in meters above sea level, were Hill 861 and Hill 881 South. There was another 881 slightly to the north, so to avoid confusion, the two were always referred to as 881N and 881S. These hills overlooked the airstrip and provided excellent observation to their west. The only thing west of Khe Sanh was a tiny outpost of Army Green Berets at Lang Vei, and then there was Laos and the Ho Chi Minh trail. Small as the Khe Sanh area was, it was a very strategic location and a lot of Marines died taking those hills from the NVA. That battle was to become known as the Hill Fights.

The Marines now owned this real estate. A company of infantry was placed on 861 and 881S and they began working like beavers to fortify them. Oddly, the NVA had barely threatened the main base even though it was the source of supplies supporting the Marines on the hills. Since most of the battalion that took the hills was now in residence on them, there were relatively few troops on the base. The brass must have felt that the location was going to become even more important, so the 26th Marines, currently in the Phu Bai tactical area of responsibility (TAOR), were being moved to Khe Sanh to reinforce. Since Bravo was the Recon company OpConned to 26th Marines, that meant we were moving with them. This move was supposed to take place in about a week, so there was much activity packing up the company office, supply, armory, and so on in preparation. Patrols were also suspended in order to allow teams already out in the bush to finish their patrols and get the company all back on base at the same time.

That patrol cycle was actually the reason why many members of the company didn't know and, in fact, never met many of the other Marines. There were three teams in each of four platoons and they were in constant rotation in order to keep at least half of the teams in the bush at any given time. Normally a patrol was expected to last five days. When the team returned to base, they had three to five days before they went out again. That "down time" was spent getting their gear ready for the next patrol, a little rest, keeping bunkers in repair and sometimes being sent out on working parties around the base as needed.

Waiting to move to our new home in the north, however, didn't mean we were lying about, smoking and joking. There were, as mentioned, the ever-present working parties, but during that week, some of us were tapped for Rough Rider escort duty. Rough Riders were convoys of anywhere from six to twenty supply trucks making deliveries to bases north of Phu Bai like Dong Ha and Con Thien. Phu Bai was Division HQ from whence all good things were distributed.

Two teams were usually parceled out among the trucks for security. We rode in the back of the open trucks and watched for any nasty little people who might come slithering out to steal our toilet paper or other luxuries. We had our rifles and wore helmets, flak jackets, and web gear (belt, ammo pouches, etc.) with canteens and ammunition. A very light load compared to a Recon patrol. The convoys were rarely attacked but it was a necessary precaution.

Remember I had mentioned how hot it was? For some inexplicable reason, I decided not to wear any socks this day. While bumping along in the truck, my trouser cuffs had shucked up a couple of inches above my boot tops. In about an hour, I thought fire ants were working on my legs. The sun had burned a bright red band around my legs just above the boots and it was painful! Luck was with me, though, because among those on my truck was the team corpsman, HN Charles "Doc" Miller. From his Unit One, Doc Miller produced a magical ointment that helped soothe the burn, but it was a few days before my skin resumed its normal pallid shade. Doc and I had become pretty good friends. He was a little skinny guy with glasses and when he laughed, it came out as a rather fiendish cackle.

This particular convoy was headed for Dong Ha. That's a little place not far below the DMZ (Demilitarized Zone) where Route 9 goes west from Route 1. All along Route 1, there are villages, hamlets and clusters of huts. Anytime we slowed down or stopped, our truck was immediately rushed by several ragged and half-naked kids holding out their hands for whatever they could get. When I say half-naked, I'm not kidding. It's quite common, especially in the more rural parts of Asia, that little kids are naked from the waist down until they are about three or four years old. I suppose it saves on diaper changing. These little mooches knew just enough English to say either, "Hey, G.I., gimme chop-chop" (food or, more likely, candy or gum), or "Hey, G.I., gimme chigarette for mama."

"No chigarette for baby-san. Chigarette numba ten!"

"Chigarette for mama. Chigarette numba one, G.I. numba one," they would insist.

The softhearted Yanks usually came prepared to banter and hand out goodies and the kids knew it. Whatever you might toss to them resulted in a spirited scrimmage and you had to be careful to toss things far enough away that they didn't wind up under the wheels of the six-by. If someone actually did throw a cigarette, the victor would immediately produce matches and sometimes even a Zippo and light up. I'm talking about five-year-old kids! Health issues aside, there is something very comical about a pint size Marlboro man strolling along "sans trou" with a Lucky Strike dangling from the side of his mouth.

Route 9 eventually winds its way to Khe Sanh and on into Laos. We rumbled into the base at Dong Ha, dismounted, and stretched our legs while the trucks went to their various destinations to offload. We had just remounted the trucks and were driving toward the front gate when there was a blast and we saw a column of smoke rising from an area about 75 yards away. The trucks slammed to a stop and we all bailed off looking for cover. After a moment, we looked over to where the explosion had been and noticed people casually walking around. Then someone nearby hollered to us that some engineers were blowing up a dud NVA mortar round that had landed the previous night. Who knew?

We got back to Phu Bai without further incident and continued with preparations to move north. The big day came and Bravo departed for Khe Sanh. I was a little surprised when the convoy of trucks we had loaded with the company property left without us. A couple of teams were assigned Rough Rider duty to the convoy but the majority of the company fell into formation after chow with just our web gear, helmets, flak jackets, and rifles. Were we going to hump all the way to Khe Sanh? I wasn't sure how far away it was but I knew based on the Rough Rider convoy to Dong Ha that it was many miles.

The C.O. turned the formation over to the Company Gunny, and we marched off in a column at route step. I was not looking forward to the torture to come. We left the old company area, now just an empty tent ghost town, and headed in the general direction of Route 1 somewhere in the distance outside the base. We arrived at Route 1 but instead of turning left (north), we crossed it and continued toward a number of hooches and Butler buildings. Sounds of helicopters whacking their way overhead became more noticeable. We soon found ourselves in front of a building with a sign that read something about "The Home of MAG" followed by a number. Be still, my heart! Could it be? Were we to be saved from some kind of death march?

We dropped our gear, stacked arms (a means by which three or more rifles could be placed in a tripod-like configuration so they didn't lie around on the ground to get dirty or stepped on), and waited for *the word*. Team leaders turned lists of their team's names over to the Gunny, who then turned them over to the C.O. These lists of names were the flight manifests, or sticks. We were going to fly up to Khe Sanh! Oh, joy! Oh, rapture! The zoomies had just become my favorite people.

After a bit, the Company Gunny came back and told us to grab our gear and form into a single file by sticks. We were led around the building and beheld a C-130 running up its engines on the taxi pad. The C-130 is a large four-engine prop-driven cargo plane. Officially known as a Hercules, they were also called Herkybirds. C-130s are capable of landing and taking off from surprisingly short runways. They are incredibly reliable, tough, and versatile, and are still much in use today.

We filed up the rear ramp and got seated. The seats were aluminum frames with nylon webbing, something like a lawn chair but much less comfortable. The seats ran down both sides with another row of seats back to back down the center. We stuffed as much of our gear as we could under the seats and then fastened our seat belts. With four engines running, the noise level was such that talking was difficult. The interior walls had no sound insulation. All the C-130 was meant to carry was cargo and Marines so who cared about insulation? I heard a whining noise and looked back to see the ramp closing. Immediately, the plane began to move. Only a few lucky ones could see out because there were only a couple of round windows on each side. We taxied for a few minutes and then stopped with a lurch. The engines revved up to take-off speed and the plane jumped forward. We bucketed along for only a few seconds and then popped into the air amid much thumping and banging of landing gear being retracted. We were off!

About a half hour later it was apparent that we were descending and as soon as the wheels touched the ground it felt like the plane was standing on its nose in order to come to a stop. Later flights on C-130s were the same no matter how long the runway was. That was just the way the Herkybirds came to earth.

We rolled to a stop and filed off the plane into a noticeably cooler and dryer, but still hot and humid, climate. While Phu Bai was situated at sea level, Khe Sanh was in the mountains. The plateau that the base and airstrip sat on was one of only a very few relatively flat pieces of terrain in this corner of South Vietnam. After counting noses and getting saddled up, we formed into platoons and route stepped down a dusty dirt road parallel to the airstrip. Around us were the usual hooches but more often we saw squad tents and a few other small, nondescript buildings. There was clothesline and comm wire strung everywhere between tents and from short poles running in every direction. Sandbag emplacements were near every building and tent. It had the general appearance of a refugee camp in a war torn central African country. The tallest structure on the base was what appeared to be a watchtower. It was probably 35 feet tall and had a little roof over the platform on top. I would learn more about that later that night.

A ten-minute stroll brought us to our new company area. There was a row of hooches along the road and on the other side of them was a row of squad tents. The Gunny saw to the assignment of hooches and tents and we began settling in. There were no cots or anything and even the company office was bare because we had to wait for the convoy to arrive. Route 1 allowed traffic of about 30 mph maximum, and Route 9 was even slower, so we knew it would be a few hours' wait.

Khe Sanh was surrounded by higher terrain, especially to the north. A massive ridgeline ran roughly west to east. On the western end was Hill 950, a sharp hump that stuck up all by itself. There was a Marine radio relay post on 950 defended by a few radio operators and a platoon or so of grunts. To the east and about midway along the ridge was a bigger, broader hump that was Hill 1015 and considered the main observation post of the NVA. In fact, except for Hill 950 the entire remainder of the ridge belonged to the NVA. What kept the NVA from rolling right over 950 was the fact that the south, west, and north sides of the ridge dropped off almost vertically while the only way in to the east side of the position was a ridge top trail only feet wide. Hill 950 was so pointed and small that there was very little room for a resupply chopper to land. There was a small landing zone (LZ) that a Huey or a 34 could squeeze into, but I doubt that a 46 would fit.

Beside each hooch or tent in our company area was a shallow ditch surrounded by sandbag walls about two feet high from ground level. We would use these bunkers in case of artillery, rocket, or mortar attack. Having no experience in that area, I didn't think much about it, but I noticed some of the old hands casting critical looks at them.

There was electricity at Khe Sanh, a luxury I didn't expect after seeing the place. Khe Sanh was a little, shall we say, rustic. There was one bare bulb hanging from the overhead and one outlet on each side wall. One novel thing was that the light was wired to a switch on the door so that when the door was opened, the light went off. This was so that minimal light escaped at night. Khe Sanh was a blackout base because any steady light at night could draw fire. In the tents, there was no solid door to attach a switch to so standing operating procedure (SOP) dictated that the door flap toward Hill 1015 was not to be opened at night unless there was an emergency. The other end of the tent was pretty well screened by many other buildings and tents across the base.

Later that afternoon, the convoy rolled in and we unloaded the trucks and made ourselves at home. All the officers lived in one hooch, all the staff NCOs in theirs and all the sergeants likewise. It was a tiny concession to their ranks and responsibilities. Corporals and below stayed with their team. The sergeants' area took up about two thirds of a hooch and the company supply occupied the remainder. There was a wall between the two sections, so that left only one entry-exit door to each part. It turned out that I was to stay with the team I had been with, which was in the second platoon under Lt. Pfeltz.

When it gets dark in Vietnam, it gets *dark*. The nearest civilization was the village of Khe Sanh, a couple of kilometers away. It was commonly called Khe Sanh Ville to differentiate it from the base, for which the official name was Khe Sanh Combat Base (KSCB). There was not much electricity in the Ville that I know of, so there was no glow of neon or any other light in the night sky except stars. It was just *dark*.

It was also very quiet. You could hear the occasional conversation hundreds of feet away. The quiet that night didn't last though, because about 1:00 A.M., a siren awakened us followed a brief moment later by a descending whistle. Any John Wayne fan knew that sound. It was something unpleasant falling out of the sky! The explosions sounded some distance away but in seconds, we had our boots on and, with little else, scrambled out and dove into the bunkers. It was terrifying and exhilarating at the same time. Somebody was actually shooting things at me and they were coming closer! After a few minutes of sporadic incoming, the rounds stopped. I don't think they hit nearer than a hundred yards to our area but it sure seemed closer. It turned out that these were mortars and I was to learn that each type of incoming round had a distinctive sound and that sound indicated how close to me they would drop.

The siren wailed again and people began emerging from bunkers and trenches. The siren had come from the watchtower I had seen that afternoon. It doesn't serve much of a purpose in the daytime but at night a sentry could often hear when something was launched at the base. The sentry would then crank the handle on a siren indicating incoming. When it appeared that the barrage was over, he would sound all clear. It didn't always work because sometimes the wind or rain would mask the sound of the launch. In the case of rockets and artillery, they were often fired from the far side of the 1015 ridge, or from the massive palisade to the southwest in Laos called Co Roc, and the sounds of firing were usually inaudible. A crude system, to be sure, but it was better than nothing.

Mortars and artillery whistled as they approached, while rockets shrieked. The longer you could hear the sounds they made, the farther away they would hit. A short whistle, or worse, no whistle at all, meant it was coming down close. That's probably where the old saying "You never hear the one that gets you" came from.

Someone said that the ever-watching NVA had probably seen a bunch of Marines come in on the C-130 and then the convoy arrived, so they decided to send us a little housewarming barrage. It made sense to me because anyone on 1015 with a set of binoculars had a great aerial view of the base.

I was too keyed up to sleep much for the rest of the night. I realized how vulnerable we were and it occurred even to me that the bunkers outside our tents were far less than adequate. Now I knew why the old hands had looked askance at them.

After breakfast, the company fell in for morning muster and Colors. Colors formalities are observed at 8:00 A.M. and sunset when Old Glory is hoisted or lowered from the flagpole. All personnel, wherever they are, stop and render appropriate salutes during this period. After Colors, the C.O. gathered us into a school circle. He said that he, and we, had learned a few things from last night's mortars. It was apparent to all that the bunkers we had were way too shallow and needed roofs over them. Reinforcing the bunkers would be our number two priority right after doing what we were there for ... reconnaissance. All hands not involved in preparing for patrols would be expected to fill sandbags. The engineers had been contacted and would be delivering pallets of empty sandbags and dump trucks of dirt to fill them with that morning. Another lesson learned, he said, was that immediately following any attack, the base SOP required a physical nose count to determine if anyone was missing. Not doing that could mean that someone might be lying somewhere wounded and unable to call for help.

The sandbags and dirt arrived shortly and we got busy. A couple of engineers stuck around to give us tips on how to build the bunkers to best deflect or absorb a hit and then we were left on our own.

7. Patrol Preparation

Just before noon, the word came down for all officers and NCOs to report to the C.O.'s office. We were informed that two choppers were waiting at the helo pad (where we had gotten off the C-130) to take us on an overflight. An overflight is a casual appearing flyover of the area your patrol was going into. It was only one chopper instead of the usual four or more, so it didn't look like anything tactical was going on. This was to get a good look at the terrain, compare it to your map, and select potential LZs. The vegetation on the ground did not always match the vegetation indicated on the map. Many of the maps we had were years old and even had notations in French. An LZ had to be big enough and clear enough to land at least one helicopter in, so the overflight pilots sometimes advised the patrol leader in picking them.

This overflight was not for a patrol, though. This one was a general overflight for all the potential patrol leaders to get a good look at the Khe Sanh area. We grabbed rifles and web gear and straggled to the helo pad. There were two CH-46s sitting on the pad and as we approached, the rotors began slowly turning. In seconds, they were a blur and creating a terrific down blast of hot air and JP-4 fumes. The exhaust from the chopper's turbines is searing and not meant for humans to breathe. The rear ramps were down and we filed inside. Even sitting still, there was a fair amount of vibration. As the pilot began to lift off, the vibration became worse. I looked around and no one seemed concerned at all. As in the C-130, there was so much engine noise it was difficult to converse. Directly above our heads were two 1500 horsepower turbine engines.

Just behind the cockpit were the crew chief and a gunner. Each of them manned a .50 caliber machine gun that was mounted in a doorway on the right and a window on the left. As soon as we were airborne, they were both very intently watching the ground. Khe Sanh is small enough so that anything in the air above the base is still well within range of enemy heavy machine guns outside the perimeter. The barbed wire, concertina, and other obstacles extended outside the trench lines surrounding the base by about 50 meters.

The vegetation had been cleared away for about another 100 meters past that but it still left the whole rest of northwest South Vietnam for the bad guys to hide in.

As we gained altitude we could see down on hill 881S. The top was dotted with bunkers, lean-to's and other crude shelters, and I could see trenches and bunkers encircling the summit. The rest of the hill was an ugly, naked, twisted mass of burned and blasted trees and craters. Mountains that we could not see from the base came into view. Some of them were enormous and the peaks of a few of them disappeared into the clouds. The countryside surrounding the base was pockmarked with hundreds if not thousands of various sized craters caused by artillery and mortars from the NVA and us. I could see the Ville, a cluster of small, nondescript structures straddling Route 9. Closer to the base were a few small groups of huts indicating Bru settlements. There did not appear to be any rice paddies. Most of the area was too mountainous or irregular and the climate did not lend itself to that type of agriculture. Beyond that was green jungle and expanses of elephant grass as

Khe Sanh terrain with bomb craters.

Hill 950 to the left and Hill 1015 at the center. The lighter color is elephant grass 3 to 8 feet high (courtesy 1st Lt. Fisher).

far as the eye could see and it was all owned by the NVA. I began to feel very small.

When we got back to the company area, some of the patrol leaders were summoned to the company office. They were going on patrol tomorrow and needed to make preparations. The team I was in would probably go out in about three days and Lt. Pfeltz said I should go with one of the team leaders who were going tomorrow and start learning what I would need to know soon.

Sergeant Bill Blum was a team leader in another platoon and he took me along with him to the office. I had a notebook with me so I could take notes on what I saw. First, Capt. Hudson gave each team leader in turn his warning order. The warning order can be as simple as "You're going on a patrol tomorrow to grid squares such and such to see if there is any enemy activity." Military maps are gridded off into 1000-meter squares. Each square has a four-digit number unique unto itself. Each grid square is then broken down by eye into 100 10-meter blocks, each with a number. With experience, you can find a spot on the ground accurate to within 10 meters on the map. A normal patrol zone consists of six adjacent grid squares, which translates to an area of six square kilometers. "Report to the S-2 at C.O.C. right away for your briefing," said the captain. "The Gunny will show you where it is."

Blum sent his APL back to the team tent to let them know to start preparing for a patrol. We followed the Gunny to the Combat Operations Center, which turned out to be just up the road from the company area. We were approaching a cleared area near the base of the watchtower among the hooches and all I could see was what appeared to be a cluster of various types of antennae sticking up from the ground. Then right in front of me, someone popped up out of the ground. Now I could see a hole about four by eight feet and a steel stairway going down into darkness. We were going underground.

We descended about 10 feet into a concrete structure that had narrow corridors and small rooms branching off in all directions. I never did see how large it was. The ceiling was a bit short here and there so I had to stoop a bit. There were no doors but the entrance to some areas had a curtain that could be closed if needed. The rumor was that it was an underground command center built by the French in the 1950s. Later I found out it was built by U.S. Army Special Forces in the early 1960s.

There were no luxuries but there were basic military furnishings and electricity for lights and radios. The largest room was full of activity and each team leader was directed to a different area for briefing. There was, in fact, no particular order involved as long as you went to them all.

Besides S-2, there was artillery liaison, air liaison, and communications all working in the same room. This might seem a bit chaotic but it meant that when the need arose, everybody concerned was getting the same information at the same time and support or comm efforts could be coordinated quickly.

Blum and I went to the S-2 first. There was a wooden frame several feet square on the wall on which was fastened a map covered by clear plastic. The map covered an area around Khe Sanh that would have qualified as a county at home with the Khe Sanh Combat Base at the center. The plastic had arrows and other geometric shapes as well as cryptic notations in grease pencil all over it. Its purpose was to plot the location of every friendly unit and enemy activity (suspected or confirmed), and it was updated as necessary around the clock.

The S-2 lieutenant asked Blum's patrol call sign and I think it was *Primness*. He checked it against a clipboard and, pointing at the map, said, "Here's your RZ [Recon Zone]. The terrain is mountainous and mostly jungle covered but with patches of elephant grass here and there. The map shows two streams, and there have been no recent sightings by Recon patrols. Two other teams will be in RZs such and such but there will be no other friendlies anywhere near your area." That, quite often, was all the 2-shop knew about an area. Finding out more was our job.

Then we went over to arty (artillery) where Blum picked four coordinates on his map that looked like possible LZs. He gave the coordinates to the arty officer, who assigned a registration number (for example R123) to each position, plotted them with a grease pencil on the big arty map, and then relayed them by field phone over to the artillery battery on base to make calculations in advance. This is so that if a patrol gets in trouble near one of those registration numbers, they can call it in and request a fire mission. The battery will already have made the calculations and it takes only a few minutes for the cannon cockers to set the fuses on the rounds, move the guns into position, and fire. The guns can also use that info to shoot (at the team leader's option), prep-fires on potential LZs in case there just happens to be an NVA unit there.

The NVA were known to have counter-recon patrols whose specific job was to find us. They would occasionally stake out likely LZs after seeing choppers conducting overflights on the off chance that a recon team would be coming sometime soon. At other times, we just plain got unlucky and landed on the bad guys' toes. In addition, each night as the team sets in to their harborsite, the team leader will pick several places on the map, such as known trails, and any other likely avenues of approach to the harborsite, radio those coordinates back to base and arty would assign registration numbers to them. During the night, arty would fire occasional H&I (harassment and interdiction) fires and, if the harborsite were threatened, they would be reference points from which to adjust fire on the enemy.

Next was air liaison. The patrol was not going out until the next morning but Blum still had to arrange for an overflight. (If he had known about the patrol earlier, he probably could have had it included in the group overflight we had just taken. Oh well.) The zoomie officer had him scheduled for a 4:00 P.M. overflight today and tomorrow's insertion would be at 9:00 A.M. give or take an hour (or so). The wingers had a more relaxed sense of the passage of time. On the other hand, when it got nasty they busted their butts to support us. We also got the call signs for helicopter gunship and fixed wing support if needed. Gunships are helicopters; usually UH-1C/Ds ... Hueys. They look like a cross between a Volkswagen Beetle and a dragonfly bristling with machine guns and rocket pods. UH-1Es, also called Hueys (a Huey was a Huey to us), were known as slicks because they were without weapons and used for moving troops or medevacs. The gunship's only job is overhead protection of ground units. Fixed wing is any airplane other than a helicopter. They were usually fighter-bomber jets like the F-4 Phantom and were used for close air support like the gunships but bigger, louder, faster, and nastier.

We moved on to communications. There, we got the brevity code, shackle code, and radio frequencies. There were two frequencies, one primary and one secondary. In case the primary was unusable due to bad weather, our location, or for security reasons, we could change to the secondary and hope for better results. If other frequencies were necessary, they could be sent to us using the shackle code. This was a code used normally to transmit numerical information that you didn't want the bad guys to know about. It was based on a ten-letter word with no repeated letters. Below the letters were the numbers 0 through 9 in any order. Of course, both the sender and receiver had to have the same combinations. Oddly enough, the only example I can remember is...

FORNICATES

1 2 3 4 5 6 7 8 9 0

So, if I were given Romeo, Tango, Foxtrot, Charlie, over the radio I would know that the new frequency was to be 38.16. Frequencies on the AN/PRC25 radio were always two numbers followed by a decimal point, followed by two more numbers. Indicating the decimal point in code was unnecessary. I could do the same with map coordinates or any other number. The radioman on the base would say, "*Primness*, (Blum's patrol call sign) change freq to shackle November, India, Oscar, Oscar." Blum's radioman would acknowledge, make the change and then immediately call the base on the new frequency to confirm that he got it right and the frequency was working. If not, the base would continue to monitor the original frequency and give Blum another set of numbers until reliable comm was established.

Another version of shackle code was sort of the reverse of the 10-letter type. It looked like:

1 2 3 4 5 6 7 8 9 0

A B C D E F G H I J

K L M N O P Q R S T

U V W X Y Z

The letters could be in any order but, again, both ends of the conversation had to have the same set of codes in order to communicate. If I said Whiskey, Mike, or Charlie, they would all mean the number three. Conversely, I could spell out simple messages, for instance, GO FISH, by saying 7, 5, 6, 9, 0, 8. I would read down each column until I made words that made sense. Obviously, this code does not apply well to emergencies.

The brevity code wasn't necessarily very sophisticated. It was designed to confuse anyone eavesdropping but its main purpose was to keep messages short. Any time you needed to send a message of more than about fifteen seconds, you would stop transmitting, even if it was mid-sentence, and then resume transmitting after a pause of a second or two. The operator at the other end knew you weren't through talking until you said, "Over." This pause was done in order to defeat an enemy RDF (radio direction finder). An RDF is an electronic device that can detect a radio signal and indicate what direction it came from. Two or more RDFs can triangulate and pinpoint the location of a radio transmitter. The longer you transmit, the better the chance that a RDF can home in on you.

A typical brevity code was as follows:

Moving = any dog	Stopping = any State
North = Packers	South = Cowboys
East = Giants	West = Raiders
Helicopter = Mixmaster	Enemy = black hat
Smoke = any cigarette	Observation post = glass

A message saying "We are now Poodle, Packers, Raiders, and will Utah at Romeo, Charlie, Alpha, Tango, Sierra, Sierra to Glass, Black Hat, Lucky Strike" would mean, "We are moving northwest and will stop at [coordinates] 367800 to check out some enemy smoke." Smoke from cooking fires drifting up through the trees often gave away NVA camps. "We are Chihuahua, Packers, Raiders, and will Arizona at Mike, Foxtrot, Zulu, Romeo, Juliet, Tango, to Glass, Black Hat, Marlboro" would mean exactly the same thing. After a while, it became a second language. Brevity codes had 30 or more key words in them and were changed about every month or so.

One other means of encoding was to use the Tango Lima, or TL. This was short for thrust line. I'm not sure where the thrust part comes from but that's what it meant. S-2 would pick a grid intersection in your RZ as the TL. Each grid square can be divided into 10-meter square subdivisions, so if I wanted to indicate a point on the ground without going through the shackle code I would say, "From Tango Lima, right two decimal one, down decimal six." That meant the indicated spot was, from the TL, 2100 meters to the east and south 600 meters. Since the enemy didn't know where my TL was, they would not be able to decipher the location I gave unless they could see me. They have maps, too. Camouflage discipline at all times!

The patrol leader carried these codes on paper because there's too much room for mistakes if he tried to memorize them. For that reason, as part of the patrol order, he made sure everyone knew that the codes were in his top right pocket, for instance, so that if he went down, someone could grab those codes to use them or, at the very least, keep them out of enemy hands. Of course, if the codes were lost, the 2-shop would conjure up new sets quickly. If that happened, though, things had probably reached such a level of unpleasantness that codes were out the window and transmissions were in the clear. In other words, no longer coded ... spoken in plain, blunt English.

8. Settling In and Environment

We now had all we needed from C.O.C. and headed back to the sergeant's hooch. Blum's APL had already gone to supply to draw chow for the patrol. We carried C-rations on patrol and each meal came in a little box. Inside were three or more tin cans of various sizes containing an assortment of food-like material. The C-rats were bulky and heavy so we discarded the boxes and packing materials and saved only what we needed. Each man generally carried two meals a day (except for the real chowhounds but if you want it, you carry it), even though we were provided at least three. This again was to cut down weight. When I detail the load we carried, you'll see why that was important.

The team's two radiomen reported to the Bravo Company comm chief, Sgt. Del Weidler, to draw their radios and spare batteries. The AN/PRC-25 radios — Army Navy/Portable Radio Communications (model 25) is a backpack radio that was the workhorse of infantry communications. It weighed about 20 pounds with a battery and accessories. It didn't have the longest range and was affected by mountainous terrain and weather, but it worked fairly well most of the time. Batteries for the AN/PRC25 radio came in the shape of a block of 18 dry cells wired together and encased in wax to produce 15 volts of power. They were heavy and nobody liked to carry them. When the battery wore down, we would break them apart and bury the pieces in several locations. A drawn down, but intact, battery block still contained enough voltage to trigger command detonated booby traps if the gooks found them.

While that was being done, Blum prepared his patrol order. The Marine Corps has an acronym for everything and the patrol order, officially known as the Five Paragraph Order, is shortened to SMEAC. That stands for Situation, Mission, Execution, Administration and logistics, and Command and signal. Situation also covers three subparagraphs called HAS — Higher, Adjacent, and Supporting units. A typical five-paragraph order that I would write up to brief the team would be:

Situation: There have been no recent enemy sightings in the area and S-2 wants to know if there are any signs of new or recent activity.

Higher: We will report any findings by radio to regimental C.O.C.

Adjacent: Team Ridgerunner will be in RZ such and such. Team Broadweave Two will be in RZ so and so. No other friendlies will be closer than seven klicks to us.

Supporting: Artillery support from either Alpha or Charlie battery of the 13th Marines' 105 mm howitzers, gunships and fixed wing as needed.

Mission: Conduct reconnaissance and surveillance in assigned area to determine nature and extent of enemy activity. Be especially watchful for (trails, old or new campsites, etc.) Utilize supporting arms for the destruction of enemy forces and installations. (This was typical wording for almost every patrol mission.)

Execution: We will be inserted by helicopter at map coordinates 169568 at 0900 tomorrow. We'll cover as much of the area as possible on foot or by using OPs. We will engage targets of opportunity as deemed necessary.

Administration and logistics: Smith and Jones will carry the primary and secondary radios respectively. Smith is normally with Team Beekeeper but he's taking Brown's place while Brown is on R&R. (We often traded team members around to fill in for people on sick call, or on orders for training, etc.) The Doc will have his Unit One, and he has your medevac numbers. The codes and patrol leader's notebook (the patrol leader takes detailed notes throughout the patrol including date, time and coordinates of all sightings or non–sightings. After the patrol he refers to them while being debriefed by S-2), will be in my upper right pocket and the maps will be in my right trouser cargo pocket. I will also have the 7 × 50 binoculars. You will all have your Geneva Convention cards[i] and dog tags. I will be third from the front followed by the primary radio and the APL will be third from the rear followed by the secondary radio. Doc will be behind the primary radio. The APL has distributed chow for five days and we will leave the base with six full canteens each and replenish with natural sources as needed. In addition to water, each of you will carry your M-16, 600 rounds of ammo with at least half of that being in magazines, six fragmentation grenades, 1 CS (tear gas) grenade, gas mask, and Ka-Bar or bayonet. The APL will take a couple of men to the armory and draw out and then spreadload the following items throughout the team:

4 Claymore mines

4 sticks of C-4

Blasting caps

Det cord

2 LAAW rockets

1 M-79 grenade launcher and 50 rounds of 40mm ammo

2 each of red, yellow, green and purple smoke grenades

3 pop flares (An aluminum tube about a foot long that launched a variety of illumination or colored flares a couple hundred feet into the air. The colored flares were generally used as signals and the illumination flares had a small parachute on them to slow their descent.)

2 Willie Peter frags

1 Starlight scope

(Plus any additional special equipment required for a specific task).

Command and signal: The chain of command is myself, the APL (and so on down the line). The primary radio will be on frequency 56.98 and the secondary will be on 77.20. The Recon radio relay point on Hill 950 is Rainbelt Bravo. There will be an inspection at 0815 tomorrow morning. (Patrol inspections were not for seeing if you have polished brass and sharp creases. They are necessary to insure that each man has all the equipment he is supposed to have and that everybody knows the mission.) Any questions?

It was so mountainous around Khe Sanh that without that relay team we would have had almost no radio comm. The PRC-25 is primarily a line-of-sight transceiver. Rainbelt Bravo relayed every transmission to and from teams in the bush and the C.O.C. This added a few seconds to transmissions but it worked 95 percent of the time and sure beat the alternative.

It was getting close to Blum's overflight time so while the team busied itself with preparations, he headed for the helo pad. I sat and studied the notes I had taken and wondered if I could get this all straight. We had gone over the basics of patrol prep at Recon School but this was real, practical application and it was somewhat bewildering.

Dear Dad,

I got your letter today that was mailed May 12th. We are at Khe Sanh.... I don't know if it's shown on the map you have. While at Phu Bai I went on a few patrols. On your map find Hue (pronounced Way) right next to Phu Bai. The patrols we ran were to the N.W. of Hue about 2 or 3 miles.

Where we are now is really on the front lines. Remember the fight they had for hill 881 & 861? Well we can see 881 from here and there are gooks in the hills all around the area. At Phu Bai we were against the freshmen, up here we're against the varsity. The gooks they were fighting at Phu Bai were the black pajama gang. Up here they are hard core NVA or north Vietnamese Army.

I may be running my own patrols very soon now. There is a radio relay station on a mountain top just a few thousand meters away. A couple of minutes ago I heard firing up there then a flare went off and then I could see tracers going back and forth. It's about stopped now but I still hear an occasional shot....

As far as the M-16 goes, mine has never jammed on me and I've fired almost 400 rounds through it [at this point it was all famfire — familiarization fire — on a crude rifle range at Phu Bai so I could get the sights adjusted and just get used to how it functioned].

The people that say it jams because we don't keep them clean is talking thru his hat. [We kept them clean.] Of course they require more care than the M14 or M1 but it's also because the bores have a tendency to pit easily, it feeds too fast sometimes which results in a double feeding and there has also been a lot of trouble with the extractors not keeping a grip on the cartridge so it doesn't eject....

Well I guess that's about it for now.

Steve[2]

I recall that soon after arriving at Khe Sanh we were all issued the new, improved M-16A1. We still called them M-16s though. It wasn't as if you didn't add A1, people didn't know what you were talking about. It was eventually determined that the original M-16 had a lot of manufacturer's defects. To remedy the pitting problem the A1s had certain internal parts chrome plated so the corrosive burnt powder would not build up. There was a major problem with defective ammunition then, too. If a bullet doesn't have enough powder in it, there isn't enough gas energy generated to make the rifle function correctly. A lot of guys died trying to fire useless weapons and not one politician or arms maker went to jail.

I think I should give you a description of the area immediately surrounding our company position. Imaging the face of a clock lying on the ground with twelve at the northern position and six to the south. You are standing at the center of the clock on the dirt road that runs from 9:00 to 3:00. Facing north, or twelve o'clock, and starting at about eight o'clock (to my left rear) is the regimental command post with its underground combat operations center. Near it is the watchtower that is manned at night, mainly to listen for the "thoonk" of a mortar, or the deeper "boom" of artillery being fired at us from the hills. Rockets were harder to hear but if it was very still they made a sharp "Sssssh" when they were launched and sometimes at night you could see the flame of the afterburner. Rockets, especially, move very fast and the screaming noise they make is a real motivator to find a hole to crawl into.

To the left and straight down the road that you are standing on which runs from nine o'clock to three o'clock is the mess tent, Charlie Med, and the helicopter taxi area where we boarded choppers for our patrols. Across the road at ten o'clock and a bit closer to me is the tiny PX that never had much in it and next to the PX is the equally tiny post office. Moving from ten o'clock across to about two o'clock is our company office followed by the two rows of hooches and squad tents that house Bravo Company. The last hooch down to the right in the row next to the road is where the sergeants lived. They have two-thirds of the hooch and company supply has the rest. The next area down is the 1/26 C.O.C.

Crossing the road and coming around to four o'clock is the shower tent. A crude affair, but better than nothing. It consisted of a large, green canvas tent about 40 feet long and 20 feet wide. Inside there was a framework of 2-inch steel pipe supported at a height of about eight feet. There were holes drilled on the underside of the pipes at intervals of about four feet. Water was pumped into this grid from outside and then gravity caused the water to dribble out of the holes onto the grubby Marine standing below each hole. There was no control over the water temperature. That was up to the bored snuffy outside who ran the pump. The water temperature varied from scalding to I-didn't-know-water-that-cold-could-flow! Wooden pallets formed the floor so we were up out of the mud. Scrubbing off several days of grime and ground-in cammie stick could take quite a while under that anemic trickle of water.

Going to the shower tent during the monsoon was always an adventure. There were two ways to do it. One was to go more or less fully dressed in the filthy utilities you had worn for days on patrol. The problem was that after you got squeaky clean from your shower you had to wear the same foul rags back to the hooch unless you brought a clean uniform with you. If you did, the rain hammered down so hard that your clean, dry utilities were soaked and mud splattered by the time you got back to the hooch. Raincoats were nonexistent and most ponchos were full of holes and offered only minimal protection.

The other way to go to the shower tent was the common sense way. Usually we just put a towel around our waist, stepped into our shower shoes and strolled across the road. We would arrive drenched and shivering from the cold. Some, to keep their towel dry, just rolled it up under their arm and walked over in their skivvies. There was absolutely no need for modesty. The best part was in returning to the hooch. Wet shower shoes are slippery and there was mud everywhere. Watching people exit the shower tent was almost a spectator sport because a large number of clean people wound up prone in the mud and rain when they slid out of their shower shoes. Of course, that meant another shower. Sometimes in the monsoon it rained so hard, we just stepped out of the hooch and took a "natural" shower on a wooden pallet placed by the washstand.

Behind you, from four o'clock to eight, are mostly just supply and admin facilities. There was quite a bit more to the base than that, but it's about all I ever saw. We were off base on patrols so much that when we were here, the time was spent maintaining bunkers and equipment and preparing for the next patrol.

9. Lizards and Leeches and Bugs ... Oh, My!

Flora and fauna are what make ecosystems tick. During one Khe Sanh area patrol, we had moved up into some low hills where it was heavily forested. I have mentioned before how it seemed that everything in Vietnam bit, stung, stabbed, or cut. One of the most annoying bits of flora I found was the "wait a minute" vine. They grew up and down from every direction. I don't think I ever actually saw the source of one of them. I'll describe them as best I can. Imagine the vine part as being green (duh) and varying from one-eighth to three-eighths of an inch in diameter and very flexible. About every eight inches was a set of thorns. They were arranged around the vine in sets of three, like a fisherman's treble hook, and they pointed backwards. Each thorn was about the size and shape of a cat's claw and just as sharp. As you move through the bush, these things snag anything they touch and you would finally have so many of them hooked to you that your forward progress would stop dead. You had to back up a bit and unhook each and every thorn (hence, wait a minute). The thorns never broke off the vine and if they hooked bare skin, they would sink in like a fishhook.

When we stopped for a harborsite one night, I noticed a rather exotic looking fungus growing nearby. It was ivory colored and had a mushroom-like stalk several inches tall. The cap was perforated like lacework and draped down around the stalk almost to the ground. I had never seen anything like this so of course I poked it with a twig. The next thing I knew, I was repelled by the foulest odor you can imagine. It almost brought tears to my eyes. I retreated a few feet and the smell eventually went away. One of the guys asked what I was doing so I explained. He went over to the mushroom, picked up a twig and said, "Did you poke it like this?" After he got through gagging, nobody else was curious about the mushroom.

Do you like animals? Little fuzzy, cuddly critters that climb in your lap, or lay on their backs for a tummy rub? Well, I didn't see any. Okay, I saw two. Make that one and a half. Both of them were in Quang Tri later on in my tour when I was in Echo Company. The one was a Vietnamese puppy that wandered into the company area and nobody knew where it came from. He was a little brown thing with a curly tail and he loved the attention we gave him. He was fed the finest C-rats available plus the occasional bite of fruitcake from home. He was around for about a week and then he just wasn't there anymore. I prefer to think he moved in with the "in the rear with the gear" headquarters people. They lived better than we did, anyway.

The one half-cuddly fuzzy critter was Stormy. He was a large, lean German Shepherd scout dog that was attached to Echo. He was not necessarily attack trained but you still didn't go too near him if his handler wasn't around. He had a big, toothy "smile" and a couple people got nipped when they ignored his warning. Before a patrol, the handler would walk him around the team. The theory, I guess, was that once we got in the bush, if he smelled anything that didn't smell like Marines, he'd bite it. He even had his own personal bunker. I never went on a patrol with Stormy so I can't say how effective he was, but I heard from some of the guys who did and their complaint was that they had to carry extra water and dog food for Stormy. An extra canteen or a couple of cans of Alpo doesn't weigh all that much but after days of humping those hills, every extra ounce felt like a pound. Stormy didn't have any 782 gear so he couldn't carry it and the handler couldn't carry all that was needed.

The biggest spider I saw was hanging in the center if its web and I almost walked right into it. It was a dark day under a high triple canopy and I didn't really see the web until I was within a couple feet of it. It was at eye level with me and probably three feet in diameter. The spider was in the center hanging head down. Its body was long rather than bulbous ... about the size of my index finger, and was black and bright yellow. We gave it a wide berth and went on our way.

Another patrol found us in an area west of Quang Tri that was commonly called the "back yard." That's because there were vast expanses of only two to five foot elephant grass. Here and there were copses of trees and there were also large forested areas, but a lot of the back yard was wide open and dangerous to cross in the daytime. Therefore, we often moved at night with the aid of a Starlight scope. The point man carried the Starlight and he would scan the area in front of him, move, maybe 50 feet, and scan again. Depending on how dark it was to the rest of us, we would each actually hang on to the pack of the man in front of us.

While slowly traversing a small rise between tree groves, I, and some others became aware of an occasional scuffing sound or the crack of a twig being broken. It was consistently to our right rear and seemed to stop when

Top: Me with the puppy that we had for about a week at Quang Tri. *Bottom:* Stormy in his bunker at Quang Tri.

we stopped. A common tactic when following someone is to move when they move so their sounds mask yours. I was concerned because whoever was there wasn't being very careful. If the bad guys don't care if you know they are there, that means they think either they are in the superior position, or they're too stupid to live long.

I stopped the team and whispered to everyone to get flat on the ground because, even though it was very dark, we were exposed. I crawled up to the point man and took the Starlight. Just as I scanned to the area I'd heard the sounds from, something moved and my heart stopped for a second. I couldn't believe my eyes. There, standing at the edge of the tree line about 75 meters away was what appeared to be an elk! It was much larger than a deer, weighing probably 300 pounds or more. Moreover, it had, in my opinion, a real set of trophy antlers. It looked right at us several times and didn't seem unnerved by our presence at all.

I passed the Starlight down the line so everybody could have a look. Years later, I did some library research, found that the animal is native to eastern Asia, and was most commonly called an Asian wapiti. In other words, an elk. The 1/26 chaplain, Navy LCDR Ray Stubbe, suggested to me in a recent telephone conversation that this animal might have been a kouprey, as he knew of an instance where a Marine captain was pinned against a tree by a kouprey. I did a little research and found that the kouprey is native to Asia but is an ox-like animal with a single, thick, forward pointing horn on each side of the head ... more like a water buffalo. The animal we saw clearly had tall, multi-tined antlers much like a mule deer. Further, the kouprey is diurnal and our critter was obviously very comfortable in the dark.

Maybe this was a previously unknown species. Too bad I could not have gotten a picture of it. Just think; zoology books might now contain a description of *johnsonicus scarethefudgeottaus.*

It seemed to be content to mosey along as we moved. I guess when NVA elk get bored they find a recon patrol to sneak up on. It was getting on towards 0300 by then so I began giving thought to a harborsite for the rest of the night. After crossing the rise, we came to a dense thicket at the edge of the tree line. The location gave a good view (with the Starlight) of the area we had come from and the bush gave us good concealment. I called in arty registrations but didn't bother with Claymores. I wanted to keep our moving around to the minimum and it would be light in just a few hours. We set up watches and rolled up in our blankies.

I woke up at first light to a lot of bird noises. That's good because birds clam up if they are disturbed. I was lying on my back and my left arm was across my chest. I gave myself a minute or so and then moved my arm to sit up. ZAP!! It felt like lightning had struck the underside of my wrist! I looked down and there was a scorpion about four inches long sitting on my shirt with his claws and tail up in the air. It must have been partially under my wrist when I moved. My corpsman on that patrol, HM2 Sid Rosser, saw it at the same time and flicked it off of me with his Ka-Bar. He then had to smash it several times with a rock to kill it. Those things die hard!

My arm was instantly on fire and the pain was spreading up to my elbow. The Doc said there was not much he could do, and he was concerned because the sting site was right on top of the blood veins in my wrist. That's probably why the pain spread so fast. Within minutes, it was up to my shoulder. Doc told me it would continue to be painful but he didn't think I'd die right away.

Any movement caused a burning sensation and my whole arm began swelling up. We had to get moving so Doc Rosser put my arm in a sling to support it. He then gave me two aspirin and as he did so, I looked him right in the eye and said, "If you tell me to call you in the morning, I'll shoot you!" The sling did not hinder me too much because my hand wasn't terribly affected and, the back yard, wherever there was canopy, wasn't jungle. It was more like tropical forest and pretty easy to move through. I figured if I had to use my rifle, I'd overcome the pain in my arm.

Somebody asked if I should be medevacked but Doc said we should just keep an eye on it. I agreed with that because a medevac would probably be more trouble than it was worth. My arm felt like raw meat for the rest of the day but within 24 hours it was almost back to normal.

Lt. Pfeltz took a two-team patrol out to the northeast of Khe Sanh. Due to the terrain in the Khe Sanh area, communications could often be a problem. This patrol involved leaving one team at a specific high elevation location to act as a radio relay for the other team, who would continue the patrol farther away from the base. We had about 18 Marines on this one and it was the biggest patrol I ever went on. I was the APL to Lt. Pfeltz. We had been humping along a ridge under 100-foot canopy and it was hot work. The lieutenant called a break so we all flopped down in patrol order. Lt. Pfeltz was to my left and the radioman, L/Cpl. Garry Tallent, was to the lieutenant's left.

As we lay back on our packs we heard some noise above us and noticed a troop of rock apes swinging through the treetops directly above us. Rock ape was a generic label we applied to every type of monkey. Most of the monkeys we saw were gibbon-like animals. These were VC ... Varmint Cong! They saw us at about the same time and they all stopped and hung by one hand. We studied them and they studied us. A few seconds later, I heard Lt. Pfeltz softly cursing. I looked at him and he had a streak of monkey poo on his left shoulder. Tallent, with his customary big grin on his face whispered, "That's the first time I ever saw an officer get shit on."

Those of us in the proximity of the lieutenant were doubled up trying not to laugh out loud. Lt. Pfeltz was not especially amused. When we resumed the patrol, the lieutenant put Tallent on the point. After about thirty minutes, he put the regular point man out front again.

Most of my encounters with fauna seemed to occur while on a break. One interesting incident was when I noticed a little tree, hardly more than a stalk that was growing straight up for about three feet. It was covered with what looked like small white flower petals but the petals were slowly moving. I moved a little closer and the petals erupted into hundreds of little butterflies or moths with wingspans of only about an inch. They fluttered around in a cloud above the stick for a minute and then they all settled back onto it again. I could not tell if they were getting some kind of nourishment from that plant but they were definitely there for a purpose.

West of Phu Bai, when I was still an observer, I was the next to last on a patrol. Tail End Charlie was from the New York City area and sounded like it. We were moving through a fairly open area and approaching a thicket of taller elephant grass. The first couple of guys got through it but the next few began jumping around and flapping their arms. It was a bunch of those NVA bees! They were really more like hornets or wasps that they had stirred up and were big, aggressive, and black and yellow. Everyone else had hurriedly gotten through them leaving Noo Yawk and me looking at the very ticked off swarm that was buzzing around in front of us. Noo Yawk turned to me and whispered, "If we buzz loik bees, dey won't bodder us." I looked at him for a second and realized he was serious. Then I thought there was not much to lose because we had to catch up and I didn't see a way around them.

We both began quietly saying, "Bzzzz, buzz, brrr." And, if I'm lying, I'm dying ... we went slowly through that swarm and didn't get stung once!

There is a very large, tall tree with a rather smooth bark that is, I believe, a member of the Kapok family. The roots start growing away from the trunk like buttresses anywhere from five feet off the ground to over ten feet but they extend solidly all the way to ground level before disappearing. Each tree had five to six of these walls, partitions if you will, around the base of the tree. I suppose they helped support the trunk that, in most cases, I would estimate at six to eight feet in diameter. These compartments were big enough so that sometimes if we took a break under one of these trees, we could each settle into our own little alcove for a few minutes.

We had been under an enormous canopy for a full day and I was navigating by dead reckoning. If you carefully observe the terrain as you move, you can compare the contours on the map to what you see on the ground fairly well. However, there's nothing like an azimuth or two to pinpoint your little piece of real estate. An azimuth is simply a compass heading toward, or from, an objective or target.

I asked for a volunteer to climb a tree, look out of the top, and take a bearing on a distinctive terrain feature. The branches of these trees will support someone right to the very top. One of my little green monkeys said he'd do it, I gave him my compass, he dropped his gear, and up he went. He was gone for at least 15 minutes when suddenly we heard a muffled shout and moments later, he came half climbing, half falling, down the tree. He got to the ground and sat down and covered his face with his hands saying, "Oh jeez, oh jeez, oh jeez!"

I shook him and asked what was wrong. He began to calm down and as he looked at me, he started giggling in embarrassment but he muffled it behind his hand. He explained, "It was a long climb but there were lots of branches so it was going okay. I got to the very top and as I poked my head up out of the leaves, I was almost hit by the biggest, ugliest bird I've ever seen! It looked sort of like a very big owl with a flat face and it was flying right on the treetops. When I popped up, it was coming straight at me and went 'Awwrrk, awwrrk,' and it scared the hell out of me! I couldn't get down the tree fast enough." I didn't even ask him if he took an azimuth.

Well into the monsoon season, probably around late November, my team, Broadweave Two, was on patrol northeast of Khe Sanh. In 24-hour rain, it was impossible to stay dry. Wearing ponchos would make your gear hard to get at and they were noisy moving through heavy vegetation. I doubt if the temperature ever got much below 50 degrees, but it felt a lot colder when we were soaked to the skin all the time.

Due to difficult terrain and weather, I was alternating point duties among the regular point man, the secondary point, and myself. I had just taken over the lead in approaching dusk and began looking for a good harborsite. Moving around a large bush, I suddenly came nose to nose with an NVA. An NVA lizard, that is! Right out at the end of a tree branch and about six inches away at eye level, it almost made me jump out of my skin.

Despite my presence, it didn't run away. In the cold, and being a reptile, it remained on the branch. It looked sort of like an iguana about 18 inches long. I carefully pried its feet away from the branch and pondered on what to do with it. I mean, I had to do something, didn't I?

A good spot for a harborsite was nearby, so we settled in for the night. I carefully curled the lizard into a ball and tucked it into my 7 × 50 binocular case. After setting out Claymores and giving nighttime artillery registrations to Rainbelt Bravo, I made a sort of closed basket cage out of sticks and vines and put the lizard inside.

After an uneventful night, we prepared for extraction from the LZ about 300 meters away. We could see the base at Khe Sanh but a deep river gorge in our path meant it would have taken the better part of a day to hump back so we happily sat in the rain and mud to wait for choppers. When the CH-34s came, I popped a smoke and as they landed, we lowered our heads against the prop wash and began boarding through the right side cargo door.

As patrol leader, and last to board, I anticipated difficulty in getting in the door with all my normal gear plus the lizard. I handed the cage to the door gunner while I got in. Behind his flight helmet and goggles, I could not see his reaction to possibly the most interesting prisoner of war that ever boarded his chopper. On the other hand, with Recon's reputation of being "snake eaters," he may have thought I was saving it for a snack later on.

After debriefing and turning in our gear at Khe Sanh, I went to the sergeant's hooch, took my prisoner out of its cage, carefully straightened it out and set it on the cot next to mine. The hooch was comfortably warm from the wood stove in the center of the room. It didn't seem to affect the lizard, or so I thought.

After about 20 minutes while I cleaned my rifle, the Spam hit the fan. Someone came in the door, which made a sudden noise. It startled the now thawed-out lizard, which bolted the length of the cot, banked off the wall, and screamed past the bug-eyed Marine as it went out the door, never to be seen again. Perhaps the thought of having to eat C-rations with Marines was too much for its saurian mind.

Mosquitoes were enormous at Khe Sanh. I heard that one landed on the helo pad and the airdales pumped 100 gallons of JP-4 into it before they realized that it wasn't a Huey. Okay, so they really weren't that big, but there were a lot of them, and they were voracious. In the summer I think their breeding areas dried up some but when it was wet out in the bush, they were all over us day and night. Depending on the tactical situation, rather than swat them, sometimes we just had to let them chew on us. The bug juice we were issued was some help but the smell of it almost made the cure as bad as the illness.

Rats were also a problem on almost any base. They lived in the nooks and crannies of the sand bags in our bunkers. They came out, mostly at night, to scrounge for food. Sometimes that food was a Marine toe or finger, and there are many documented cases of rat bites.

One of our team leaders, I think it was Sgt. Cargroves, came up with the idea of a rat safari. Since the rats usually came out at night, his plan involved the use of flashlights and Ka-bars. The scheme was that each of us would sit cross-legged on our cots with our backs up against the wall. Under our butts would be a folded up flak jacket. You'll see the genius of this in a moment. On our heads was a helmet. We also wore a flak jacket but we put it on backwards with just our hands sticking out the armholes. In one hand was a Ka-bar and in the other, a flashlight. Bait, in the form of woof cookies, was left in the middle of the floor. Woof cookies was what we called a round, hard cracker that came in C-rations. They were usually accompanied by gorilla spread ... a small tin of jam-like substance. The light was put out and everyone assumed their positions. After a while we could hear the rustling of little rat feet as they moved toward the bait. As Cargroves shouted, "Now!" we flicked on the flashlights, threw our Ka-bar at the spot-lit rats, and then ducked, turtle fashion, into our flak jackets while knives ricocheted off walls and floors. Now you know why we sat on flak jackets because the canvas cots would have been no protection against a blade bouncing up from the floor. Hardly anybody ever got hurt and it should be noted that not one rat was harmed during these events.

Speaking of rats, I got trampled by one. It was a couple of hours after setting in to our harborsite, and under the canopy, there was stygian blackness. The only things visible were the bits and pieces of phosphorescent vegetation lying on the ground. I don't know what kind of rotted plant parts they were or how they acquired phosphorescence, but they at least gave you a sense of where the ground was in the darkness.

The rat in question was not the kind of rat we saw on base. They were opossum sized nocturnal creatures that we called tree rats. They may well have actually been an Asian opossum of some kind. This particular night, I was lying on my back in my sweat soggy, smelly utilities trying to imagine what fresh air tasted like when I heard furtive noises approaching from my right. It was obviously not of human origin and it didn't make a slithering kind of sound so I wasn't very worried about it. I knew it was either a small mammal or lizard, neither of which is dangerous. As it drew closer, though, I began to think that it was rabid and was coming right toward me, as rabid animals are wont to do.

As that thought ran through my head, the animal ran across my chest. I believe it realized right then that I was not a log but in fact was a large animal that could harm it. When I say it was tree rat, I am basing that assumption on the size of the animal as it ran over me. It shrieked in alarm, causing me and the rest of the team to sit bolt upright as it tore off through the undergrowth. I'm not sure who was the more startled.

My last critter encounter involves that most disgusting of all things, the leech. They were everywhere in Vietnam. There were water leeches but we didn't run into them very often. They were long and flat and you had to be careful that you didn't suck them into a canteen while you filled it from a river. The land leeches were dark brown striped things and, when empty, about an inch and a half long. On the bases where the ground had been completely cleared of vegetation, you never saw a leech. In the bush, though, they could be found on the ground, in the bushes, and in the trees. When we stopped for a break, within minutes, the leeches would be seen marching toward us. They would drop out of trees or we'd pick them up brushing against leaves or elephant grass. They moved like an inchworm and often stood on their tails and seemed to be sniffing the air. I think they could pick up the carbon dioxide we exhaled. The leeches were cold blooded so when they got on your body, they assumed your body temperature and didn't feel cold or hot. Unless you saw one, the only way you knew you had a leech was if you felt an itchy sensation a little like a mosquito bite. They have a circular mouth with saw teeth and when they chewed into your skin, they injected an anti-coagulant so your blood flowed freely. Even after you pulled one off, the bite mark would continue to bleed.

Early one morning, on our last day out, we were scheduled to walk up to 881S and then get choppered off the hill later on. It was a rainy, chilly day and as we got ready to move out and climb the hill, I felt an itch behind my right ear. I scratched at it but since I was soaked, I could not feel the soft, squishy leech that I didn't realize had attached itself there. We moved out but after a few minutes, my radioman behind me whispered, "You've got a leech behind your ear." We stopped for just a minute while he put a couple of drops of bug juice on the leech, which immediately curled up and dropped off. By then it was bloated to about the size of my thumb.

I thought nothing more of it. Leeches and bugs were just part of what you had to get used to. We started the climb up the hill. We made it in much better time than we would later in the summer on a patrol where we ran out of water. An officer met us at the concertina wire perimeter and right away, a look of concern crossed his face. He asked me, "Did somebody get hit?"

I gave my standard response to an officer's question. "Huh?"

He repeated his query and pointed at my chest. I looked down and was very surprised to see the front of my utility shirt covered with blood. Then it dawned on me. The leech bite! When the leech fell off, the bite continued to bleed and the blood had run down my jawline and dripped off my chin. It was a little embarrassing. Doc Miller taped a piece of cotton on the spot so it would clot.

We took some preventive measures against leeches. While on the move, we squirted bug juice on our boots and trouser cuffs. That usually kept them from hitching a ride because they were actually quick enough and in such numbers that they could attach themselves to your boot for the second or two it was on the ground as you walked. At night in the harborsite, we dribbled a perimeter around our individual sleeping spots because the leeches were really repelled by that stuff. That didn't stop them from dive-bombing off a tree or bush, though.

When I got back from Vietnam, all the girls were wearing miniskirts and for a while, it was *de rigueur* to wear panty hose that were a dark brown with lighter brown vertical stripes. Their legs looked exactly like 40-pound leeches. It really was a turn off.

Water leeches were especially vile. If you stuck your canteen into a stream, it was easy to suck a water leech into it without noticing. We got used to using a bandana over the mouth of the canteen to act as a filter to keep the leeches out. Water leeches were anywhere from two to four inches long and flatter than land leeches. The risky thing about a water leech in your canteen was that it was very easy to ingest one of them while drinking from it. They could flow right down your throat as if they weren't there. Once inside your stomach I suppose stomach acid

South of 881S — Blood from leech bite running from behind my ear down my jaw line and then dripping off my chin.

would eventually kill them but I imagine they could still do some internal damage, not to mention the messy result.

Okay, just one more. Ticks were a nuisance, too. I got one once on the top of my left shoulder near my neck. I didn't notice it until it was about the size of a small marble. It was so disgusting to have that thing sucking my blood that I just took my Ka-Bar and shaved it off. Of course, that left the tick's head still imbedded in my skin. It bothered me for a couple days and then I forgot about it. However, every now and then over the years, it gets itchy. It's still there.

PART THREE

IN WHICH I CAN DEFINITELY
SMELL THE ELEPHANT

10. Could'a Been Worse!

The Fourth of July celebrates our country's independence from tyranny. We were in Vietnam to try to help South Vietnam achieve the same goal. Americans observe the Fourth to one degree or another wherever they are and war zones are no exception. The Company Gunny had arranged for us to have a barbeque in the company area. No doubt similar events were taking place all across the base and up on the hills. We had a box full of steaks and I'm not sure what else but the idea of cooking steaks over a grill sounded like fun. It didn't even cross our minds that all the food was provided by the mess tent where we would otherwise eat the same chow, but it somehow tasted better this way. Fireworks were no problem either and were provided for free on many nights by the NVA. In fact, we usually got to see more of them than we cared to.

We also had many loaves of fresh baked bread. Bread was one of the things the mess cooks did well. The bread was lying on a table that had been dragged out into the company street and one of our staff sergeants was slicing it up with a big knife. He was a little guy that always seemed to be worried about something. I was lounging nearby as he was slicing and the company commander, Captain James Williams, walked up to the staff sergeant to ask him something. The staff sergeant looked up from his labors and was talking to the captain when, maybe it was the thought of that tasty bread, a gob of spit fell out of his mouth onto the bread he was slicing. No one but me seemed to notice. All the bread slices were dumped back into the box they had been delivered in and placed on the chow line. I didn't have any bread.

By now, I was the APL and my patrol knowledge was increasing. We had a shortage of sergeants but I was still kind of green so Lt. Pfeltz continued to lead the patrol. Besides, as I said, he liked it.

Dear Dad,
Well, the stuff hit the fan yesterday. On the second of this month we went out on a patrol. They took us by helicopter 7½ miles out. The area we went into was hilly but very little cover. There was 2 to 3 foot elephant grass and that was all.

82

We moved about 100 meters from our LZ ... and found about 5 bunkers. There were 40 foot craters all over the area from a B-52 bombing mission.... We moved on up to a hilltop to spend the night and there found several bunkers that appeared to be emplacements for anti aircraft guns. We also found a small shovel and some sneakers. The next day we didn't see much and only moved about 1000 meters. Late that afternoon we came to a spot where we spent the night. In this area was a small bench made of sticks lashed together and we also found a small pick. The next morning we moved up to the top of the hill and found 17 bunkers. We searched each one and came up with 3 gook hats, a rifle case, a canteen pouch, a pack, an ammo box, links for a machine gun belt, rice bags, medicine bottles and in one we found writing on the wall which I climbed into and copied down. The lieutenant decided we'd stay there and set up an O.P. [observation post].[1]

All the hats we found were beat up, but one of them, a pith helmet, was at least in one piece and it still had the commie star on the front of it. I thought the hat would make a nice souvenir. We took off our packs to get a little more comfortable and Lt. Pfeltz told me to take two men and do a little reconnaissance around the hilltop we were on to determine if there were any other trails or bunkers we should know about. The hill was oval with the long axis running east and west. The top and three of the sides were covered with chest high elephant grass but the south slope looked as if it had been burned off right to the ground at some point. The deteriorating condition of the bunkers indicated that this site had probably not been used by the NVA since the hill fights a few months earlier. The burned off elephant grass on the south slope was probably the result of a napalm strike. Since the hilltop was not very big, a circumnavigation of it would only cover a couple of hundred meters in length and take about ten minutes. For a few minutes of that time, we would be out of sight of the O.P.

Just about my only item of personal comfort on patrols was a black sweatshirt with the sleeves chopped off at the elbows. After a sweaty day of patrolling, I would take off my nasty utility shirt and put the sweatshirt on. That little bit of comfort made a lot of difference. I usually kept it on all night so my utility shirt could dry out some.

Since I knew we'd be there a while, I changed shirts and, for the heck of it, put on the pith helmet I had found. I had the other two guys fall in behind me and we went down off the hilltop about 30 meters and began our circle of the hill. As we came around to the O.P. side I could see Lt. Pfeltz' head and shoulders above the elephant grass looking at us with binoculars. We completed our circuit, found nothing except the trail we already knew about and came back to the O.P.

Lt. Pfeltz turned to me with a very exasperated look on his camouflage painted face and said, "You scared the hell out of me!"

I said, "Huh?"

"When you came around the hill with that black shirt and pith helmet on, I thought, that's the biggest f**king gook I've ever seen! The only thing that saved you was that you and the other two idiots were carrying 16s."

Only then did it hit me what a bonehead stunt that was! You learn things.

We had a trail running along behind us so we put 3 men on one end of it and 3 men on the other end about 40 feet away. Myself, the lieutenant and the radioman set up the O.P a little ways down the hill. The area we were watching had a view that covered more area than you can see from the front porch.[2] Anyway about 2:30 I was crapped out, when the radioman woke me up and said something about moving out. I got up and went back to tell the rear man to get everybody ready to go soon. I didn't know why we were moving but when I went back down the hill to the O.P. I found out. There were 40 gooks in column (single file) headed straight for us and waving to us! [They were less than 100 meters away. Lt. Pfeltz had the presence of mind to wave back at them.] Needless to say we broke all records for getting our gear on. We at first were going to head for the hilltop and make a stand but then decided that running away was a little better idea. [Recon's role was not to engage at close quarters unless absolutely necessary.] In the confusion, 3 men did not get the word that we were going down the other side of the hill. As assistant patrol leader I had to stay there till I was sure everybody was on the way. Five people passed me and I stood there waiting for the other three. Well they didn't come and I decided they must have gone down behind me. About that time I heard the gooks talking and decided I'd better leave. I headed down the hill and as soon as I got within sight of them [the patrol] I saw that we were still missing three. [I signaled to Lt. Pfeltz that we were not all there.]The lieutenant held us up and he and I headed back up the hill to find them.[3]

The realization that there were three of our people unaccounted for was electric. The urge to get as far as I could from the enemy that I knew were very near and the need to find those three Marines was titanic. Every second felt like an hour.

Just then we heard 3 bursts from an M-16 and a few seconds later 3 men came out of the brush onto the hilltop [about 100 feet away]. We almost opened fire but then we realized they were the three missing men.

They still hesitated, not sure who we were. I then held up my rifle so they could clearly see that it was an M-16 and not an AK-47.

I stood up and waved at them and when they saw me they came flying down the hill. We all got together again and kept moving.[4]

My relief at finding those guys was almost dizzying. We had just experienced the same phenomena that had kept the NVA from shooting at us thus far. Everyone involved thought (or knew) that everybody else was a gook. We ran down the hill through knee high brush that had grown back since it had burned. You would think that with gravity on our side, going downhill would be easy. The load that we carried on our backs actually served to push us down the hill so we had our "brakes" on most of the way to keep from accelerating out of control while still maintaining all possible speed. After descending about 80 meters of a 40 degree slope, we reached the small valley at the base of the hill and our thighs were beginning to burn from exertion.

All the way down I expected to hear rifle fire from behind us. That anticipation made my ears feel like they were standing straight up. I wanted to look back but I had to concentrate on keeping my balance. At the bottom, we did not pause for a second. We were completely exposed and had to reach cover! I was panting hard along with everyone else as we started up the other side of the valley. Here the brush was thicker because it had not been burned off but we were still visible and moving. Why the gooks had not fired at us yet was beyond my imagination because we were pretty much sitting (or scrambling) ducks. As we climbed, we slowed down. The undergrowth, the weight of our gear, and the laboring of our hearts and lungs were taking their toll. I began to wonder what would kill me first, the hill or the gooks.

I chanced a look back and several of the NVA were standing where we had started down the hill gesturing and calling to us. They still did not fire at us even though we were well within rifle range. We stopped at the top of the hill in a small tree line and threw ourselves on the ground behind some downed trees. Our lungs and legs were on fire and we were sucking air as if it was on sale. As the crow flies, we were only about 300 meters, maximum, from our former position, but we were absolutely winded from the exhausting run with all that gear in that heat.

As we reached the top of the hill, Lt. Pfeltz had just finished calling for a fire mission from the artillery. Artillery was the nearest and quickest form of support and we could usually count on its arrival in a matter of minutes. As we hunkered down behind what little cover there was, Doc Miller was to my right and Lt. Pfeltz and the radioman were to Doc's right. I've heard the sound of approaching artillery variously described as a rustling noise, like a freight train, or whistles. In fact, it can be any or all of these sounds depending on size and proximity. At the relatively close distance we were to the target it sounded like a squirrel scrambling through dry leaves, but with a descending tone. The first two rounds hit just to the east of the hilltop. The lieutenant radioed a quick adjustment and added, "Fire for effect!" That meant that he was happy with where the adjustment rounds were going to land and he wanted the battery from the 13th Marines to fire three rounds each from however many guns were in the battery ... usually three. A total of nine 105mm artillery rounds were about to drop into Mr. Ngyuen's back pocket. And they did.

The hilltop erupted in flashes and geysers of dirt, smoke, and NVA. The lieutenant hollered (no need to whisper now) into the handset, "Rainbelt Bravo, Broadweave One, outstanding coverage! Repeat fire for effect, over!"

> When we got there the lieutenant started calling in artillery and that [hilltop, 300 meters away] is too close. There were chunks of steel as big as my fist landing all around us. Then he called in an air strike. First the Hueys came in.... They strafed the hilltop. After that came jets with bombs, rockets and napalm.[5]

The artillery fired three fires for effect. That was a total of 27 to 36 rounds depending on the number of guns firing. There was a lot going on now. Back on the base, the C.O.C. knew that with contact of this nature the team's mission was compromised and the men would normally have to be extracted. For some reason, the people back on the base in the concrete underground bunker didn't want to pull us out. After some "negotiations" with Lt. Pfeltz, they scrambled two troop ships and two gunships to come and get us out. At the same time, Lt. Pfeltz was on the horn calling in an air strike. With any degree of stealth gone, I could clearly hear the lieutenant's end of the radio conversation. From experience, I also knew what Rainbelt Bravo's responses were as he relayed our transmissions to Khe Sanh.

"Rainbelt Bravo this is Broadweave One, over."

"Broadweave One, Rainbelt Bravo, go ahead, over."

"Rainbelt, request fixed wing at this location, over."

"Roger, Broadweave One, send your traffic, over."

"Rainbelt, Broadweave One, Grid 700445, troops in the open. My observer/target line is 340 degrees magnetic, approximately 300 meters. Danger close, over."

"Roger, Broadweave, standby."

All of that meant that we needed jets for close air support and the enemy was at map coordinates 700445, in the open, about 300 meters from us. Danger close means that we were well within the recommended 750-meter safety radius for air delivered ordnance. Danger close for artillery is 600 meters. The observer target line is the compass azimuth from our position to the target. This line is what the arty and air people use to calculate adjustments, if any, from those that we call in as the ordnance hits the target.

By this time, the artillery had finished its business and the Huey gunships from Khe Sanh had arrived overhead. We could also hear the deeper throbbing of the CH-46 troop ships approaching from the east. The Hueys orbited the target area but then angled off a bit to the west. The lead gunship came up on our frequency...

"Broadweave One this is Grassflat Lead, over."

Lt. Pfeltz answered, "Grassflat Lead, Broadweave One, go ahead, over."

"Broadweave, Grassflat, the target area is pretty well torn up and we can see people down. There are some survivors running west on a trail. We'll keep them occupied until the fast movers get here, over."

"Roger, Grassflat Lead, thanks. Out."

The gunships began running machine gun and rocket passes at the fleeing NVA. It takes only about 20 minutes to scramble a pair of jets from Da Nang and have them arrive on station in the Khe Sanh area. Right on schedule, we got a call from Grassflat Lead.

"Broadweave One, this is Grassflat Lead. Fixed wing is on station." (We couldn't see them because they enter the area at about 20,000 feet.) "We will mark the target with Willie Pete and bring them on in if that's OK, over."

"Roger, Grassflat, thanks for the assist. Out."

At some point, a gunship fired a Willie Peter round at the target to mark it for the air strike. WP gives off an intense white cloud and makes it much easier for the jets to spot the target in a sea of green. Then they cleared out, joining the extraction CH-46s orbiting about a mile away.

It was very handy having helicopter support on hand because, as in this case, they could talk directly to the jets and speak aviation to them. Our AN/PRC25 radios did not have the frequencies necessary to talk to the jets. An air strike is an extremely complicated affair, best left to the people who know what they are doing. That doesn't mean that if we needed jets but had no FAC with us, or no air assets overhead, we could still call in our location, the target location, and target description and the air liaison back at the C.O.C. would make it work. It would be clumsy but it would work.

In this case, there was a lot of choreography involved. The Fire Support Coordination Center — FSCC — was directly involved in the combined arms support we were getting. I don't know where the FSCC was located. It may have been at Khe Sanh but I think it more likely was at Da Nang. The FSCC monitors all air traffic and artillery at all times. If there might be any conflict at all, the FSCC takes control of who does what and when. When an artillery round is fired, no power on earth can bring it back. It will go where it will go. Aircraft, however, can change their direction of travel, so it is up to the FSCC to tell the various pilots where they need to be so that they don't wind up on the gun-target trajectory and get blown to bits. Jets fly high and fast, choppers fly low and slow, but artillery just goes. These are three different dynamics that must not conflict each other.

The artillery is the quickest support so it has the right of way. While the gun bunnies are doing their thing helicopters are lifting off and heading for the same target the artillery is shooting at. The choppers are told by FSCC exactly how to approach our extraction LZ so that they do not cross the gun-target line. The jets are the last ones to arrive at the dance but they come in very high above the vulgarities taking place nearer to earth. Depending on the urgency, the choppers will orbit away from the LZ or target so the jets can get right in there and do a little landscaping. Sometimes it's the other way around ... choppers first after artillery and then fixed wing.

Whatever the order of things, once Lt. Pfeltz turned the fixed wing over to the gunships we just laid low and watched several million dollars worth of aircraft and ordnance perform at our beck and call. For a few moments, it was quiet except for the distant thunder of the 46s and the "wopping" of the Hueys. Then somebody spotted a dark smudge on the horizon. F-4 Phantoms had notoriously dirty exhaust signatures. The smudge got bigger and closer but we still couldn't pick the jets out. Slowly the scream of jet engines became louder and just as we could make out the shape of the jets, they rocketed overhead and dropped their bomb load.

The bombs were called Snake Eyes. At the rear of the 250-pound bomb were four fins that, when released from the plane, flipped open to catch the wind and slow the bomb so it dropped almost straight down. This made them very accurate. You haven't lived until one or more F-4s thunder overhead at about 400 feet off the deck at 600 miles per hour! The noise is earsplitting!

As mentioned, we were down behind some trees and we placed our packs in front of us for a little more protection from the artillery and bomb fragments. This was my first action with supporting fires and since it was obvious the gooks were preoccupied with getting killed, I thought it was an excellent opportunity to take a few snaps. I got up on my knees and aimed my trusty Kodak Instamatic at the hilltop. Amidst all the other noise, I heard sounds like large, angry wasps buzzing by just over our heads but it didn't instantly sink in what it was. The corpsman, Doc Miller, was beside me, grabbed me, and slammed my face into the dirt whilst commenting as to my obvious lack of I.Q. and the legality of my parentage. He'd been that close to an air strike before and knew what those noises were!

The jets made two bomb runs and then made two passes with napalm. Napalm is a jellied gasoline mixture in a large aluminum drop tank. When the jet lets it go, it tumbles through the air, thoroughly mixing the napalm, which ignites in a huge orange ball of flame upon impact. Whatever does not burn is suffocated by the elimination of oxygen in the immediate vicinity of the fireball. We could feel the heat from a few hundred meters away.

> When they were through, that whole hilltop was all black and smoking and nobody was moving up there. Even while the jets were making runs, the helicopters came and got us out.
> When we got back to the air field, the base commander was waiting there to congratulate us.
> The reason why those gooks were waving to us as they came toward our position was because they thought we were gooks too. They were wearing jungle uniforms and equipment much like us (except for rifles). The firing we heard later was one of the three men who got separated. He was waiting by the trail we had been on because he didn't know where we were. The first gook came up the trail and started

to say something to him but all he got in reply was lead. He also killed the second man.[6]

That Marine's name was, I believe, Hernandez but I'm just not positive. He was of Mexican descent and being of that persuasion, and wearing dark face paint, he looked, at first glance, very gook-like. That probably also explains why they did not pursue us by fire as we went down the hill. I think they were still convinced we were NVA and even the shooting was a case of mistaken identity. Either that or they were dumber than a box of doorknobs.

> They [the zoomies] estimated at least 30–35 kills ... which is very good.... Also I wonder if you could send me some fizzies. Anything but cola or root beer. And maybe some dried fruit.
> Well I guess that's it from this part of the world. So long for now.
> Steve[7]

Remember Fizzies? They looked like a small, colored, Alka Seltzer tablets and came in various flavors. You drop them in a glass of water and they fizz up to make your own soda pop. Sometimes, as kids, we would just put one in our mouths. They would quickly foam up and we would run around foaming at the mouth and growling. Fizzies would come into play later in yet another personal debacle.

11. Sergeant of Marines

At Khe Sanh, there were few amenities. I know this will come as a shock to those of you who have seen all the Hollywood versions of what Vietnam was "really like." Off duty hours were spent in a large, well-lit urban area with street after street of curio shops, sidewalk cafes, and bars with exotic Asian bar girls. The G.I.s were either in casual civilian attire or starched and pressed uniforms. Up to date American rock 'n' roll music blasted from jukeboxes. Well, Pilgrim, I wanna tell ya those weren't Marines. Granted, some Marine bases like Da Nang and Phu Bai were somewhat civilized but up in the north country of Dong Ha, Gio Linh, Con Thien and Khe Sanh, it was more like the western front of World War I.

From other Khe Sanh veterans, I have heard over the years that there was some kind of enlisted men's "club" on base. The closest thing I saw to a "club" was a little shack in the regimental HQ area. In fact, it was right across from the small Air Force detachment's hooches. Well, wasn't *that* convenient. The "club" had a plywood awning that could be swung up to reveal what would otherwise look like a snack bar. In the immediate vicinity were a few lopsided wooden tables and benches. In my many months at Khe Sanh, it was open only once that I knew of. I repeat, ONCE! All of us, at some time, had been issued ration cards for beer. The ration was two beers and two soft drinks *per day*. Did I mention it was only open once to my knowledge? You couldn't have four beers or four sodas. It had to be two and two or none at all. On that day of days, I went over to the "club" and stood in a jubilant line of parched Jarheads waiting in the blazing sun. Jarhead, by the way, is a pejorative term for a Marine when used by non–Marines. One account suggests that it refers to the Marine high and tight haircut, which is cut almost to the skin at the ears with a bit left on top giving one's gourd the appearance of a jar with handles. Another legend says that during World War II the Mason jar company stopped making jars and made the helmets for Marines.

A mighty cheer went up as the awning was propped open and the line began to shuffle forward. Within minutes, I could hear what sounded like cries of dismay and outright anger but I didn't know why. When I got to the window, I handed over my ration card, which was closely inspected for authenticity and then duly punched by a stern visaged supply-type guy. There was no charge for the drinks but it was clear that the manner in which the supply guy glared at me with his good eye that it was he who had actually paid for them. I was handed my spoils and almost burned my hands! The cans were blistering hot! The "club" apparently had no refrigeration at all and the sodas and beers had been sitting inside the closed hooch for who knows how long. This explained the verbal outbursts I had heard before.

I traded my two beers to another guy for his two sodas and felt I had made a good deal. Many, as did I, took their booty back to their hooches to, at the very least, sit in the shade for a couple of hours to let them cool down to a temperature that wouldn't burn their lips. Others, though, having been deprived of this nectar of heaven for an insufferable length of time, slowly and painfully sipped down the molten brew. The biggest problem was that when they opened the cans, nearly half of it exploded out on themselves and anyone nearby. There were several minutes of foamy little geysers erupting around the tables. Maybe the "club" was open much more often and maybe the beer was cold on those occasions but I never saw it.

I tend to rag on the supply-types because they could be very exasperating. However, I do have to say that without the hard work that many of them did, we line troops would have had nothing to wear, nothing to eat, and nothing to shoot people with.

There actually was a tiny PX on base and it was right next to our company area. Its main inventory was razor blades, soap, soap holders, Barbasol shaving cream, stationery and envelopes, sometimes some towels and washcloths, laundry detergent, and little else. Now and then, a few cases of potato chips came in but even at one bag per man they were snatched up in short order.

Dear Dad,
    This last patrol was really hairy. I was supposed to have been the patrol leader but they just got a staff sergeant in the company and they gave the patrol to him. Navigation is not his best skill. He can read a compass but since he can't read a map and [see] the contours of the land, he shoots an azimuth and follows a course straight cross country. He doesn't take into consideration the hills, vallies and thickness of the growth and as a result we covered only 1000 meters in two days! I was doing [a lot of] his map and compass work and everytime we took a break or stopped for the night, I usually had to show him where we were.[1]

This staff sergeant struck everyone as a little different. He was a nice enough guy but sometimes took his recon tactics to an extreme. On this patrol, at one point, he had us follow a river. *In* the river! We were about thigh deep and our movement, if kept slow, was surprisingly quiet. The problem was that the heavy jungle was overhanging into the water on both sides and towered above us. Once we got in the water, there was no seeing out of the river channel and no ready escape from it. If we had been seen, we'd have had nowhere to go.

One evening he was looking for a harborsite in a very erratic and contorted piece of terrain. I saw several acceptable places but we wound up staying on the side of a hill that was so steep we literally had to tie ourselves and our gear to small trees to keep from sliding down the slope. We hung there like cocoons all night and I don't think anybody slept. I'll say this; no one could possibly have snuck up on us. Even monkeys have better accommodations than that.

One of the sergeants had a transistor radio. Armed Forces Radio used to broadcast music and news from, I think, Saigon. The music was dopey and the reception that far north was bad anyway. So what did we listen to? Why Hanoi Hannah, of course. She was the Vietnam equivalent of Tokyo Rose. The commentary was laughable ... predicting doom and destruction for this or that American unit. She even mentioned 3rd Recon Battalion once just after we moved to Khe Sanh from Phu Bai. The music was the most current American stuff, though, so we laughed at Hannah and listened to her tunes.

Another short-lived attempt was made to entertain the troops. A special tent was put up to house a television set. Yes, a TV! It got three stations reasonably well; one of them being Armed Forces TV, and the other two were Vietnamese or maybe Thai. Apart from AFTV, we could not understand a word being said and aside from talking heads all the other programming was of elaborately costumed and choreographed historical dramas and dance routines. The music that accompanied these productions was like cats yowling with a lot of gongs and crashing cymbals. Once I watched what appeared to be a Cambodian soap opera. At least I think it was a soap opera. It was in Hindi, or something, so I could not keep up with the plot very well, but it seemed that Ravishandihar had been stepping out on her husband Mahandapur, with Jondalar. However, Mahandapur's friend Shanafanaful saw them and told Mahandapur about it. Mahandapur doesn't believe Shanafanaful so now they're on the outs. Meanwhile, Ravishandihar suspects that her daughter Madubandifra has been sneaking out with the Amapoto boy two rice paddies over. At least, that's what I got out of it. One night, while taking some incoming artillery, the TV became *hors de combat*. Its demise was not mourned.

For the first couple of months at Khe Sanh, we even had outdoor movies. Despite the savage fighting for the hills just weeks before, the base was somehow considered safe enough to show films. In our company area, a movie screen from Special Services was put up. Special Services is a part of the supply system that provides recreational or sporting equipment to the troops when possible. Volunteers ran the 16mm projector and we watched old movies. I ran the projector a couple of times but, while standing on frequently muddy ground, I got shocked when I touched the projector. I handed in my resignation from the Motion Picture Projectionist Union.

A couple of days before the staff sergeant's "cliffhanger" patrol we fell out for morning formation as usual. After roll call, instead of dismissing the company, Captain Williams said, "Corporal Johnson, front and center." Startled, I hesitated for a second and then presented myself in front of the captain. He took a piece of paper out of his pocket and began reading, "To all who shall see these presents, greeting." That's the wording that begins all promotion warrants. I was picking up sergeant! I had no idea. I had a relatively short time in grade as a corporal but I guess somebody saw some potential. That same day, I moved my cot and gear into the sergeants' hooch, as was now my privilege. While doing so, Corporal Lister came around the hooch from the supply end and saw me. He immediately came over, shook my hand and said, "Congratulations. I thought you was a boot." A boot is a recruit, a rookie, a newbie. From a supply-type that was an abject apology to anyone he had thought held inferior status to his. Of course, items from supply were still being bought and paid for personally by the corporal and his colleagues but at least I didn't get any more noise about the proper use of liquid resources.

The empty cot in the sergeants' hooch upon which I established residency was in a corner against the wall separating us from the supply end of the hooch. That actually made it rather cozy because I had a wall to put nails in and hang stuff on and I didn't need to procure a chair because I could sit on my cot and lean back against the wall. I had acquired a little "nightstand" made from wooden ammo boxes and had all the comforts of home. Our bedding generally consisted of the sleeping bag, a pillow and sometimes even a pillowcase. What? No sheets? Well, no. Can you imagine how hard it would have been to keep sheets even semi clean? And don't forget that our laundry service at Khe Sanh was a bar of Ivory soap, a bucket of cold water, and our own two hands. If you wanted it clean ... you washed it. There were clotheslines between the hooches and tents for drying but during the monsoon, we hung things inside. They never got quite dry even then, so along with the constant rain we varied between soaking wet and mildly damp all the time. Sometimes we would sleep in our clean but damp utilities just to dry them out. Mildew became our friend.

Against the outside wall of the supply end of the hooch was a large wooden bin into which we were all expected to toss our unwanted cans of C-rations. Not everybody liked everything but some liked certain menus, almost to the exclusion of most of the other selections. (There were 12 different meals in a case of C-rats.) The bin was for allowing anyone who wanted to paw through the cans in search of specific delicacies. This was way before dumpster diving became fashionable.

Ham and lima beans were almost universally hated by Marines. They were too salty, full of grease, and had huge lima beans entombed in the lard. They weren't called, among other things, Ham and Hockers for nothing, but the locals loved them. There were very few local Viets or Bru allowed on the base. That was for security reasons. However, some of them were trusted to act as maintenance workers, picking up trash and general manual labor. Sometimes we would catch them in the bin with just their feet sticking out rooting for the Ham and Hockers. Occasional scuffles broke out if there was only one can and two scroungers. I was rather partial to the pound cake so it was not unusual to see me digging like a badger for those morsels.

12. A Day in the Life

We got hit on the base with rockets and artillery for the most part. Mortars are relatively short-range weapons. The Chi-com 82mm mortar has an effective range of a little over 3000 meters and to get close enough to the base to use them meant taking a chance of being seen and quickly erased by grunts on the perimeter or by mobile U.S. Army quad–50s. There was a detachment of them on base and they were truck-mounted contraptions that consisted of four .50 caliber machine guns controlled by one trigger. They could rip up an entire acre in a matter of seconds. They were designed as an anti-aircraft weapon. The Geneva Convention limits anti-personnel weapons to .30 caliber so these four .50 caliber rifles could only be used on aircraft and other equipment. Right! Russian 122mm rockets were the most terrifying, partially due to the screaming, whooshing sound they made as they descended, and also because they were murderous when they detonated. Their range was more than three times that of the mortar.

One afternoon I was strolling down the main road near the company area when the incoming siren cranked up. I waited a second until I could hear what was coming so I'd have an idea which way to run and how fast to do it. The sounds I heard told me it was already too late. The shorter and higher pitched the whistle or shriek, the more vertical the round is descending. These were short! Fortunately, I was pointed in the right direction because the first rounds landed about 100 feet behind me. The sound of the blasts and a maximum surge of adrenalin propelled me so that I barely felt my feet hitting the ground. Other people were scurrying from wherever they had been to the nearest bunker. For some reason, I had a real desire to jump into my own bunker at the sergeants' hooch, which was still about 50 feet away.

Rockets were still hitting behind me but my mind was telling me that they were rapidly closing on my heels. The closer I got to the bunker the less sure I was that I would make it. I took a giant flying leap toward the bunker opening just as a rocket detonated somewhere behind me. My momentum, probably aided to some extent by the concussion wave from the blast, flung

95

me right through the opening to land hard on my face inside. I was a bit stunned and for a few moments, I didn't know if I was hurt or not. After a bit, I sat up and looked around. Several faces looked impassively back at me in the dimness of the bunker. When a brief break in explosions occurred, a voice from the gloom at the rear of the bunker said, "Nice of you to join us. May we serve tea now or were you going to perform some more tricks?"

Later, as I dusted myself off, I noticed a couple of short tears on the left thigh of my trousers. After further inspection, I found three fine slices, hardly more than paper cuts, across the side of my left thigh. There was practically no blood and I was mainly irritated because now I had some needle and thread work to do on my trousers. Doc Miller noticed me checking my leg and said, "Looks like you got nipped. I'll make out a casualty tag."

A casualty tag meant that a record of my "wound" would be made and I would, at some point, by regulation, be awarded the Purple Heart Medal. Some would have jumped at the chance to get a PH so easily but I was well aware that a lot of Marines who had lost arms, legs, and worse rated a Heart one hell of a lot more than I did. I wasn't trying to sound noble but I told Doc that that just wasn't right and declined a casualty tag.

On another occasion, three of us were sprinting for a bunker. I dove in first and was immediately pile driven by the other two. They were, of course, wearing helmets, flak jackets, and all manner of other sharp and or hard accoutrements. Even though I had my flak jacket on, it didn't do my back any good. I blame some of my current arthritis problems in my back on that incident.

Once during a mortar attack, I got caught too far from a bunker to do myself any good. I took what little cover I could behind a trash filled burn barrel. The protection was more mental than physical. At one point, rounds were impacting within about 100 feet and shrapnel was flicking up little clots of red clay no more than 20 feet away from me. I tried and almost succeeded in fitting my entire body into my helmet.

Having nothing much to do one afternoon, I had spent an hour or so sorting my sock collection by color. That didn't take long because I only had black or green socks. My social calendar was, oddly enough, uncluttered until teatime, so Doc Miller and I decided to stroll around the base to see what was what. As we were returning to the company area, I spotted a sergeant, formerly of the *Albany's* Marine Detachment. He was from Alabama or some place and would generally fit the description of a redneck. He pronounced "oil" as "awl" and "hour" as "ore" and the rest of his command of the English language went downhill from there. On the ship, he treated everyone junior to him as some kind of recruit and was not especially well liked or respected.

I introduced him to Doc Miller and found out that he was in Vietnam as a dog handler and he hated it. I wondered how the dog felt about the situation. He kept glancing at my collar upon which was affixed the rank insignia of sergeant. The last time he had seen me, only a few months before, I was a very new corporal. I told him I was in Recon and he looked at the dog as if to say, "And I got *you*." The dog returned a similar expression.

We chatted a few more minutes but we each had places to go so we moved on. I never saw him again but I presume he survived his tour.

In that same time frame, I got a letter at mail call from another MarDet Marine. It was from John Huggard. When we all left the ship he had been a corporal but was now, according to his return address, a sergeant. He had been one of my best friends on the *Albany* and was one of those guys who always had something going, if you know what I mean. He loved to play cards and I was terrible at it. Best friend or not, it didn't stop him from relieving me of $38.00 over a brief period of time playing 500 rummy at a penny a point. Do you understand how bad a card player you need to be to lose $38.00 that way? And that was when I was making about $80.00 a month! I have never played cards for money since then. Fortunately, John put me on a convenient installment plan.

John's return address showed that he was farther south somewhere in the 1st Marine Division. He enclosed a photo of himself in utilities and a helmet. I have no idea how he found out where I was, but then John had a way of finding stuff out. Intending to write back, I tacked the envelope to the wall of the hooch above my rack. A week or so later after returning from a patrol, the letter was nowhere to be found. I am sure that no one removed it for any reason. I could only assume that it fell off the wall and was blown or swept out the door by accident. I never did get back to him. I have found out that he got home okay and in the years since has made quite a success of himself. I expected nothing less from a guy whose *Albany* nickname was "The Fox."

There was a situation that was somewhat amusing to those not directly involved. In my team, there were two Italians. For some reason they were at constant odds over which of their families would have been of the higher class in the old country. I have no idea if either of them was from, or had ever even been, to Italy, so I don't know how the conflict began. They used two terms. If I heard it correctly, I believe the "higher" class was Genovese and I think the "lower" class was Calabrese. They were actually close to fisticuffs a few times over this issue. I don't think they ever did get it resolved but it did relieve a little boredom for the rest of us.

13. Trenches and Bunkers

The environment was tough on equipment as well as men. In the summer, the heat and humidity just sapped your strength. During the monsoon, the constant rain keeps everything, if not soaked, at least sodden. Imagine the hardest rain you've ever seen almost nonstop for 4 to 5 months. Metal rusts, canvas rots, and there is mildew everywhere. Our maps were made of thick paper but it was by no means waterproof. If it wasn't water, sweat made them soggy. Some people had gotten acetate map cases made for weekend hikers from home but they would eventually crack or leak. I had a plan for something a bit more durable so I wrote home and asked my dad if he could manufacture something for me: "If you could get 2 sheets of Plexiglas 6½ by 6½ inches. In each corner put a screw and wing nut and around the edge, a fairly watertight gasket about ¼ inch wide. This is to put a map in and keep fairly dry."[1] I based these measurements on the size of the cargo pocket on my trouser leg. That's where I always carried my map. Making the map case took a little while but my dad came through.

> That map case is just exactly what I wanted. Two officers in the company have seen it and they think its quite a thing. One grunt lieutenant saw it and asked if Recon is issuing that kind of map case now and wanted to know where he could get one. When I told him it was one of a kind, he looked sort of disappointed. If you have enough plexiglass left I could work up a little business here for you. How would $2 apiece sound? Several patrol leaders in the company have said they'd kind of like one. The last patrol I took out, it rained for 5 straight days but not a drop got inside the case.[2]

That map case served me well for several months. I would fold the map down to fit in the case so the recon zone was visible in the center and then secure the cover. On the back, I wrote backwards on the inside with a magic marker the various elements of a call for fire including direction adjustments. Then, when I wanted artillery, I would make my calculations, write them in the appropriate place on the back of the map case with a grease pencil and hand it to the radioman. He would then just read it off to Rainbelt Bravo, while I kept my eye on the target. As the rounds came in I would then just give the corrections verbally to the radioman and he would send them. Corrections were very brief and would sound like, "Right 200 [meters], drop 100, fire for effect." When you get the first few rounds adjusted to where you want them to hit, fire for effect means the entire battery of three 105mm howitzers (or whatever artillery is shooting for you) fires three rounds each. Nine rounds will impact the target almost simultaneously.

The waterproof gasket in the case eventually became dried out and leaked a little. My dad made me another one and I still have both of them.

Another item that wore out quickly was gloves. We wore them all the time in the bush because everything out there bit, stung, dug, scratched, or cut. We cut off the fingers at the second knuckle so we could still put our fine motor skills to work, but the gloves otherwise offered good protection ... mostly against the elephant grass. Supply, however, took a dim view of us cutting up their gloves and then having the temerity to wear them out and ask for more.

> I want to thank you for the package you sent.... I haven't used the gloves yet because I have another pair that I'm going to wear out first. I hate to wear my sleeves rolled down [we used the cammie stick to cover our bare arms] so as a result my arms have been pretty well slashed up by elephant grass. Now I have little white scars on my arms where the cuts were and for some reason they won't tan....
>
> Except for the rain, the weather is getting a little more to my liking now. Quite often it gets down to about 60° and that's the way I like it. The heat over here just makes me wilt. Everybody else is running around complaining about how cold it is and thinking that I'm crazy because I like it.[3]

There were three sectors around the perimeter of the base that were manned by the grunt companies of the 26th Marines. Each sector had a color assigned to it and the sector that bordered the northern side of the base was Blue Sector. It ran parallel to the airstrip and was relatively straight. Physically, it was a trench with M-60 machine gun emplacements every few dozen yards, interspersed by heavier bunkers containing .50 caliber machine guns. In front of the trench line were a series of concentric rows of concertina wire, and double apron barbed wire. Imagine several rows of barbed wire strung horizontally in the shape of a pup tent about four feet high and you have double apron. There was also tangle foot, a maze of barbed wire strung tightly between stakes about eight inches off the ground and extending out from the outer row of wire for eight to a dozen feet. It was extremely difficult to walk through in the dark. In addition, there were Claymore mines and buried drums of foo-gas — commonly a 55-gallon drum of electrically detonated napalm. Its detonation causes a sheet of fire to shoot up and out. In and among these obstacles were pop flares, Bouncing Bettys, and various other pyrotechnic devices. During daylight, this defense is difficult enough to get through but at night, it was a very effective barrier.

Bravo Company Recon was part of the reaction force for the Blue Sector. At any given time, about half of the company would be on base between patrols. That amounted to a force of about 40 to 50 Marines that could be called upon to reinforce any part of the perimeter in an emergency. Depending on intelligence received, Bravo would, now and then, be tasked with providing a couple of teams to supplement that sector. We were also responsible for the defense of the 26th Marines HQ area.

The alert level on the perimeter was normally 50 percent. Every other man was on his feet and had eyes to the front. No chatter, no smoking. It made for a long night even if the watches were broken into one-hour turns. If there was intel that there might be an attack soon, the alert level was 100 percent until we were told to stand down.

Those long nights on the line were tedious and boring but two occasions stood out. One night, right at midnight, a half dozen colored pop flares went into the air to the west of our piece of the trench. In the dark, it was hard to tell but it appeared to be over towards regimental HQ. A few minutes later, I could hear shouting from over that way. When I could finally make out what was being said, I thought I heard, "It's over, it's over!" My first thought was, "What was *IT*?" Then it struck me that maybe the war was over! By the time that thought had sunk in, *the word* had gone past me and was headed east.

There was a lot of chatter on the line but no more flares went off. Then somebody came walking down the line behind the trench telling everyone to, "Knock it off, shut up, keep your eyes open!" Could it be? Was the war over? Many thoughts whirled through my mind. One of them, oddly enough, was disappointment. I had seen some action (but nothing like what many other Marines went through) and emerged relatively unscathed. After several months in Vietnam, I felt confident in my abilities and did not especially fear the thought of facing enemy fire again. On the other hand, I knew the feeling of the "pucker factor" and didn't much like it. That was the measure of the stress in any situation. A high pucker factor means high stress. It is a reference to what happens to your sphincter when you are well and truly scared. To say this was an anticlimactic situation would be an understatement. I mean, to have the war be over was a major relief ... the end of the great adventure, and yet...

Excitement and rumors filtered up and down the trench line all night long. Somebody tried calling C.O.C. on the EE8 field telephone to find out what was going on and he was told that the phone was for tactical use, not idle chitchat. The next morning, no one seemed to know who fired the flares, or why. It certainly did not signify the end of unpleasantries. It merely resulted in another round of contradictory feelings in most of us. Oh well.

On another night in the lines, we got a genuine scare. It was probably 0300 or so and I was more or less asleep in a cubbyhole that had been carved into the forward wall of the trench. These cubbies were for shelter from the elements or incoming fire as needed. They were not living accommodations. A short distance to the east of our position on the blue perimeter there was a sudden burst of M-60 fire. In a belt of machine gun ammunition, every fifth round is a tracer. It leaves an incendiary streak as it flies through the air and the gunner can use the stream of red to keep his bursts on target. The communist tracers were green. I jumped out of the cubbyhole and stood up in the trench in time to see the tracers from a second burst flashing out into the darkness and I could hear some shouting from that part of the line. The gun position that had fired was about 100 meters down the trench to the right so I couldn't really see much.

Two hand held illumination pop flares went up from the line. I could see the trail of sparks as they arched up and out over the wire. At the top of the arc, they both gave a muffled pop and then ejected the illumination element, which slowly descended on a small parachute. The whole area was bathed in a rather sickly light. As the flares descended, they swayed back and forth under their chutes, which caused the shadows on the ground to move accordingly. I could not see anything moving but there was then another flurry of machine gun and small arms fire. By this time, all hands were standing to in the trench and I could hear rifle safeties clicking off on either side of me.

Within a couple of minutes, 60mm mortar illumination rounds were going off above us. These things really lit the area up and made it almost like daylight. Sporadic fire continued for a few more minutes and then died down. Eventually the mortars ceased fire but during the rest of the night, they launched an illumination round every now and then. The big problem with illumination flares is that when they burn as they drift to the ground you are completely night blind for several minutes from the glare. This is not a good thing because if the enemy has any smarts, they will shield their eyes until the last flare goes out and then attack. They will have night vision and you will not. On the other hand, the illumination is fired so you can see if there's anything out there, so you need to look. Catch 22.

The word drifted quickly back to us from the direction of the commotion that an attempt to infiltrate the perimeter had been made by sappers and we went on 100 percent alert. Sappers were usually almost naked and unarmed except for the demolitions they carried. A sapper's mission is to breach the defensive perimeter, neutralize tactical and strategic positions, and thus prepare for the attack of the main body. They were adept at snaking their way through the wire obstacles. Unfortunately, they picked a spot on the line occupied by an alert Marine. Just before daybreak, we were relieved off the line so we wandered down to get the straight scuttlebutt on the night's activities.

The grunts who had stopped the attack were sitting up on the lip of the trench smoking their first cigarettes of the day and heating up C ration coffee. With little prompting they recounted the adventure of a few hours before. One of them had heard some noise in the wire. There were no patrols out so it could not be friendlies, but there was still the possibility that it was an animal of some kind. You don't open fire on the perimeter at night unless you have a target. It isn't as if the bad guys don't know where the trenches are, but why give them any help?

The Marine had quietly fixed his bayonet onto his rifle and waited until the furtive sounds were right in front of him approaching the trench. Due to the proximity of the sapper, the Marine could not make a sound in an attempt to let the others know he had a problem. He said that he could hear the sapper slide his hand down the inside wall of the trench less than an arm's length from where the Marine silently waited. The sapper now knew he was at the lip of the trench. The Marine knew it too and brought his bayonet right up into the sapper's upper chest. The sapper screamed, the Marine hollered, "Gooks in the wire!" and the Spam hit the fan.

The sapper was able to crawl away for a few feet. In the feeble pre-dawn light, I could just see a body lying out near the wire. The grunts were waiting for the EOD — Explosive Ordnance Disposal — people to come by and remove the demolitions the sapper carried. Then I guess the body would be turned over to the S-2 guys. Had the sapper just happened to arrive at a spot between sentries, he might have gotten onto the base and caused some real hate and discontent.

Generally, we were shelled at night. I suppose the NVA thinking was that the darkness added to the confusion and, at the very least, caused us a lot of sleepless nights. On the other hand, their muzzle flashes could be more easily seen at night and if they were awake and shooting at us, they weren't getting any sleep either. We had piled into the sergeants' bunker at the outset of a rocket attack and were settling down for a lot of noise and concussion. I noticed one of the guys messing around near the bunker entrance and he was half exposing himself to fire in order to manipulate something on the roof of the bunker.

In the cloud of dust that invariably filters down from the roof and seems to levitate from everywhere else due to the concussive effect of near hits, I lost track of what he was doing. When the all clear was signaled, I asked him what he had been doing and he showed me a small, battery-powered tape recorder and, during the attack, he had placed the microphone outside to record the rockets screaming overhead. We gathered around to listen to the playback and were surprised at the clarity of it. We could hear the rockets long scream as they passed over the area as well as the short shriek that indicated they were coming down very close to us. One of them was close enough that we could hear the debris that had fallen on top of our bunker after the blast (the crater was about 50 feet away). In the background, we could hear what was probably .50 caliber counter-battery fire from one of our perimeter positions.

I asked him if he could make a copy of that tape so he found someone else with a tape recorder and transferred it to a small reel of tape for me. I still have that copy and on the rare occasions when I listen to it, it still makes the hair on my arms stand up!

When we received incoming, if anyone thought they saw a muzzle flash or launch signature (smoke) from rocket launcher or mortar, the .50s would quickly try to lay down suppressing fires to keep the gook gunner's heads down. Our own 105mm howitzers would also fire counter-battery fires if a target could be plotted by crater analysis. That sometimes took a little while, though, and if they were firing rockets or mortars, they could be packed up and gone before our guns could be brought to bear.

Outside the perimeter, at the northwest extremity of the base was a large open expanse. This was the drop zone for parachuting supplies to the base in the event that the runway became unusable. A favorite target for the NVA gunners was the airstrip. Helicopters can land just about anywhere but fixed wing aircraft need runways. If there is even a minor disruption to the runway surface supply planes take great risks trying to land. Therefore, even when the runway was intact, we would occasionally get supplies airdropped, I suppose for practice. On one of those days, a couple of the Recon teams were detailed to go to the drop zone to provide security. As I mentioned, the drop zone was outside the perimeter but there was jungle within rifle range of one side of the DZ that bad people could hide in.

The idea was that we would fan out around the tree-lined sides of the DZ and keep our eyes open for any activity. The big drawback was that while we were observing the trees, many tons of supplies were rapidly descending above us and pinpoint accuracy on the DZ was difficult, at best. Having eyes on the top of our heads would have been handy. Even with three parachutes, a pallet of artillery ammunition probably weighed over a ton and was hitting the ground at about 35 MPH. They often penetrated as much as 12 to 18 inches into the ground. Sometimes a pallet would fly apart on impact, hurling its contents like a bomb. The worst was when there was a "streamer" and the parachute didn't open. They hit the ground at terminal velocity! There were occasional injuries and I heard of one death on the DZ.

14. Harborsites and a Little Travel

Several more patrols went by without much fanfare. We fired artillery at suspected NVA camps based on our observation of smoke from cooking fires coming up through the jungle. We couldn't really see the result because of the jungle but there were occasional secondary explosions because our artillery hit, and ignited, larger types of ordnance stockpiled at some of those locations.

The monsoon rain, even under that canopy, was driving down and the noise of the rain drowned out all ambient sound. We had been moving through very difficult terrain for two days and we were soaked to the skin, tired, and miserable. We had seen neither hide nor hair of the bad guys. In fact, the few trails that we came across were overgrown and looked unused for years.

We stopped for a break on a piece of high ground under some tall canopy. There were often three distinct layers of growth in the jungle. The tallest were up to 150 feet and were truly mighty trees festooned with stout vines and parasitic plant life. There was also a lot of bamboo and nearer to the ground were many banana palms. They were anywhere from six to twenty feet tall but the leaves on all of them were huge. The biggest were seven or eight feet long and as much as two feet wide.

It had been hard slogging so, for this break, I decided we'd just stay put for a couple of hours and rest up. I set up security watches just as if it were a nighttime harborsite and those not on watches tried to take a nap. Tired as we were, it was impossible to doze off with the rain pelting down on us. Finally, I passed the word to make minimal shelters from the banana palm leaves. These were not elaborate at all ... just a bit of overhead cover. Within 15 minutes, each of us had tiny, primitive hooch to sit under more or less out of the rain and suddenly the whole situation became more tolerable. Sometimes the smallest comfort can be worth its weight in airplane tickets home.

When it came time to move on, we carefully restored the site and carried the banana leaves along with us, stuffing them one at a time out of sight into thickets that we passed every 50 feet or so.

Toward the end of each day on patrol, I had to start thinking about where to set up the harborsite. Our normal tactic was to study the map for a likely location, based on terrain and vegetation, and then pick a spot that would be very difficult for anyone to approach at night without difficulty. As a result, we spent many nights in thick, thorny brush or even perhaps, oh, I don't know, dangling from a tree on the side of a mountain.

Whatever the case, our routine was to stop before dusk somewhere near to the proposed harborsite. While there, and while we could still see fairly well, we ate chow. We rarely used heat tabs because there was a slim possibility that the flame could be seen and the smell of cooking can carry a surprising distance. Heat tabs were made of trioxane ... little blue tabs that when lit with a match burned with a small, intense blue flame that would boil a canteen cup of water or a can of C-rats in a few minutes. The fumes were awful and really irritated your eyes if you weren't careful. C-4 worked well for cooking too. Believe it or not, a small ball of C-4 will burn but not explode when lit with a match, but the flame was brighter.

I don't think there has been a foot soldier since the days of the Roman Empire who didn't complain about the field rations. Our C-rations were heavy, bulky, and not exactly a gustatory delight. After several days of this fare, the result was often either constipation or diarrhea. I did have one favorite, though. It was the beans and meatballs ... very tasty. The pound cake was unusually well made, too. The worst was, of course, the aforementioned ham and lima beans. However, tactics and survival usually dictated that we eat whatever we had cold, grease and all. All trash was carefully buried and camouflaged.

There was one thing I never figured out. The little pasteboard box containing each meal was a dull, vaguely beige color. The various cans inside were all painted olive drab green or brown with black lettering describing the taste delights contained within. A foil packet with condiments, matches, gum, powdered coffee, a 4-pack of cigarettes (Pall Mall, Camel, Lucky Strike — all unfiltered), and toilet paper was also in the box. The foil packet was dark brown, the toilet paper was a neutral color, and even the matches were green. The plastic spoon that came in the packet was white. *White!* How — what — who?

On rare occasions we were issued what we called long rats — long range rations. These freeze-dried meals were very lightweight and very tasty. All you do is add a half a canteen cup of water (hot or cold, but hot was best), let it sit for five minutes and chow down. There were no extras like crackers, bread, fruit, or cheese spread as in the C-rations but there was enough there so you didn't really need them. The army's LRRP — Long Range Recon Patrol — teams were supplied with all the Long Rats they could carry. We were lucky to get three or four of them every few patrols. The Marines have always seemed to be the illegitimate stepchildren of the military.

I might as well cover hygiene, too. First, we did not wash or shave on patrol. Marines in the field do not "freshen up." The smell of any soap, deodorant, or shaving cream is instantly detectable in the bush to anyone downwind. That we did not have the water to spare, especially in the summer, goes without saying. The call of nature was accomplished by digging a "cat hole" with an entrenching tool or Ka-bar, squatting over it, and then carefully covering it over. Certain plants, when pulled up by the roots, left just the right size hole. Business done, you stuck that plant back where you got it, and everyone, including the plant, was happy. No, we did not use leaves to clean up. There were small rolls of toilet paper in each C-ration meal. Can you imagine grabbing something like a poison ivy leaf?

At the pre-harborsite, weapons were given a rudimentary cleaning and radio watches were assigned. Two men awake, one hour at a time, all night. I would select coordinates for night defensive fires around the proposed harborsite and call them in. The arty guys would assign a registration number to each of them and I noted them on my map case with a grease pencil. Artillery would use those same registrations for H&I fires at night.

Just before it got dark, we would very carefully move to the actual harborsite. This was so that if we had been spotted earlier, there would hopefully be some confusion as to where we really were. Many teams had their butts saved by this tactic. If, after arriving, I wanted to change a registration, for instance, I would call in the correction. Otherwise, we were fed, watered and tucked in for the night. We slept in a 360 degree circle with the primary radio in the center and our feet nearly touching. Our packs and other gear were placed behind our heads. The smaller the harborsite, the better.

The only other business left was to put the Claymore mines out on any possible avenue of approach to the harborsite. If we were probed at night, and I felt they had us pinpointed or were getting too close, I could blow one or more of the Claymores. The effect of those things is devastating and while they recovered from that shock, we would be organizing a defense or making our escape. There was the danger, however, that if we had been careless, and the gooks knew exactly where we were, they might be able to slip in, find a Claymore, and turn it around. They would then create enough of a disturbance that might cause me to set the Claymore off but we would be on the receiving end. Even though we camouflaged the Claymores with leaves and debris, we still had to keep the possibility in mind that they could be turned against us.

Staying alert at night was, literally, deadly serious. It was said that Charlie (as in Victor Charlie — VC) owned the night and it did seem that they had a knack for moving around in complete darkness. Two men awake with one of them on the radio and the other listening to the night was pretty much S.O.P.

There was no gabbing and joking between the watch standers. Noise discipline was critical at night. No lights except for red lens flashlights under a poncho and only if absolutely necessary. No smoking was a no-brainer at *any* time for several reasons. However, if it had been an especially exhausting day of moving through what seemed to be giant, green steel wool in 100 degree heat and 100 percent humidity, I would set one-man watches instead of two. Of course, that meant that the man on watch had to keep one ear on the radio handset and the other on the jungle. Oh, and stay awake, too. Aye, there's the rub. (Shakespeare — *Hamlet*, don't you know.) Marines are mostly human and as such, they can reach a point where the body just pulls rank and closes up shop for a while.

We've all been there ... too tired to keep our eyes open. Realizing, with a start, that we had just let several minutes go by in total unconsciousness. Doing that while driving is often fatal. Doing that while in a harborsite at 0300 with the distinct possibility of people who mean you harm being nearby could also be fatal. Getting up and taking a walk is out. Singing and whistling is out. Heating up some coffee over a cheerful fire is out. What it came down to was discipline and the knowledge that other Marines slept safely while you watched over them.

That being said, we still dozed off sometimes. Probably more often than I am willing to admit. We just couldn't help it. Recon S.O.P. at night is for Rainbelt Bravo to call each team every hour or half hour, I don't recall now. The small, tinny voice of the radio operator up on Hill 950 would say, "Broadweave Two, Rainbelt Bravo. If you are alpha sierra (all secure) key the handset twice, over."

If everything really was normal, the man on radio watch would squeeze the transmit button on the handset twice, which Rainbelt Bravo heard as two scratchy bursts of static. This means of communication was crude but nearly soundless. If Rainbelt did not hear two clicks he assumed one of two things. There was trouble near the harborsite and the team could not risk even the tiniest sound or movement, or the guy on radio watch was asleep. The Rainbelt operators were always cool. Instead of assuming the worst (the Rainbelt radiomen were all qualified Reconners and had experience in the bush) he would then say, "Broadweave Two, Rainbelt Bravo. If you are *not* alpha sierra key your handset once, over." If that was the case the radio watch was obligated to press the transmit button once very carefully. If we were about to get in trouble it was imperative that Rainbelt knew it.

If there was still no click from the patrol it was a fair bet that somebody had dozed off. Or they were all dead. It was rare but a sleeping team could be hit so hard and fast that there was no chance of communicating.

Rainbelt Bravo radiomen were patient and tried calling every couple of minutes. They were always greatly relieved when they finally received two belated clicks. Actually, I don't know how the Rainbelt operators stayed awake. They weren't exactly holding pajama parties on Hill 950. I even heard of one instance where a team had not been heard from for a few hours and, when notified of it, the Recon company commander ordered the artillery to send a round out to impact within a couple hundred meters of the harborsite coordinates. There was an immediate response from the errant team.

One night, because of very difficult terrain, we had to set in within a dozen feet of a trail. It didn't look heavily used but we always avoided trails because it was too easy to get surprised. I had with me a small anti-personnel mine called an M-14 concussion mine. It was approximately the size of a tuna can and had a plastic body. The idea was to dig a small hole, put a flat stone in the bottom to make it very firm, remove the safety clip from the mine and set it on the stone. A thin layer of dirt or some leaves would disguise it. It was placed where someone would be likely to step. It was designed, upon detonation, to shatter the bones in the foot and lower leg by concussion. There was almost no shrapnel from it.

I went down the trail about 30 feet and found a thick branch lying across the trail. I placed the mine where I thought someone would place their foot after stepping over the branch if they were coming toward the harborsite. I returned to the harborsite and told everyone precisely where the mine was.

About a half hour later, my lower intestine said, "I'll bet you can't hold it all night." Security is a high priority so, on patrol, even big bad Marines take a partner when they go on a potty break. In the gathering gloom I poked the guy next to me (Lance Corporal Garry Tallent, my radioman) and told him I had to go to the gent's. I led the way down the trail past the mine (after pointing it out to him) where I found a convenient spot. As we headed back, I came to the fallen branch and casually stepped over it. My foot was about six inches above the mine and coming down when I realized what I was doing. Did you know that levitation is actually possible? I don't know how I did it but my amazing gymnastic ability kept me from putting my foot down right there. I stopped and turned to Tallent behind me. He had noticed where I was about to step at the same instant I did, and he was pale as a sheet even through the cammie paint! I was in a cold sweat and it's a good thing I had just emptied my bladder because there was an almost overwhelming sensation to do it again. I was stunned at how careless I had almost been! I never carried an M-14 mine on patrol again.

It may have been a night on that same patrol about 0200; someone yelling out loud shocked me and everyone else awake. Lying on my back there was just enough difference between the darkness of the jungle around us and the dark sky above that I could make out the silhouette of someone standing above me. He was reaching up over his head and yelling, "Okay, bring it over. A little more. A little more. Dat's good. Dat's good." Two or three of us tackled him and slammed him to the ground. Startled, he began thrashing around but we held him down and covered his mouth until he relaxed. It was Lance Corporal Noo Yawk. It turned out he used to work on a construction site and was having a dream where he was guiding a crane or something. Needless to say, we were all wide awake the rest of the night.

We were occasionally provided with experimental equipment to test. I don't know if it was experimental government issue or if came from civilian suppliers, but we were expected to try it out and give our assessment of it. One was a very lightweight mummy type sleeping bag. It was hardly more that a sort of nylon shell with a zipper up the front. I guess they were intended to be used for fair weather camping. Besides the fact that they were somewhat flimsy, zipping yourself into a bag in the bush is an excellent way to get killed. If we got jumped during the night, we'd never get out of them in time. Besides, our ponchos, if we even used them, were just fine. We never even took those sleeping bags on patrol.

A far more sensible item was a tube of some kind of silicone jelly. It was essentially water proofing for your feet. The object was to smear it all over your bare foot and ankle and then pull a sock on over it. Getting the sock on was a chore but once in place, and you got used to the squishy feeling between your toes, this stuff really worked. I used it from November and into the monsoon until I ran out and had little trouble with immersion foot. One thick application generally lasted for a whole patrol. Of course, you had to peel your socks off like a banana when you got back, but that was a small price to pay. When the silicone was gone we tried to get more but apparently what we got was all there was. I never again saw that stuff nor have I ever seen it in camping supply catalogues.

First Lieutenant Carl Schlack, the company executive officer, was a former enlisted man who had been commissioned as an officer and, while probably only in his early to mid 30s, was the oldest man in the company while holding a rank usually associated with someone in their early 20s. In the Corps, these guys are referred to as Mustangs. Lt. Schlack was known as "Pappy," but not to his face. Mustangs have come up through the ranks and have seen life in the Marines from both sides. Their experience was invaluable and we looked at Pappy with a certain degree of reverence.

One day as I returned to the sergeants' hooch I was met by Pappy coming out the door. He had with him two young Marines from my platoon and he was not pleased.

"Ah, Sgt. Johnson. I've been looking for you. I just caught these two try-ing to swipe some long rats from supply and they claim to belong to you."

The two miscreants were standing at attention and had "hands in the cookie jar" looks on their faces.

I said, "Yes Sir, they're mine."

After giving them a withering look, he said, "They are thieves and I can't stand thieves but I'll leave their fate to you." With that, he turned and left.

If we were starving, stealing food could be considered a capital offense. As things stood, though, it was a relatively minor transgression. Pilferage of building materials, or surplus equipment from supply units (preferably some-one else's and otherwise known as midnight requisitions) was fairly common and sometimes the only way to obtain things outside the glacially slow supply system. Their biggest crime was getting caught and especially by an officer.

I asked, "What the hell did you think you were doing?"

One of them said, "We just really like the long rats." (I couldn't fault that. They *were* tasty.) "We knew supply wouldn't give them to us and we didn't think they'd be missed."

I walked around behind them without saying anything and stood there for a few moments. I had learned this trick from one of my D.I.s. They didn't know what I was thinking or doing and it made them sweat. Stepping back in front of them I said, "Here's the deal. You will each eat two cans of ham and lima beans. You will eat them in front of me and you will eat them cold!" I was counting on the fact that ham and limas were almost universally hated and I was right. They pleaded with me to make them fill sandbags or dig bunkers. Anything but Ham and Hockers! I told them to procure two cans each from the C-ration dump box beside supply and report back at 1700 for chow call. I added, "Bring a John Wayne[1] and a spoon."

At the appointed time, they both reported to the sergeants' hooch to await execution. There was even a small crowd present to watch the torture. They opened the cans and there on the top was the usual half-inch layer of pure lard that made the ham and limas so greasy. The C-rat cans are always filled right to the top and are too full to mix the ingredients without spilling. If we had to eat them, we tried to scoop off the lard and tossed it away.

I said, "Eat. Lard and all. Begin!"

They grimaced and dug in. One of them gobbled both cans as fast as he could, figuring to get it over with. The other one tried to take it in small doses until I told him he had 10 minutes to finish or I would add another can to the punishment. When the last spoonful was down the hatch, the onlookers gave them a round of applause.

Later that evening I bumped into Pappy and he said, "Johnson, I heard what you made those two do this afternoon."

I thought he might be mad at me because I didn't write them up on a formal charge sheet. He just grinned and said, "Okay."

I had been having headaches for a few weeks and sometimes they were quite severe. I went to the company chief corpsman and he sent me up to Charlie Med. The doctor there thought for some reason that it was because I needed glasses. My vision then was better than 20/20 so that didn't make any sense to me. Then he told me I had to go to the Naval Hospital in Da Nang for an eye exam. I figured he was a doctor and what do I know? He got me orders releasing me from the company for a day and handed me my health records. I went back to my hooch, got my rifle, helmet, and flak jacket, checked out at the company office and went to the airstrip to hitch a ride to Da Nang.

The only thing headed for Da Nang right then was an Air Force helicopter. This was the strangest aircraft I had ever seen. It was a very boxy looking chopper that you entered through a good-sized door at the rear. The twin rotors, instead of being fore and aft like any respectable helicopter, were situated side by side but tilted outboard at an angle allowing the blades to intermesh like an eggbeater. There was no tail assembly to speak of. There were seats down the sides for about four people each. There were, besides myself, several Marines and one ARVN. Pronounced Arvin, it denoted a soldier of the Army of the Republic of Vietnam. As I got settled in the seat beside the ARVN, he turned to me and asked, "Da Nang?" I gathered that he was asking if the chopper's destination was, in fact, Da Nang, and I nodded that it was.

This was not a very fast chopper so it took a while to get there. I really don't know what its main function was and I have never seen another one like it since. We landed at Da Nang and as we got off the chopper, I noticed that one of the other Marines was hobbling with a bootless and heavily bandaged foot. He was trying to hop along using his rifle for a cane and not having much luck. I told him I'd give him a hand so he put one arm around my shoulders and we made our way to the terminal. I asked him if he had been wounded but he said that he broke something in his foot when some heavy object fell on it. We both got into a jeep that was shuttling back and forth from the hospital but when we got to where I needed to go he had to go on to another area.

After reporting to the eye doctor, I was given a thorough eye exam. The doctor asked me how long I had been having headaches and I told him that it had been for a few weeks. He then told me to have a seat in the waiting room. About a half hour later, he came out and handed me two pair of glasses! There was a pair of dark glasses and a pair of clear ones. They were bifocals but only the bottom part was a reading lens. The upper lenses were just clear glass (or plastic). Military issue glasses at that time were clunky looking dark rimmed things that those who had to wear them called BC glasses. BC stands for birth control because no self-respecting female would ever go near someone wearing them. I asked him what they were for and he said that he thought the headaches were caused by eye strain, maybe from reading maps. I pointed out that my vision was very good and he gave me some explanation, mostly in four syllable medical terms, and told me to wear them when I was reading and see if the headaches go away. I put them in my pocket and left.

As I recall, the hospital was not on an actual military facility. It was a large building that stood alone in downtown Da Nang and was more like a clinic than a hospital. This was the largest example of civilization I had yet seen, so I strolled around a bit. There were people, Vietnamese, and American military, everywhere. Scooters and bicycles clogged the streets. I took a few pictures of the street scenes but it wasn't much to write home about. (As a matter of fact, I didn't.) The noise and bustle of Da Nang was actually rather annoying. I found myself missing the relative quiet of Khe Sanh. (Quiet, that is, between rocket and artillery attacks. But then, you can't have everything.) I caught the jeep shuttle back to the airstrip and checked in at flight ops. This time, the next aircraft going to Khe Sanh was an Army plane they called a Caribou. This twin-engine plane held about 30 people in inboard facing seats that went down the sides of the fuselage, which was hardly wider than a CH-46.

Those of us who were waiting for the flight found a spot to flake out against a section of chain link fence near the air terminal. Across a large parking lot was a good-sized PX and several of the guys went over and loaded up on pogey bait. While we were lounging, a special services bus pulled in with a number of passengers. There was a sign on the side of the bus indicating that it was carrying a USO troupe. Among the several people who got off the bus were some females of the American species. I don't know if any of them were celebrities but it didn't matter, as they waved and shouted to us. Then one girl broke away from the group and headed directly for a six-holer that was about 100 feet away. It was obvious where she was going. In a flash, we all had the same idea. When she was about half way to the head we shouted in singsong unison, "We know where you're going." She instantly stopped, put her face in her hands, spun around and hotfooted back to the bus. Even her own group got a laugh out of it. I don't know how far they were going but I hope there was another rest stop scheduled soon.

Having done our mischief for the day, we soon boarded the Caribou and winged (wang, wung?) our way north. As we approached the runway at Khe Sanh, we began to bounce around a lot. I had heard that there was often a tricky crosswind there and we must have been in a good one. As we got to within a hundred feet of the ground, I could look out one of the windows and was shocked to see that I was looking down the length of the runway! We were coming in damn near sideways! I think pilots call it "side-slipping." Everybody had that "deer in the headlights" look until we banged down on the runway. We slowed to a stop very quickly and soon I was strolling back to the company area with my new spectacles in my pocket. I tried the glasses out but could not see any improvement to my vision while wearing them for reading so I never used them again. By the way, the headaches went away soon after. Go figure.

15. On Patrol

On a patrol southwest of Khe Sanh, we came down a small hill probably three klicks from 881S. Near the bottom of the hill was a little flat spot that looked like it had been used fairly recently, as the grass was flattened out and there were cleared areas. We carefully explored it because our natural first inclination was that it was an active NVA campsite. When I was satisfied that it was not an active campsite I decided we'd take a break. After settling down one of the guys noticed that the dirt in a spot about a yard across appeared to have been disturbed.

We cautiously dug into it and a few inches down struck something metallic. It seemed an unlikely place for a landmine but we treated it as such until we uncovered a couple of C-ration cans. Further excavation revealed 30 or 40 intact C-rat cans that had been buried. The cans had no holes or rust on them, indicating that they hadn't been there long, so when some of the team selected a few favorites I let them go ahead. The remainder of the cans was reburied after we punched holes in them so the contents would rot. The site was covered and made to look like it was never there. Our own garbage was disposed of likewise. Empty cans in a pack can clank and rattle. It's much easier to bend them as flat as possible and bury them.

The RZ continued to the east and on the last day we followed a narrow ridge downward toward a tiny hamlet of Montagnards that straddled the road coming out of the base toward the Ville. My point man suddenly stopped and pointed to the right and left down off the ridge a few feet. I moved up to him and he pointed to a couple belts of machine gun ammunition on one side and some pop flares and hand grenades on the other.

It was all American ordnance! I examined it carefully to make sure it wasn't booby-trapped and then we picked it up and put it in our packs. The brass on the ammo was still shiny so even though there had been no rain for a while, it obviously hadn't been there very long. I noted the coordinates in my patrol book and we moved on.

We came out on the road and started toward the base. On the way, we passed through the hamlet. These people were actually Bru, a tribe of the Montagnards. The hamlet looked like something out of *National Geographic*. There were, maybe, 25 huts made of sticks and bamboo with thatch roofs and were held up off the ground by stilts. They appeared to be just one room and they had small cooking fires on the ground in front of each one. Little pens were beside each hut and in them were an assortment of pigs and goats. Undisciplined chickens ran rampant everywhere. Men and women both wore a sort of kilt made of grass. Both sexes went topless. During the monsoon, they wore a woven reed cape under a wide conical reed hat. They were small, dark brown people and they all completely ignored us. They hunted with bow and arrow and were deadly with handmade crossbows.

We were soon back on the base and I went to the C.O.C. for debriefing. Our job is to report everything we see as well as reporting seeing nothing. The C-rats and ammo were about all we saw on this patrol so as part of my report I included the location and description of the C-rats and ordnance we found. Not knowing where it came from, and being still serviceable, the ordnance was turned in to our armory along with our own grenades, gas, Claymores, etc.

Three or four days later, I was in my team's hooch giving them a new patrol order when the door flew open and in stepped a gentleman I had never seen before. He was large, hairless, and ticked off. A fierce red handlebar mustache adorned his face and captain's bars graced his collar points. He looked around the hooch and said, "Who is Sergeant Johnson?"

I stood up and stammered out, "I am, S-s-sir."

"Come with me." It was not a request.

We went outside and he said, "Did you find chow and ammo out in such and such an area a few days ago?"

I said that I did and he glared at me for a second and then seemed to calm down a bit. He introduced himself to me as Captain John Raymond, company commander of Alpha Company, 1/26. That grunt company lived along the northern perimeter of the base in the Blue Sector. He explained that he had just come from a weekly briefing from the base commander and it was brought up that Recon had found perfectly good C-rats and serviceable American ammunition. No grunts had been in that area for about ten days except for a patrol from Capt. Raymond's company. It was quite apparent that some of his troops, in order to lighten their load, dumped some of this heavy stuff along the way.

That explained to me where it had come from but I could not think how anybody could be so stupid as to throw away food and especially ammo. The goofy part was that they buried the food and left the ammo in plain sight. I can only guess that the ammo was tossed while on the move and the cans were buried while they took a break. At any rate, Capt. Raymond was furious that any of his people could be that knuckleheaded. He said he wasn't mad at me and, in fact, appreciated my conscientiousness in destroying or retrieving those items and reporting it. He then thanked me and left. He was not a happy captain but at least I was no longer the target of his wrath. I expect a small mushroom cloud erupted over the Blue Sector shortly thereafter, and I was destined to meet Capt. Raymond again in a very unexpected way.

I was talking with a team leader from 1st platoon one day about an area that he had been in recently and that I was about to take a patrol into the next day. While talking with him, I heard someone nearby mention Tyrone, Pennsylvania. Tyrone is a small town, even smaller than Jamestown, and it was only a little over an hour away from home. I looked around and saw the speaker, a blond haired sergeant with a very confident air about him. I said, "Hey, Tyrone." He looked over and I said, "Jamestown, New York." He immediately got up and came over to introduce himself as Albert Lumpkin. He said he never expected to see anybody who knew where Tyrone was. Lumpkin was actually in Alpha Company, 3d Recon, that had already been at Khe Sanh for a few months. Bravo Company had relieved Alpha in June and I believe Al's team was OpConned to Bravo, and then it was just sort of absorbed into Bravo Company.

My next patrol took us quite a way west and a bit north of Khe Sanh. The farther away from the base that we got in that direction, the heavier and thicker the jungle seemed to be. The mountains got steeper, too. I checked in with air liaison and scheduled an overflight. At the appointed time I was at the helicopter pad and within a few minutes I noticed a Huey slick (no guns or rocket pods) heading straight for me from the helicopter revetments on the other side of the airstrip. It was moving at about 20 mph and maintaining its "air taxi" at about two feet off the ground. Hueys don't have wheels like other aircraft. They have landing skids much like sled runners. On the ground, maintenance crews can put dollies on the skids to maneuver the Huey around with a tow motor, but to move from one place to another under power, but not really fly, is called air taxiing.

This Huey was making a beeline for me and I began to wonder if I should move. Hueys, although small, have a very predatory look to them and I could not help but feel kind of like a bug being zeroed in on by a giant dragonfly. The Huey slowed and turned sideways to me about 50 feet away. It settled to the deck and the pilot motioned to me to jump in the back. Now I realized this was my overflight bird. My first Huey ride!

Hueys have a good-sized sliding door on either side of the bird so climbing into the cargo-troop compartment was hardly more difficult than getting into the back seat of a minivan. Almost all Marine Hueys flew with the side doors removed for both visibility and quick access. The co-pilot pointed to a crew helmet on the bench seat behind me and I put it on. Now I could talk with both pilots over the intercom system. I knelt on the deck between and behind the pilots as we lifted off. Riding in a Huey is like being in a sports car compared to the much bigger 34s and 46s.

Kneeling where I was, I had almost as good a view out the front windshield as the pilots did. This was fun! We flew out to the vicinity of my RZ and I compared the ground with my map. I chatted back and forth with the pilot about the suitability of two or three potential LZs and then we headed back. The sky was darkening with storm clouds so the pilot headed back to Khe Sanh a bit faster than we had come out. I was looking over the bewildering array of gauges and dials on the dashboard trying to find the speedometer. Giving up, I asked the pilot what the top speed of a Huey is.

He said, "In a slick with no load, we can do about 130 knots flat out but we normally cruise at about 100 knots." Pointing to one of the gauges, he said, "Right now we're doing 104 knots because I want to beat that storm back to base."

Arriving all too soon at the chopper pad, the pilot flared the Huey up slightly and settled to the ground. Before taking off the helmet, I thanked the pilots for the ride and stepped out. As I moved away, the pilot lifted into the air taxi mode and scooted back to the revetments.

Based on my overflight, I had picked an insertion LZ near the edge of some heavy looking jungle, the theory being that as soon as we landed we could melt into that greenery and leave the immediate area unseen. We always moved cross-country and avoided trails like the plague. We also never chopped our way through the bush. We just had to slither through it as efficiently and quietly as possible. We were often in lower level growth that was so thick you could lean against it without falling through. It's hard to believe anything requiring sunlight for photosynthesis could survive as thick, green, and prolifically as it does under a dense overhead canopy.

I went back to the sergeants' hooch to collect the rest of my gear and then went to the team hooch and told them to mount up. After a few minutes of grunting into their heavy packs and web gear, we straggled up the road to the chopper pad in front of Charlie Med. Two CH-46s were sitting there with their rotors turning. The ramp was down on the nearest one, indicating that was the one we should board. Leaning into the rotor wash, holding our breath for a few seconds as we went through the hot, and nauseating (to me), exhaust from the rear turbine, we filed into the chopper. The interior of a 46 is fairly roomy with seats down each side made of aluminum tubing covered with web mesh. They vaguely resembled lawn chairs but weren't anywhere near as comfortable. There were seat belts but we never used them because we did not take off our gear and with those huge packs on our back, the seat-belts weren't long enough to go around us anyway.

The fuselage of the chopper was aluminum with no inside lining. Plumb-ing and wiring of all kinds snaked and wound its way down the overhead and sides from front to back. There was a myriad of electrical junction boxes, fit-tings, valves, couplings, and gauges. There was also a pervasive odor of JP-4, hydraulic fluid, and machinery grease. As the pilot cranked up the revolutions to the rotors, the chopper began a rhythmic shimmy until we lifted off. Then it just shook all over. This was all perfectly normal for a Phrog.

As we clattered our way west we passed over Hill 881S. It looked just like an anthill with green bipedal ants crawling around on it doing whatever bipedal ants do. Although a 46 can outrun a Huey gunship, they usually chuffed along at a relatively sedate pace on our insertions. Looking out the round Plexiglas window, I saw the gunships churn past us on the way to chew up our LZ if they saw any signs of enemy activity. Somewhere far above there were probably a couple of Phantoms on station.

Upon nearing the LZ, we began a sharp spiral down from a couple thou-sand feet. The rear of the chopper dropped as the pilot picked up the nose to flare to the ground. The rear wheels hit with a thump and then the nose wheel settled down. Most of us were on our feet hanging on to whatever was handy even before touching down. As the crew chief lowered the ramp, we ran out under the rotor wash and quickly established a 360-degree defensive position around the chopper. With the roaring turbines and lashing vegeta-tion, we could neither see nor hear much of anything.

Often, at that point, the only way a team knew that they had landed in a hot LZ was when the chopper's gunners opened up with their .50 calibers. You can hear a .50 caliber over *anything*. Sometimes there was time to get back on the chopper and make an escape and sometimes the pilot felt that he was taking too much battle damage and had to get into the relative safety of the air immediately. In that case, the team had to defend itself (with the deadly support of the gunships) until the backup chopper came down for them. If the team felt they could break contact, they would quickly move out of the area to either continue the patrol or be extracted elsewhere. In any event, insertions were highly risky, dangerous operations involving the coor-dination of many people and a number of large, expensive machines.

From the air, it's tough to tell two-foot elephant grass from eight-foot elephant grass. When the rotor wash flattens it down, then we know. This time it was about six feet high and very thick. After dropping us off the chop-pers pulled away from the area so we could sit still, listen, and watch for the presence of enemy activity. It soon appeared that we were alone so I had the radioman contact the choppers.

"Lucky Strike lead, this is Broadweave Two, over."

"Broadweave Two, Lucky Strike lead, go ahead, over."

"Lucky Strike lead, Broadweave Two. We are Alpha Sierra (all secure) and will beagle igloo raiders (move northwest), over."

"Roger that, Broadweave Two. Have fun. Lucky Strike lead, out."

The birds then headed back to Khe Sanh. If we needed them, though, they would have been right back, and I mean pronto!

We eventually moved out of that heavy stuff into slightly more open but steep terrain. That night we set in to our harborsite on top of a tall ridgeline in some thick brush. The side of the ridge fell away quickly covered by three-foot elephant grass so we had limited visibility outside our thicket. We made our usual night preparations and settled down. Sometime after midnight, one of the radio watches woke me up to tell me he had seen lights down in the valley below. I woke everybody else up and we awaited developments. Within a few minutes Doc Miller whispered, "There's one!" Now we could see what appeared to be the light from something like a Coleman lantern. The total darkness around us and the considerable distance to the valley floor made it difficult to determine anything except the fact that there was a light and it was slowly moving from south to north.

Even binoculars didn't reveal any additional detail. Before that light passed out of our sight, another one came from the south. In a few minutes, one more was seen. I called in a SALUTE report. This is another of those acronyms that we use. The letters stand for *S*ize (of the unit), *A*ctivity (what they are doing), *L*ocation (map coordinates), *U*niform (what they are wearing, and yes, the phonetic word for uniform is uniform), *T*ime (of sighting), and *E*quipment (what they have with them) and it pertained to enemy, not friendly, activity.

Since there wasn't much to tell in this case, my SALUTE report sounded like:

Sierra — lights in the valley

Alpha — moving south to north approximately 100 meters apart.

Lima — grid 774585 (Enemy locations were usually given uncoded. If they could hear our transmission, and they knew where they were, they could decipher a small part of the shackle code.)

Uniform — Unknown

Tango — 0140

Echo — Lanterns

Rainbelt Bravo repeated it back to me for confirmation and then relayed the report to the C.O.C. The Rainbelt Bravo guys were all Recon radiomen who rotated that duty a month or two at a time, so they, at least, had an idea what was going on out there. There was nothing else to do. A Starlight scope at that distance would have been no help. It was *dark*, we were some distance away and moving closer would have been noisy and hazardous in the *dark*.

A few minutes went by and then Rainbelt Bravo called and said that S-2 wanted us to call in a fire mission on the lights. I took the handset and, through the relay, explained that it was *dark*, we can't see what we're shooting at because it was *dark*, and the lights were far enough away that adjusting the artillery at that distance in the *dark* would be nearly impossible. At night, there is no frame of reference. Judging distance accurately for a fire mission is critical. Not only that, but artillery barrages landing right on top of you do not just accidentally happen. Someone has to control it, that someone has to be within visual range, and the bad guys know it.

Sanity somehow prevailed and we did not call a fire mission that night, although we counted eight lights moving through. The next morning, I was a bit leery about leaving our little nest until I had a better idea of our surroundings. While the team cammied up, I called the base and asked for an air observer to come up and have a look around. An AO is an unarmed light plane used for spotting artillery and air strikes and piloted by certifiable crazymen. AOs were often called Bird Dogs. If, as I suspected, it was a large unit moving north, who knows but what they might have decided to stop for the night just a couple hundred meters away from where we saw the last light. I really hate surprises like that.

It wasn't long before we heard the drone of the little single engine prop plane headed our way. Over the radio came, "Broadweave Two, you still down there?" I assured him we were and asked him to check out the area. He then went on to fly lazy circles at an altitude of a few hundred feet above the mountaintops. About ten or fifteen minutes later he called back and said, "Well, Broadweave, it looks like a circus followed by a herd of elephants passed up that valley. The grass is trampled flat several feet wide and disappears into the jungle at the north end of the valley. A lot of people went through there."

I thanked him and he buzzed away. Was I ever glad we hadn't called a fire mission! The NVA would have known that no one but Recon would be out that far calling in artillery at 1:30 in the morning and a unit that size could have fanned out to every likely O.P. looking for us. We would have had to run for our lives and not accomplished much. By the same token, we had observed a large enemy unit movement that would otherwise not have been detected, and that was our job.

We moved out and had an interesting day. About mid morning, we came across an area that had been arc lighted. Arc light was the term for a flight of B-52 bombers dropping their entire load of bombs (typically 105–500 pound bombs) on suspected concentrations of enemy troops. The craters were anywhere from thirty or more feet across and fifteen to twenty feet deep depending on the density of the soil. One of our occasional duties was to take a device consisting of a steel rod with a torque gauge attached to it and push it into the ground as far as it would go and then read the gauge. This indicated how dense the soil was at various depths. We did this in three places one meter apart several times during a patrol. The results were recorded and given to S-2 for data on how effective bombs might be in that area. We also did BDAs (bomb damage assessments). We would go to the site of an arclight and measure such things as crater depth, diameter, and extent of the debris field. The Air Force likes statistics.

This area had once been an expanse of elephant grass but now it looked like the moon. There was no indication of what the intended target might have been. PFC Gary Scribner motioned me over to the edge of one of the craters. He was pointing to a pile of rags at his feet. Upon closer inspection, I saw that it was a human skeleton, in very bad shape, still in an NVA uniform. The body had been there long enough so that it had completely decomposed except for the bones. The skull had an NVA helmet on it but it was crushed around the skull. What was he doing here by himself? Was the target totally destroyed except for his body? He was wearing a helmet but had no other gear, not even boots. Had he been stripped of useful items after death? If so why wasn't he buried? Very strange.

Moving on, and nearing the top of another mountain, the point man stopped and motioned me forward. Just in front of him and barely visible under the debris on the jungle floor was a brass disk about four inches across. My first thought was that it was a mine of some sort. We were in the middle of a lot of nothingness. A mine made no sense. I looked closer and could make out lettering engraved into the brass. I carefully brushed it clean, read in French, and English the elevation, a bunch of other data, and the date it was placed there many years before. It was a surveyor's benchmark. It was secured to a granite block the size of a paving brick and sunk in flush with the ground. I had never seen one before.

I checked my map and sure enough, there was the symbol BM+ right where we were standing. I knew precisely where we were. This was long before GPS technology came along so it was weird thinking that at some time a surveying party had trekked through this country, stood right in my footprints, and planted this benchmark. I don't remember the date on it but it may have been there for 75 years or more and probably hadn't been seen since then. I'd bet the farm that it hasn't been seen again to this day.

I have been asked if I was scared in Vietnam. Well, yes and no. On base, the stress level was usually very low. Sure, a rocket could land in your back pocket at almost any time but there was generally a few seconds' warning.

There were also many pretty safe places to take cover. You were among many other people and the setting was familiar. In other words, take away the threat of incoming and it was kind of like being at day camp with lots of sandbags and automatic weapons.

On patrols however, I was on one of several levels of scared all the time. They varied from somewhat apprehensive to eye popping. Scared keeps you on your toes. Any combat veteran who says he was never scared is lying. Anticipation of the unknown is the most nerve wracking. Once you can see the problem you can start to overcome fear with reason and faith in your training. That's why the old adage "The more you sweat in training, the less you bleed in war," is dead-on accurate. I paid attention to guys like Blum and Lumpkin whenever I could. They always seemed very professional.

Just about the highest compliment I have ever received came from Corporal Kevin Macaulay, one of Bravo's radiomen. In an e-mail to me he said,

> I always felt that you had more of a handle on things than did some of the rest of the men in the company. You were more mature and took your job more seriously than others. Some of the guys were always playing practical jokes on one another and grab-assing all the time. I think you realized the gravity of the situation and were always prepared when you went to the bush. I remember watching inspections before you went out on patrol and you seemed much more squared away than others. I remember Lt. Schlack pointing at you and telling us that was the way he wanted us to be when we went on patrol. We watched and those of us who got what was going on emulated you and the others who looked like they knew what they were doing.

Kevin also said that Lt. Schlack stated that if he (Schlack) was going to the bush, he'd want to be with Johnson's team. Accolades like that mean more to me than all the ribbons and medals a large mule could carry.

Another patrol a week later brought us back to the same general area where we had found the benchmark. Lots of steep hills, heavy jungle, leeches, mosquitoes, and maximum humidity and heat. The second or third night out while in the harborsite, we received a radio message telling us that we could expect an arc light about five klicks to our south at about 0200. The message didn't say what the target was but they wanted us to be aware so that it didn't come as a big surprise.

As 0200 approached, I made sure everyone was awake. I had never seen an arc light before and I was pretty sure no one else had either. After a while, somebody whispered, "Listen." Very faintly, we began to hear the roaring of jet engines but they must have been very high. Somebody said he thought B-52s bombed from about 25,000 feet. It was a clear, starry night and somebody with sharp eyes spotted the tiny flame at the rear of the engines far above. The flames did not match where the sound appeared to be coming from until it occurred to me that at that altitude, it takes several seconds for the sound of the jets to reach the ground. That made the noise appear to be far behind the actual position of the bombers.

I thought that the location of the arc light must be farther to our west because we could see that the bombers were now considerably past us. Just then, we heard the whistle of the falling bombs. Lots of them! The whistling was still sounding like it was quite high in the air when the first of them hit the ground and then all hell broke loose! There was a string of bright flashes that probably stretched for 1000 meters from east to west. The roar of all those bombs exploding was incredible and then the vibration hit us. We literally bounced around on the ground and the concussion wave rolled right over us! It was truly impressive. However, it was not five klicks away, but more like half of that. For an arc light, that's right next-door.

The shock wave moved on and the ground stopped shaking, but we could hear very large chunks of Vietnam raining down on the jungle below us for several minutes. I began to worry that we would be within the debris field but the nearest sounds of impact we heard were a couple of hundred meters away. It's hard to believe that anyone could live through something like that.

The next morning, we could see some of the damage done to the jungle but there were no signs of any enemy activity and the craters were outside our RZ anyway. I half expected to be sent down there for a bomb damage assessment but we never heard anything more about it. It was often so hot, even at night, that we'd sweat the camouflage paint off our faces. After a delicious breakfast of a can of cold C-rat scrambled eggs, I passed the word to cammie up and we left the harborsite.

The patrol continued through the day encountering the usual unbelievably thick growth under the canopy. We often saw ferns that looked like they belonged in the Triassic era. They looked just like the ones in your garden but the fronds were two feet wide and up to five feet long.

Besides being incredibly humid, greenhouse hot, and not a breath of a breeze moving, it stunk. Sometimes the layer of decaying vegetation on the jungle floor was inches deep and stunk like any rotting matter would. It probably makes world-class compost. If you have ever been out in the woods in late fall and kicked up a soggy mass of dead leaves, you know the smell. You just need to magnify it by a factor of 10 to really appreciate it. After coming back from some patrols, it took two or three showers to get that stink out of your skin.

We worked our way around through the RZ for the next two days making some possible smoke sightings, but visibility was difficult due to the heavy jungle. When everything around you is as much as 100 feet tall, you can't see out. Now and then, we came across small clearings on the side or top of a mountain and the view across the valleys far below was incredible. Under that canopy, however, you had to literally bump into enemy troops and, even though it was very likely that there were one or more base camps in the vicinity, we just couldn't see them.

Late in the afternoon of the fourth day, we got a call to find an LZ and stand by for extraction. We weren't due to get pulled out until at least the next morning but who was I to quibble? Problem was, there weren't any bare spots big enough for a chopper to land on. Well, there were, but they weren't horizontal. The only jungle free areas within sight or on the map were on the sides of some of the steeply sloping hills and were impossible to land on.

I radioed that fact to Rainbelt Bravo and was eventually told to get to the nearest, best spot and the choppers would come out and assess the LZ. They must have wanted us out of there bad! That made me nervous. I gave the coordinates of a spot that was not the best, but was in fact the only place that had just three to five foot elephant grass on it.

Before long the sound of large machines beating the air into submission reached my ears and, over the radio, I talked the lead gunship to our location. The troop carriers were CH-46s and I could not see how they were going to do this. The slope of the hillside we were on had to be nearly 40 degrees and the open area, while large, was surrounded by 80-foot trees. The lead 46 cautiously flapped his way closer to the LZ and then the pilot put the chopper into a hover and just hung there in noisy serenity. I could see him and the copilot giving it a very careful examination from a couple hundred feet out. The gunners were hanging out each side of the chopper intently eyeing the ground below for enemy activity. My team was on the edge of the tree line on the upper end of the clear area and, I don't know why, but I waved at the pilot. Not a two-handed "Here we are, come and get us!" wave, but more like a "Hi, how ya doin'?" thing. The pilot just as casually waved back and smiled.

We mark LZs with a colored smoke grenade, to identify the LZ and to give the choppers the wind direction. We carried a variety of colors so when the pilot tells me to pop a smoke, I then ask him what color he sees. That's because sometimes if the gooks are monitoring your frequency, they may have smokes with them. If I say, "I'm popping a yellow," the gooks might also throw a yellow and the pilot might land on the wrong one and be in real trouble. But if I pop a smoke but don't say what color I'm throwing and the pilot says, "I see a purple and a green about 500 meters apart," I would say, "We're the purple one. Get here fast!"

The pilot told me to pop a smoke, which I did. With the chopper's proximity to the LZ the smoke was not to show him the location but rather to indicate the wind condition. The grenade promptly rolled right down the hill and out of sight in the trees. I then held up my bandana in one hand and the wind caught it showing the direction. The pilot said that was good enough and that we should move down the slope and off to one side. He said not to move from there until he told us to. While this was going on, the second troop ship and both Hueys were orbiting above the area. Under that canopy, though, who knew how many gooks that commotion was attracting?

It was then that I thought I was seeing things. The pilot turned that 46 around so it was butt first to the hillside and started backing up! Remember that a Phrog is the size of a school bus and has two big rotors, one forward and one aft. The arc of the rotors sticks out above and past both ends of the bird by probably 20 feet. Then consider the angle of the slope and do the geometry. The team was now slightly below the tailgate and off to one side and we and the elephant grass were being flattened by the rotor wash. My radioman had the handset screwed into his ear so he could hear the pilot over the roaring turbines when he told us to get aboard.

The rear rotor was almost nipping the elephant grass above us and the tailgate ramp was roaming up and down several inches above the slope while the pilot settled his beast into a hover. No part of that chopper was actually touching the ground. The word came to get in and we started crawling up the slope to the tailgate. This pilot was either certifiably bonkers or just plain muskrat crazy ... one or both!

One at a time, we clawed our way up the slope to the ramp. The rotor wash, the roar of the engines, and the swaying of the chopper was an almost surreal situation! The rear of the ramp averaged about two feet away from the slope so it wasn't just a matter of stepping on board and having a seat. Each man had to take off his pack and heave it to the crew chief who was standing on the ramp, and then he tossed it into the troop compartment. The crew chief was actually the pilot's eyes and ears in this maneuver because the pilot doesn't have the luxury of throwing his arm over the passenger seat, looking out the back window, and backing the family sedan into the garage. The pilot sits about fifty feet in front of the rear end of his bird.

As each man scrambled into the chopper, his weight would cause the pilot to have to adjust his hover position. If he dropped only a couple of feet too low, the rotor would have hacked into the hillside, or a tree, and we would roll down the mountain in a ball of fire. I was the last one in and even as I lay sprawled on the ramp, we were powering away from the hill.

Once in the air, I went forward to the cockpit and stuck my head in. The pilot turned and I gave him an emphatic thumbs up gesture. He just gave me a wave as if to say, "Aw shucks." That was, in my uninformed opinion, a superior example of piloting. I believe the helicopter units at Khe Sanh during most of the summer of 1967 were HMM-363 flying UH-34s, HMM-164 flying CH-46s, and VMO-3 flying Huey gunships. They were detachments from Marine Air Group 16.

After arriving back at Khe Sanh, I went to C.O.C. for debriefing and learned that the reason for our hasty extraction was because the Air Force was going to run an arclight through our RZ that night. In that bush, S-2 wasn't sure we had enough time to get out of harm's way before dark. This display of official concern over our health and welfare was genuinely touching.

16. A Real Mess

Sergeant Bob Mullaney, another team leader in Lt. Pfeltz's (my) platoon. was a rather quiet guy but he could play a guitar and had a singing voice to be envied. From time to time, Chaplain Stubbe took groups of Marines and corpsmen to the Ville to conduct a MEDCAP, or Medical Civil Action Program, and provide a little entertainment, mostly for the kids. Doc Miller and Mullaney sometimes went along if they were between patrols. Chaplain Stubbe was a familiar sight at the base at Khe Sanh as well as on the hill outposts, but he was most often found at Charlie Med administering to the spiritual needs of the wounded and dead. He was never without words of encouragement and optimism. A couple of the Marines swore that they once saw him walk across a water puddle and not get his feet wet. I don't know. I wasn't there.

Mullaney had another talent, too. He was a hypnotist. Not the clinical kind, mind you, but the party type. His technique was to sit in front of the victim while holding a quarter about six inches from the victim's eyes. This made the coin out of focus and the victim's eyes were somewhat crossed. An accomplice stood behind the victim holding a flashlight beam on the coin making it a bright focal point so that after a few minutes of soothing talk from Mullaney, the victim's eyelids would get heavy and close in sleep. Then Mullaney would implant a post hypnotic order, usually a physical action of some kind, which was triggered by a key word. He would then bring the victim awake and usually tell him that it didn't work and that his mind was too strong to be affected by hypnosis.

One favorite victim was a lance corporal whose nickname was Tater. One night Mullaney summoned Tater to our hooch and put him under. The trigger word was, for instance, radio. The post hypnotic suggestion was that every time Mullaney said "radio," Tater was to take off his utility shirt and lay it down on the cot beside him. Without further prompting, he was then to put it back on again. He would not be aware that he was doing this. Tater was further instructed that if he, Mullaney, said, "Knock it off," that would cancel the hypnotic suggestion.

127

The hypnosis was completed and we sat around shooting the breeze for ten or fifteen minutes. Then Mullaney said, "Hey, Tater, let's see what Hanoi Hannah has on the radio tonight." Tater immediately removed his shirt, laid it down, and then put it back on. The rest of us were choking trying not to laugh and Tater looked at us as if to say, "What's so funny?" Over the course of the next half hour, Mullaney ran Tater through his paces a couple more times, then finally told him what was going on. Tater vehemently denied taking off his shirt and stoutly maintained that he was not susceptible to hypnotism.

Mullaney said, "Okay, do you want to try it again?"

"Yeah."

Mullaney put Tater under and this time he was instructed to perform the rifle manual of arms, with or without a rifle. The trigger word was "platoon." After waking up, Mullaney told Tater, "I guess you were right, I couldn't hypnotize you." Tater left shortly after.

The next day at morning formation, we were standing at ease waiting for Lt. Pfeltz. As he approached, the platoon sergeant said, "Platoon, aa-ten-shun!" At *platoon*, Tater, in the second rank, began going through the motions of the manual of arms. We don't bring weapons or equipment to musters. At the same time, Lt. Pfeltz stepped in front of the platoon sergeant to receive his report. Right over the platoon sergeant's shoulder, the lieutenant could see Tater going smartly through the manual. The rest of us were convulsing, but in a proper military manner, of course.

The lieutenant forgot all about returning the platoon sergeant's salute and said, "Tater! What the hell are you doing?"

Tater answered, "Nothing, Sir," as he continued his drill.

The platoon sergeant turned around, deduced what was happening and barked, "Mullaney!"

Mullaney, as red faced with suppressed laughter as the rest of us said, "Tater, knock it off!"

Tater immediately stopped his gyrations and looked around sheepishly. Military bearing was swiftly restored and Lt. Pfeltz sought the relative sanctuary of the company office.

On the two-team patrol that I previously mentioned, Mullaney was the team leader of the second team. I think it was on the same day that the rock ape shat upon the lieutenant that, while descending a very steep and rocky tree covered incline, Mullaney slipped and fell a few feet, landing on his back. It was obvious right away that he was hurt. The corpsman couldn't really do anything for him and Mullaney could barely stand, let alone carry all his gear. The Doc finally recommended that Mullaney be medevacked but that would be a problem. This area was nearly devoid of flat spots that were clear enough to land a chopper.

Lt. Pfeltz asked me if I thought we should bury some of Mullaney's gear because we were already loaded down like pack animals. I said that I thought we should spread load his gear because, after all, we had eighteen or twenty people on this patrol. He agreed and we started passing out Mullaney's equipment (rifle, web gear, the contents of his pack ... everything) so that all he had to carry was the utilities he was wearing.

The lieutenant called for the medevac and we tried moving Mullaney down the slope. With a back injury like this, going up on the winch was out of the question. Mullaney was in serious pain and I think Doc Miller gave him a dose of morphine. We all but passed him down the slope hand over hand. The medevac chopper and a couple of gunships soon came clattering overhead. The canopy was so thick that even when they sounded directly above us, we couldn't see them. Recon does not talk out loud in the bush unless it is an emergency so L/Cpl. Tallent instinctively spoke over the radio to the chopper pilot in a whisper. The pilot kept saying he could not hear him and finally the lieutenant said, "With three choppers overhead, it isn't like nobody knows we're here now. Go ahead and talk."

Tallent explained the situation and the chopper pilot tried to locate an LZ nearby but there was nothing. Too much jungle. The lieutenant finally had to abort the medevac. Now we had another problem. The medevac attempt would certainly attract attention to the area and we still had to get Mullaney out of there. Once we got him down off the steepest part of the mountain, we rigged up a stretcher for Mullaney that helped ease his pain a bit but it was tough going through the bush.

By this point, the patrol had lost its stealth status and we moved like a grunt patrol while still trying to maintain an element of noise discipline. With this large a patrol and as heavily armed as we were, we felt we could protect ourselves well.

The patrol was scheduled for extraction the next morning so we focused on finding an LZ. On the map, the nearest likely spot was about 1500 meters away so we headed for it. We rotated stretcher-bearer duties and tried to carry Mullaney as carefully as we could. We spent the night in a harborsite near the LZ with Mullaney in the middle with the radios.

The next morning, the extraction went smoothly and when we landed on the helo pad, Mullaney was taken directly into Charlie Med. I think he stayed there one or two days but had gotten to a point where he could not feel his legs. Someone was sent to the sergeants' hooch to pack his gear because he was being sent down to the Naval Hospital in Da Nang. After about two weeks of rest, he was able to use his legs again and rejoined the company.

There was a corporal whose name was, I think, Larry Richards who had a pronounced British accent. There were two Canadians in the company and

I thought that having a Brit was kind of unique, too. I was in the company for about three months before I discovered that he was from Kansas or some place, and had never even been to England! He just liked to affect a British accent.

Colonel David Lownds assumed command of the 26th Marines on August 12, 1967. Once you saw him, you'd never forget him. His signature cigar and waxed handlebar mustache were all over that base. It was never a surprise to see the colonel strolling down your company street or passing through the trenches at two in the morning checking on his Marines.

An informal practice in the company held that the senior man in each tent or hooch had first rights on any external decorations on their quarters. This usually only resulted in flying a flag from the front peak of the tent. Most chose their state flag or a Marine Corps flag but the tent right across from the sergeants' hooch flew a confederate flag. I wrote home and asked my dad to find a Union Army civil war hat. Somehow, he found one and sent it to me. Every now and then, just to be that way, I would take a folding chair, the latest *MAD* magazine or *Playboy* (I only read the articles), put on my union hat and go sit in front of that tent directly under the rebel flag. Hail Columbia!

On the morning of July 31, after only two days back from a patrol, I was given a warning order for a patrol that was to be inserted in a few hours. The shortness of time on base after a patrol and the very short notice of going out again was highly unusual. No reason for the urgency was given to me as I hustled over to the C.O.C. to get things organized.

ON 01 AUGUST, RECON TEAM 2B2 AT XD770385 SENT THREE MEN FOR WATER AT A STREAM. THE TEAM HEARD MOVEMENT AT THE STREAM, RECEIVED LIGHT SMALL ARMS FIRE AND SPOTTED ONE NVA SOLDIER. THE UNIT CONTINUED TO HEAR MOVEMENT OF APPROXIMATELY 10 ENEMY BETWEEN THEM AND THE OTHER MEMBERS OF THE TEAM. DUE TO THE TERRAIN AND THE SITUATION, THE THREE MAN ELEMENT WAS UNABLE TO LINK-UP WITH THE TEAM. BOTH PARTS OF THE TEAM WERE SUCCESSFULLY EXTRACTED 1500H–1530H, THE THREE-MAN ELEMENT BEING HOISTED ABOARD DUE TO THE LACK OF A SUITABLE LZ. ONE OF THESE RECEIVED A BROKEN ARM, FRACTURED JAW, AND POSSIBLE SKULL FRACTURE WHEN THE CABLE BROKE AS HE WAS BEING HOISTED ABOARD.[1]

That's the sum of the entry in the 26th Marines Command Chronology for that date. Now I'll tell you what really happened.

Due to the haste of this mission, I was directed to go straight to the helo pad for my overflight. There was a Huey waiting and I jumped in. The RZ was west and just a little south of Khe Sanh. Not being accustomed to, or being trained in, aerial navigation, we depended on the overflight and insertion pilots to find our RZ for us. Arriving over the area, I looked for one particular upside down U shaped ridgeline. It was approximately in the center of my RZ. I pointed it out to the pilot and he agreed that it was the ridge on the map. I spotted a couple of likely LZs near that terrain feature and we headed back.

I ran back down to the team hooch where my APL had gotten things pretty well organized in my absence. I hurried through a SMEAC order (by now most of the guys were so used to them, about all I had to do was hit the high points). I hastily got my own gear together still wondering what the big fuss was about.

Self-portrait with Union Army hat.

With just a little time to spare, we moved up to the helo pad and watched a couple of CH-34s trundling across the airstrip. They really do look funny on the ground. We got into the first one and joined the gunships on the way to the RZ. I used the crew chief's mike to ask the pilot if he had the coordinates of the LZ I had picked and he said he did. I settled back for the ride and a chance to catch my breath.

Arriving over the LZ, the chopper spiraled down and then flared up before settling onto the ground. At about 50 feet off the deck, the elephant grass we were landing in looked a lot thicker and taller than it had from 1000 feet on the overflight. We hit the LZ and jumped out to set up a hasty 360 degree defensive position until the chopper left. It pulled up and away as the Hueys orbited above us waiting for me to give them the word that everything appeared quiet and they could leave. We rarely stayed in the LZ for more than about five minutes because we wanted to melt away before all that racket attracted unwanted attention. It looked okay so I thanked the helos and sent them back to the officers' club. (I don't know that there was one but we enlisted swine liked to inflict pointless envy on ourselves.) I started us toward the U shaped ridge hoping there would be a place for an observation post there and to see some terrain features from which I could fix my position on the map. I was always a bit anal about knowing where I was.

The ridge was only about 300 meters away but it took a couple of hours to get there. Right where we were there was not much forest, but the six to eight foot scrub, wait a minute vines, and elephant grass was very thick. It had been a hot day and we were sweating so heavily that we felt greasy all over. When we stopped for a breather and some water, the leeches found us and began their assault. We even had to stop at one point to reapply cammie stick to our faces, necks, and arms because we were sweating it right off. Blood from elephant grass cuts was mingling with the sweat and cammie paint on my arms to make a pretty disgusting mess. By the time we finally got to the ridge top we had uncharacteristically gone through almost half of our water and the shadows were already beginning to lengthen.

I decided that we would stay on the ridge top and set up an O.P. until dusk. At just before dusk, I moved the team into a harborsite 100 meters away in the tree line on the north side of the ridge. I had plotted my artillery registrations for the night and called them in. I was having a little trouble matching some of the hills on the map with the terrain features on the ground, but that happens sometimes because the maps we had were so old that terrain features become obscured by jungle growth.

During the night, I always listen for the H&I fires around the harborsite. Arty doesn't always fire them, especially if they have other fire missions that take priority. I did hear a few impacts some distance north of us but I figured there was another team up that way, too.

The next morning, I again tried doing a re-section ... shooting an azimuth to two or more known points and then calculating the back azimuth from those points. Where the azimuths cross on the map is where you are, and it just wasn't working. I was beginning to get a bad feeling. I called back to ask for a spotter round from the artillery so I could shoot an azimuth on it. The artillery fires one round of white phosphorous (WP) at a known point and the WP leaves a bright white column of smoke where it hit so it's easy to see. You then shoot a back azimuth to the smoke column and translate it to a line on the map. If the spotter round is accurate, you are somewhere on that line. It isn't precision but it does work. However, calling for a spotter round is very embarrassing because Reconners are supposed to be masters at land navigation.

When you call a fire mission, certain phrases are used, one of which is *splash*. The arty guys are very precise and they can tell by their calculations exactly when a round will impact. Exactly five seconds before impact, the artillery calls "Splash" on the radio. Seconds after hearing "Splash," I was looking at the hilltop it was supposed to hit. Nothing. I heard a faint *wump* far to the north but could not see the smoke column. Now I was worried! I asked for another spotter round. I could imagine the cannon cockers snickering. Recon was lost! Haw, haw, haw.

The second round had the same result as the first. In the meantime, my APL was shooting resections and coming up with the same position that I had gotten. It was now apparent that we were not where we were supposed to be. In fact, I figured we were about three klicks south of the spotter round which was masked by a ridgeline. The overflight chopper had been correct but the pilot of the insertion chopper had misread the map or was given the wrong coordinates and put us down in the wrong place. I studied the map and noticed that the shape of the ridge at the right place was nearly identical to the shape of the ridge, and directly north, of where we were. There was really only one thing to do and that was start humping north. I checked our water situation and it wasn't good for what looked like a long, hot stroll through the woods. I checked the map for the best route and while doing so, L/Cpl. Noo Yawk looked over my shoulder and noticed an intermittent stream on the map at the base of our ridge to the south.

"How 'bout if a couple 'a us go down an' fill up da canteens?"

I wasn't crazy about this idea because the stream was a couple hundred meters down the hill. However, there was no water showing on the map going north. I thought about it for several minutes and then I told him to pick two men, take all the empty canteens and get down there and back fast. I also had them take the secondary radio tuned to the primary frequency so I could keep track of them. Right away, he picked Calabrese (of Genovese/Calabrese feud fame) and another idiot and off they went.

Every couple of minutes, I had my radioman key the transmission button on his handset twice. He would be answered by two clicks from the water detail. This was a standard means of non-verbal radio communications for Recon teams. Two clicks meant Alpha Sierra (all secure). About fifteen minutes went by like this and then I heard the static noise of the water detail's handset being keyed. The carrier wave stayed open for several seconds and then went off. I was about to key my handset when I heard theirs open again. After several seconds, we heard a shot, both over the handset and with our ears. What in blazes was going on?

Immediately, Noo Yawk's voice came over the radio. "Dere's gooks down here! We saw one lookin' at us!"

I answered, "Stay put, we're on the way!"

"No! Don't come down. Dey're between you and us! It'd be suicide!"

We had still only heard the one shot fired and it sounded like the sharp report of an M-16 round, not the loud, flat report of an AK-47. I had my radioman call in that we had made contact and part of the team was separated from us. Noo Yawk kept repeating that the gooks were between us and that they could not come back up the hill and we should not try to come down. He was adamant about that. If what he was saying was correct, we could wind up in a crossfire situation, or at the very least, mistake our people for the NVA.

I relayed the situation back to Rainbelt Bravo and was asked if the detail was still in contact. Having heard no firing since the one shot, I asked Noo Yawk if the NVA were still there. He said he could still hear them moving around. He also asked if a chopper could come and winch them up out of the jungle. That would alleviate the need for either part of the team to have to try to link up with the other.

I wasn't real hot about that idea either, but I advised Rainbelt Bravo and they said to stand by. That meant that a conference was taking place and decisions were being made. I told Noo Yawk to just sit tight. Several minutes went by and then Rainbelt Bravo said that choppers were on the way. The plan was to drop a jungle penetrator line to them and winch them up. Once they were aboard, the rest of us would be extracted from the top of the ridge by another helicopter. It wasn't long before we could hear the choppers and gunships coming. Then I could see that the extraction choppers were 34s. Oh, joy!

I talked to the lead gunship pilot and told him that we were Broadweave Two and the other group would be Broadweave Two Alpha so everyone would know who was talking to whom. I talked the gunship in to the approximate location of Alpha and then the gunship told Alpha to say "Mark" when the chopper was right over him. After a couple of passes, the choppers had Alpha's location. The canopy for as far as we could see was dense enough that the pilots could not see the ground except where we were on the ridge top, which was fairly open. The lead 34 then maneuvered over the spot and dropped down out of sight into the valley. All I could do now was sit and wait as the other 34 and the gunships noisily orbited the area.

The slope of the hill and the height of the jungle nearer to us were such that I could not see the 34 as it hovered over the other group, although I could hear it clearly. After what seemed like a very long time had gone by, I could hear the chopper blades change pitch so I figured they had made the pickup and were climbing out of the valley. There was an even louder surge of engine noise and a moment later, I could see the chopper laboring into the air. Whew! Due to all the noise the choppers were making, I could not tell if they were taking ground fire from the gooks the Alpha team had run into. If they were, the gunships did not seem too concerned because they did not make any attack runs on the area after the 34 left.

The other 34 then began descending onto our ridge to pick up the remaining six of us. I popped a smoke to mark the LZ and indicate wind direction. The chopper settled to the ground and we climbed in. We began to lift off but didn't seem to be going anywhere. We sort of flexed up and down on the landing gear a couple of times and then the crew chief, using hand signals, indicated that three of us needed to get off. The load was too heavy. Doc Miller, my radioman, and I got out and moved away from the chopper. It strained a couple more times and lifted laboriously into the air. It immediately went into a nosedive down toward the valley. I saw the rotor clip the top of a tree and then it went down out of sight!

I felt like someone had a death grip on my throat. I was absolutely sure that I was witnessing the crash of a helicopter and the deaths of six people.

After an eternity, and with the engine screaming, the 34 wallowed up into view and joined the others. I could not believe my eyes! I looked at Doc and he was as white as I felt. The gunship called and informed me that the 34s would take their passengers back to Khe Sanh and the gunships would stay on station above us until the 34s came back. Needless to say, the three of us were very alert despite the firepower flying circles above us.

When the choppers returned, I had an impulse to say, "Thanks anyway, we'll walk," but of course, I didn't. The bird landed and we got in. I looked at the crew chief and he just rocked his hand from side to side as if to say, "Eh." Again, we flexed up and down a couple of times (I am told, although not by a pilot, this is actually a manner of "jumping" off the ground with a heavy load) and then took off. We didn't drop anywhere near as far as the first chopper had and the rest of the flight home was routine. I also found out later on that dropping off the hill was a method of gaining air speed. I really don't think the pilot intended to drop that far, though, and he certainly didn't intend to clip the tree. With the load the chopper was lifting from the elevation we were at, it was really straining the lift capability of the chopper. Did I mention that I didn't much care for 34s?

By the time we got back to the airstrip the rest of the team had walked back down to the company area. The three of us did the same. In the company area, I noticed some quizzical looks from a few people, and when I went to the team's hooch, they were rather quiet. Noo Yawk and Calabrese were in a corner and not saying anything and the other three were busy squaring away their gear. I noticed the third member of the water detail wasn't there. I asked where he was, and to my shock was told that he had been taken to Charlie Med and then quickly medevacked out, probably to Da Nang. I went over to Noo Yawk and asked him what happened. He and Calabrese hemmed and hawed for a minute and then someone came to the door and said the C.O. wanted to see me.

Now I had a bad feeling and the thought of stripes being ripped off my sleeve floated through my mind as I walked up to the company office. I reported to Capt. Williams and noticed that Lt. Pfeltz and some officers I didn't know were there. It was clear that the captain was understandably not in a good mood and he asked me bluntly, "What the hell happened out there?"

I explained briefly that the insertion pilot put us down on a terrain feature that resembled the one I wanted but was south a few klicks. By the time I figured out the error, I decided we needed water before setting out and Noo Yawk had volunteered along with the other two to go fill the canteens. We heard a shot, they said they saw an NVA, and based on Noo Yawk's radio transmissions, C.O.C. decided to have them winched out and the rest of us picked up on the ridge.

He asked a few more questions and indicated that he thought it was not a good idea to have "split my command."

Well, that's a valid rule of thumb as far as it goes. However, the reason infantry squads have three fire teams, platoons have three squads, companies have three or more platoons, and so on up the line is to offer tactical flexibility. Each of these tripartite units are called maneuver elements. Every infantry tactic in the book employs this flexibility. My "command" was basically a nine-man infantry squad. Maybe my sending a three-man fire team for water wasn't the soundest decision I ever made, but my answer was, "Sir, we had seen no activity, there were no trails anywhere near, and they had a radio with them."

The other officers quizzed me about the patrol in general for a few minutes. I think they were from S-2. Finally, I was dismissed, sure that I would be lucky to get out of this a lance corporal. Lt. Pfeltz followed me outside and I asked him if he knew how much trouble I was in. He said he didn't really know but there would probably be some kind of investigation.

I went back down to the sergeants' hooch, sat glumly on my cot in the corner, and tried to concentrate on cleaning my rifle. I had trouble sleeping that night.

The next morning at formation, I was told that each member of my team had been questioned the previous evening. After the formation, Noo Yawk and Calabrese were told to report to the company office. I tried to find out how bad the third guy had been hurt but nobody seemed to know. I went back to my hooch and tried to make sense of this mess. Doc Miller came in looking for me and said, "Noo Yawk and Calabrese are being transferred out of the company, and I mean right now."

My first thought was that I'm next but Doc went on. He was the unofficial company spy. He knew things before the people that knew things knew things. "It turned out," he said, "that Noo Yawk, Calabrese, and the other guy had been overheard on occasion talking about what an adventure it would be to get winched up out of the jungle by chopper. Nobody had said anything because they figured it was just a lot of talk."

Apparently they were serious about it, though, and when the opportunity for a water run occurred, Noo Yawk volunteered himself and the other two for the job. When they got to the bottom of the hill, they weren't sure if a rifle shot would be heard on top of the ridge so one of them keyed the handset while the other fired. The first long key I had heard was a false start ... probably working up the nerve to carry out their plan. There never was a gook down there and the story about gooks being between them and us was to insure that they remained isolated in hopes of being pulled out.

They got their wish but that wasn't the end of it. The very non-technical explanation was that when they were extracted, Calabrese went up first, followed by Noo Yawk. That left the third guy. Remember I said that the chopper was really revving just before they climbed into sight? That was because the load and the elevation were making it hard for the pilot to continue to hover. He had to start moving forward to get the rotors to take a bite into the air. The third guy was still down in the treetops and was dragged for some distance through the canopy. The cable broke and they had to lower another one to get him out. He was very badly injured.

I had been set up! I really felt betrayed. I went to Lt. Pfeltz and asked if I was going to get court-martialed. It was my patrol and my responsibility. He said that as far as he knew, I was 99 percent cleared because if they hadn't had this crackpot plan, and we hadn't been put on the ground in the wrong place (the insertion pilot's responsibility), it's almost certain none of this would have happened. He said I probably should not have split the team, but under the circumstances at the time...

One hundred pounds came off my shoulders. I felt bad for the guy who got hurt, but I really resented having had the wool pulled over my eyes. I resolved to run future patrols tighter and to keep my head and ass wired together. I never heard another thing about that incident nor did I see any of the three again. I learned of the "official" version in November of 2007 while corresponding with Ray Stubbe.

17. Death and a Long Walk

Dear Dad,

Last week a man in my platoon was killed as the chopper they were in tried to land. They were hit from both sides by .50 caliber machine guns. One of our men took a round in the neck and in the head. He was killed instantly. Both gunners on the chopper were hit. One in the stomach and one in the leg and neck. The one hit in the stomach died about an hour later and the other one is still in critical condition. The man in our team that was killed was the first KIA the company has had in six months. The whole company is out for blood now....[1]

Other accounts supply further details:

The 10-man Reconnaissance patrol, SAMPLE CASE 1 (2B1) had been in trouble from the beginning. It was Sunday, August 20 1967, as Chaplain Ray W. Stubbe led worship at 1000H in the 1/26 mess hall on KSCB. It was well attended, and included both the Commanding Officer of 1/26, Lt Col James M. Wilkinson, and the 1/26 Executive officer, Maj R.M. Otterean. About ten minutes into the worship, about three or 4 Recon Marines, their faces all painted with dark green and black variegated camouflage face-paint, walked in. The Recon team had been playing cards in their hooch waiting for their insertion, and one of the Marines, LCPL Garry Tallent, had suggested that they go to church, and he brought them here.[2]

Shortly after noon (at 1340H), a CH-46 helicopter (#152536) piloted by 1/Lt J.W. Mahoney carrying the Recon team attempted to insert at XD904498. The CH-46 landed and the team leader, 1/Lt Albert Ritchie Pfeltz, III, leaped out followed by his radioman, LCPL Garry Glenn Tallent. The aircraft came under heavy .30 caliber small arms and automatic weapons fire from well-camouflaged positions to the east and west of the zone. Tallent was immediately killed. The gunner on the helicopter, LCPL Harold Bauchiero, returned fire and was hit, dying later. As the chopper lifted off, Pfeltz ran back on, unharmed, unscratched, as fixed wing (MISS MUFFET 115 and 109, and CASTER OIL 175) ran air strikes.[3] There had been a 60-round artillery prep of the zone plus fixed wing prep five minutes before the team attempted to insert.[4],[5]

Chaplain Stubbe unzipped the dark green outer body bag in Graves Registration and gazed through the clear plastic inner body bag at a face that seemed vaguely familiar. The face still had remnants of a few granules of camouflage face paint. The Commanding Officer of the Recon Company, Captain Williams, was visibly shaken. All his Marines know how very deeply he cares for each one of them.

138

A memorial service was held the next day within the U-shaped entrance of the regimental mess hall with over a hundred in attendance, including Col Lownds, his S-2, Capt Harper L. Bohr, Jr, and the OinC [Officer in Charge] of Sub Unit #5, 1/Lt Hester. At the time for the prayers, a floppy cloth bush hat worn by Recon Marines in the field was brought up and laid before the cross on a small wooden table. One young Private, standing in the formation, wiped a tear from his eye in the brightly shining summer day.[6]

Garry Tallent was the guy who thought it was funny that Lt. Pfeltz got dumped on by the rock ape. Tallent was one of the most well liked guys in the company and his death was a real blow.

That happened on August 20. We were inserted into our RZ to the west of Khe Sanh about an hour after the Sample Case patrol. The next day, the 21st, was my 21st birthday. Out in the bush, it was rainy and sloppy. We had stopped for a break and I remember clearly that I was sitting under a dripping banana palm studying my map when the radioman whispered that Rainbelt Bravo wanted to talk to Broadweave Two Actual. That was me, the radio call sign for commander of a unit. If the unit call sign is, say, "Brownbag," the unit commander will be "Brownbag Actual." However, the company commander would be called Bravo (for the company) 6 (commanding officer). Chaplains were unofficially called Sky 6.

It was uncommon for the patrol leader to get a "personal call" and it usually meant something momentous and not necessarily a good thing. I took the handset and whispered, "Rainbelt Bravo, this is Broadweave Two Actual, over."

"Broadweave Two Actual, Bravo 6 wanted to wish you a happy birthday, over."

I said, "Thanks very much, out." I was stunned. Bravo 6 was the C.O., Captain Williams. I just didn't expect that.

Well, there I sat in the mud with water running down the back of my neck, still thinking about Tallent and realizing that at the age of twenty-one, I was now one of the old guys in the company. Lt. Pfeltz was only twenty-three. But, hey! At least now, I could legally get a tattoo and a beer!

It rained a lot during that patrol and we made only one, albeit bizarre, observation. We had just crossed a small stream and the rain was coming down so hard that it was difficult to hear anything else. The point man stopped, looked at me, and then pointed to the ground just in front of him. I moved up and there was a single water filled boot print. It was not the tread pattern that our jungle boots had. There was untrammeled mud for several feet around but there was just the one impression all by itself. I was baffled. We never did figure it out.

On the afternoon of the 21st, while I was "celebrating" my birthday, Lt.

Pfeltz had taken Team Sample Case 1 out to a location about 1500 meters south of the area where Tallent was killed. The LZ had been prepped with artillery and fixed wing but the choppers still took ground fire so the patrol was aborted. On 22 August, the team was finally able to insert. On the 24th, just after moving into their harborsite, they heard movement nearby and soon knew that the enemy had surrounded their position. They set off Claymores and engaged with small arms as well as calling in gunships.

> The nearest extraction LZ was 150 meters away across a river so the team moved out. Upon reaching that spot it was found to be too small for 46s to land so they moved again. By that time, it was full dark and fog was moving in so the extraction was canceled until the next morning. During the night, the team received sporadic small arms fire from the NVA who apparently weren't exactly sure where the team was. Lt. Pfeltz called in over 1100 rounds of 105mm artillery (some within 50 meters) around the team's position that night. At approximately 0700 the next morning *Sample Case 1* was extracted under heavy fire with only one Marine being slightly wounded.[7]

I never heard about that patrol until I read it on the 3d Recon Web site many years later. Go figure!

By late August, the weather was very hot and finding water on patrols often became a problem. We carried six canteens apiece (each of them is a quart) but with the heat and exertion, you could easily drink all of them in one day.

Dear Dad,
  My last patrol was a lulu. We covered [several thousand] meters as the crow flies. That doesn't count up and down mountains and detours around other obstacles. We were out for six days and then we were told that there were no choppers that could come and get us so we would have to walk to hill 881 [south] which was the nearest friendly position....[8]

On the fourth day out on that patrol, we were extended for another day and directed to check out something or other that was outside our RZ and some distance from where we were at the time. That's partly what added more distance than usual, not to mention the additional day. We trudged to the designated area, found just a little less than nothing, and when I set us into the harborsite that night I called in the coordinates of the LZ I wanted to be extracted from the next day. It was only a few hundred meters from the harborsite. I was told to expect to be contacted by the birds — choppers — any time after 0900 the next morning. We usually moved, depending on terrain and bush, to within 100 meters or less from a LZ and then waited until the birds said that they were on the way. We would then move to the LZ itself and make sure it was secure and that there were no obstacles to the helicopters.

On this morning when it got to be about 10:00, I called in to ask about the extraction. We were cammied up and ready to move to the LZ. There was a longer pause than usual and then Rainbelt Bravo said, "Ah, maybe no one passed the word. All the choppers have been grounded. You have to hump back to 881S." I found out later that a structural defect had manifested itself and, over a short period of time, several CH-46s had their entire rear rotor assembly fall off in flight. Many Marines were killed. On August 31, 1967, the Marine Corps grounded all 46s!

Thank you! Thank you very much! We normally carry enough chow for five days of two meals each day. Due to the extension of our patrol an extra day, we hadn't really had much in our stomachs for about 20 hours. Some of the guys had a candy bar or something but we were essentially out of food. I took stock of our water situation and found that we had about one-half of a canteen each. We had around 5,000 meters of mountains and valleys to cover to the hill in 100-degree heat. From a health and welfare point of view, this was not good.

Farther up the larger mountains we frequently came across mountain streams that rivaled anything you may have seen at Yosemite or Yellowstone Parks. They boiled and foamed down the mountainsides over boulders the size of a car. The roar was such that you probably would not have heard a gunshot. Mist and spray was all around the course of the streams and the rush of the water made any attempt to cross extremely dangerous. Whenever we came across one of these streams, we filled our canteens because the water was cold and far fresher tasting than the chlorinated water on the base. We also did not have to worry about water leeches because they did not live in this fast water. They were mostly to be found in the lower more sluggish waterways far below us.

However, the terrain that we now had to cover was thick elephant grass with only scattered patches of overhead cover so we were getting baked as we moved. The heat was literally sucking the life from us. At one point, while traversing up the face of a steep slope, my legs just gave out. It was so sudden that it startled me and I just sank to the ground in a sitting position. I quickly made as if I was just stopping for a quick look around and then I turned to the team behind me and signaled that we would take a short break. It was as good a time as any because when I looked back some of the guys were stopped bent over and leaning on their rifles. They were gasping like fish out of water and just about no one was keeping an eye on the surroundings. Security was almost non-existent. The elephant grass was hardly two feet tall on that hillside so we had nowhere to hide. At the same time, further movement was temporarily unlikely. We hunkered down and hoped our camouflage blended into the vegetation. We stayed there for about 15 minutes until we had our wits about us and then moved on. We were showing definite signs of dehydration.

By early afternoon, the water was really a priority so I stopped to study the map to see if there was any water around. The maps we used showed "perennial" streams — a solid blue line — that ran year around as well as intermittent streams — a dashed and dotted blue line. Intermittent streams are more seasonal and this was not that season. There were no perennial streams near but I saw an intermittent stream on the map and it was in a deep valley at the base of the hill we were on. I looked down and there, far below among the brown dry vegetation was a small glob of green. With binoculars, I could see a small stand of banana palms.

I did not want to go down there because being in a valley means you have no comm. Not even to Rainbelt Bravo. We didn't have much choice, though, because we had to get rehydrated. I called Rainbelt Bravo and told them I'd be out of comm for probably an hour or more. They radioed back that that was inadvisable (duh) but I pretended not to hear it and down the hill we went.

As we approached the palms, I saw no sign of running water and was a little concerned. Once into the grove, which was not over 30 feet across, I saw a small pool. It was, maybe, three feet across and a couple inches deep. The water was clear. Doc Miller tasted it and said it seemed okay. We took turns and got about a half a canteen cup of water each, which I told everybody to drink right down. Well, that was okay for now but we had a long way to go.

The pool (actually more of a puddle) was down to leaves and mud now but all around us were bamboo shoots about an inch in diameter. Harkening back to lessons learned in Recon School, I cut one off about six inches above the ground. Making a straw out of a smaller shoot, I sucked the water out of the base of the bamboo stalk. I got two or three tablespoons of water and it was chalky tasting but otherwise not bad. The nature of bamboo is to suck up ground water quickly. That's why they grow so fast. Within minutes, the stalk had refilled itself and I got another drink. Everybody else found themselves a "scuttlebutt" and got busy. A scuttlebutt was a keg of water on board ship around which sailors and Marines would gather and swap tales and gossip. Water fountains are still referred to as scuttlebutts by Marines.

Eventually, though, even the bamboo dried up. We still had no extra water to carry with us so I carved a wedge out of the trunk of a banana palm. It was sopping wet, and by squeezing it and straining the water through a bandana into our canteens, we wound up with a full canteen each. We also took bites of it, chewed it up for the water and then spit out the pulp. Again, it was chalky but potable. If you are ever marooned in the desert, you can get water from many cacti the same way. Just watch the thorns.

Feeling somewhat refreshed, we climbed back up the hill.

When we were about 1000 meters from hill 881, the grunts sent out 2 platoons to meet us and escort us back [up the hill. By now it was late afternoon and we were out of banana water]. Usually at the end of a patrol we have about 35 lbs. of gear still left to carry and this, plus the heat, had worn us to a frazzle. We met up with the grunts and they wanted to start right back to 881. I told the Captain in charge that we just weren't up to it and asked if we could rest for about 30 minutes. He hemmed and hawed and said O.K. When we started out I asked him to keep the pace kind of slow because we were still pretty beat. The grunts carry about 1 canteen, two magazines, a rifle, and a helmet on patrols, so they usually move pretty fast.... What they consider a slow pace was practically running in the condition we were in, so it wasn't long before my people started pooping out. Finally one man passed out cold and they stopped for about five minutes. When he was able to move again I asked the Captain again to take it easy and he said, "Sure thing."

Again we took off like we were going to a fire. By this time even the grunts were crapping out but some of them offered to carry some of our gear for us. Finally we got to the top of one hill and two of my men dropped in their tracks. The grunts had stopped for a break and I went up to where the Captain was. By this time I was dizzy, I had chills all over my body and my hands and feet felt numb, a sure sign of heat exhaustion. Anyway, I saw him just ahead and I tried my darndest to walk straight toward him but everything started spinning around and I fell flat on my face. I guess he finally decided we weren't faking.[9]

When we finally got to the top of 881S, I was pretty convinced we couldn't have gone any farther. A couple of my guys were still in surprisingly good shape but most of us were done. A corpsman took us to a spot at the edge of the LZ the grunts use on top of the hill. He checked us over and decided we were mostly just badly dehydrated and sunburned. Somebody brought over a five-gallon water can and we just soaked it up. This was a far more generous act than you might think. All potable water on the outpost hills had to be flown up by helicopter. There were no springs or wells on the hills and water was not squandered. In the meantime, I had my radioman call the base to tell them we were secure on the hill and were going off the air.

An officer quizzed me a bit on what we had seen on the patrol so I briefed him, but all I wanted to do was sleep. My stomach told me it had other ideas. I was hungry enough that my stomach was in a painful knot. There was some activity right near us that I didn't pay any attention to at first but then I noticed that a fire had been built and a tall tripod with a big cast iron pot was hanging over the fire. A heart-of-gold Marine was opening a number of cans of I'm not sure what, but it became apparent he was conjuring up a Mulligan stew for us. Actually, more likely a corpsman was our impromptu chef. A Marine would defend you with his life but only a corpsman would mother us like that. We ate all we could hold and whatever it was, it tasted better than anything I could remember. Although it wasn't quite dusk yet, we crapped out right there under ponchos and slept like logs until morning. I felt safe with a company of smelly grunts all around us.

The next morning, I was surprised to find out that a chopper was coming to get us. I mentioned to someone that I thought they were all grounded. I was told that the CH-34s were being used for medevacs and other emergencies only. The point was stretched slightly and we were considered a medevac. When we got back to Khe Sanh, my team was granted the day off on light duty. After, of course, the S-2 debriefing, turning in ordnance, cleaning weapons and gear, and taking a much-needed shower.

I have mentioned S-2 debriefings but maybe I should explain what that's all about. S-2, as you know by now, is the intelligence (Intel) section of battalion and higher units up to division. Their job is, among other things, to interview patrol leaders after a patrol to find out all they can about an area. Even nothing is something they need to know. The majority of Recon patrols often result in the conclusion that there's nobody out there doing anything. That's what we called a "milk run." When talking to the S-2, I refer to the notes I kept on the patrol and the map coordinates of everything that is seen or done by the gooks or us. That information is recorded and plotted on a map at C.O.C. The accumulated info is used to compile the "Big Picture" about a TAOR as well as to advise successive Recon or grunt patrols going into the vicinity.

Believe it or not, we sometimes got word through the grapevine that the higher brass dismissed some of the Recon team's observations. There were also occasional insinuations that a team had gone out, found a comfy place to hole up and then called in false sitreps (situation reports) and Bravo reports (asking for our exact location on the map) for five days. I'm not saying it never, ever happened but I never personally knew it to be a fact. Still, it's demoralizing to beat your brains out in that bush for days living like an animal and maybe getting shot right out of your RZ and then have some REMF blow you off.

Dear Dad,

[Some] of the patrols are a lot closer to the base and some are near the villages around the base. On this last patrol we were sitting on a hill side overlooking a valley when we heard some noise in the bushes behind us. Everybody flattened out and waited. Pretty soon an old man came thru the bushes. All he had with him was a little wicker basket and a rolled up fish net. After he'd come far enough so that I knew he was alone, I stood up and he froze like a statue. Then the rest of the patrol suddenly materialized out of the ground and he started shaking like a leaf. All the villagers here carry government made I.D. cards and this guy couldn't get his out fast enough. He was shaking so bad that I almost felt sorry for him. Anyway, I checked him out and he went on down the hill to the river.[10]

The RZ for that patrol actually bordered the base to the east. I'm not sure what we could have done that a grunt patrol couldn't. We had walked out of the base the first day and before long, we came upon a rather large cement block building. There were several smaller buildings around it and it appeared to be deserted. I checked my map and then saw that it was the Poilane plantation. It had been there for many years and Mr. Felix Poilane, a Frenchman, was a well-known coffee grower. He had come from France in 1957 to take possession of a coffee plantation that his father had started many years before at Khe Sanh. The war took its toll, however, and the plantation fell into disrepair.

There were no signs of life around the buildings and the place looked run down so I decided we'd check it out. There was no stealth involved here because while the lawn area wasn't exactly manicured, it still didn't run wild and there was none of the natural cover we liked to stay in. My radioman and I moved to the main building and walked in through the open French doors. The furniture was crude and the place needed a lot of repair. There was nothing much to see so we went back out front. The team was spread out in the brush on the other side of the road and I noticed my point man was looking at me and holding his hand like a pistol across his chest. He was pointing down the road in the direction we were about to go. I thought he was asking if I wanted him to start moving that way. He wasn't. He was pointing at a man coming into view who was heading toward me!

Well, there I was. Painted up like a tree standing in the middle of a golf course. All Recon doctrine says, "Don't be seen!" Trying to disappear in some manner was pointless so I just stood there as he approached. He was a small man of Caucasian extraction so I assumed it was Mr. Poilane. He was dressed in a colorless smock-like shirt and sandals.

I said, in my best junior high school French, "Bon jour. Ou sont les V.C.?" (Good day. Where are the Viet Cong?) I could tell my flawless French and cutting interrogation technique intimidated him.

He said, "Oh, il n'y a pas V.C. ici." (Oh, there are no V.C. here.)

I said, "Merci," marveling at the fact that I had just carried on a conversation, however brief, in French, and we moved on.

As Route 9 had become unusable for commercial purposes by 1966, the Marines occasionally flew Mr. Poilane and his coffee harvest to Quang Tri. On April 13, 1968, Poilane was returning to Khe Sanh on a Marine C-130. As it landed, it blew a tire in an old shell hole and slammed into a forklift. Mr. Poilane was the only fatality. Madame Madeleine Poilane had previously been evacuated from Khe Sanh and eventually returned to France.

The worst thing that can happen on a helicopter insertion is to land in a hot LZ. That's where there are, by pure bad luck, enemy troops on the ground within rifle range of the LZ. If they are close, they have all the advantage because if they are outside the diameter of the rotor wash, the vegetation flattens down over them and completely hides them. They can still shoot up through that stuff and a helicopter settling onto an LZ is a large, noisy, slow moving and ponderous thing that is practically impossible to miss.

On board the chopper, the turbine noise is so great that unless there is a lot of heavy caliber gunfire outside, you can't hear it. On a CH-46, there are large, round windows on the sides of the chopper and we always kept an eye out as we landed. However, on the ground with the bushes and trees thrashing around, it made people with guns hard to see. About the only way you know you're taking fire is when little holes begin appearing in the fuselage. It's like shooting fish in a barrel. The chopper body is some kind of lightweight alloy or aluminum and bullets go through it like paper. It goes without saying that the fuselage offers absolutely no protection to the people inside. The interior is lined with electrical, fuel, and hydraulic lines and one bullet in the wrong place can bring a bird down in a hurry. I only went into one hot LZ. The crew chief noticed the holes appearing, told the pilot, and he powered us out of there without any casualties and only minor damage to the CH-46. Ever since then, though, I always got very antsy during the last 500 feet or so of descent into an LZ and I could not stay seated.

18. Fizzies and Nha Trang

Dear Dad,

...Things are still quiet here. The last two patrols I've run were totally uneventful. Even the last one which was number 13 was peaceful. One of our patrols a few days ago got in hot water though. They were going along a trail [a serious Recon no-no] when they stumbled upon about 5 gooks who were just sitting there. In the confusion that followed two of our people got a little scratched up from a grenade but that was it. The gooks ran one way and the patrol ran the other way.

Last night I got to thinking about how few people I know at home now and how many of them will probably be gone by the time I get back. Theres really nothing else to write about so I guess this is it for now.

Steve[1]

One clear night there were a number of us sitting around on lawn chairs and ammo boxes shooting the breeze outside the company office. It was pitch black except for the stars. Then someone said, "What the hell is that?" We stopped talking and could clearly hear the sound of a small prop driven airplane something like our spotter planes that helped coordinate artillery and fixed wing missions. To hear any aircraft engines at night except for helicopters was unheard of and helicopters have a distinctively different sound from a prop plane.

Without warning, an illumination flare ignited high in the air and we all froze. This was creepy! We had not heard a friendly mortar fire an illumination round and besides that, this flare was directly over our heads and not out over the wire where it should have been. Everybody immediately began moving toward bunkers because we all had the same thought. The gooks were lighting us up for a rocket or artillery attack. Nothing happened, however, and later on one of the guys came back from C.O.C. and said they had no knowledge of friendly aircraft anywhere near us. The NVA Air Force never came south of the DMZ. Or did they?

Dear Dad,

I am in the 3rd platoon now instead of the 2nd. I was changed to platoon sergeant for 3rd platoon because the guy who was platoon sergeant had only about 2 months in Vietnam and there was a brand new 2nd lieutenant coming to the company to take over as 3rd platoon commander.

Remember when I wrote that the runway here had collapsed because of the rain. [Khe Sanh had an expeditionary runway made of Marston matting. It was perforated steel planking that locked together and lay on the bulldozed surface of the ground. Combat engineers and Seabees could lay down hundreds of feet per day.] Well they've been working steadily on it and it should be finished in about a week. That's when we'll probably start getting rocketed again. Con Thien, which is about 8 miles from here has been getting pasted by artillery from north of the DMZ. There is an estimated NVA division massed to the north of Khe Sanh. I hope they stay there.

Would you take out a subscription for me of the paper [Jamestown Post Journal]? That way I could find out whats happening over here. With the exception of our own little area we really don't know whats going on.

I guess that's all for now. Write soon.

Steve[2]

The monsoon season generally begins in late October at the earliest but due to the elevation around Khe Sanh and the lack of influence of the proximity to the sea, it can come as much as a month later. This year the monsoon rolled in from Thailand in November in the form of the *crachin*. The *crachin* is a weather phenomenon that exists between the torrential downpours that last until about March and consists of a constant drizzle and widespread fog. The ceiling rarely got higher than 1000 feet, putting a definite crimp in any air operations. We were accustomed to the morning fogs of the rest of the year but the sogginess of the *crachin* made it that much more miserable. Those non-monsoon fogs were a bit spooky. They were usually present at daybreak and were often as thick as a smokescreen. They even muted sound. It was sort of like walking around with fogged glasses and having cotton in your ears.

At Khe Sanh, we groped our way around the base environs until the sun burned the fog away by about 0830 or 0900. On patrols, though, we were most often high above the elevation of the base and the entire world looked like the mountain tops were islands in a sea of white cotton. If we descended from above the fog to below the fog on a mountainside, we went from bright sunlight to a dusk-like gloom. Passing through the cloud layer was the dangerous time because we had even less visibility than usual in the thick jungle.

Almost everybody thinks that Bob Hope and the USO shows went to every command in Vietnam. Well here's breaking news. They didn't! The USO and the celebrities that traveled with them were super patriots and I'm sure they boosted the morale of the troops they performed for, but mud holes like Khe Sanh didn't rate that kind of attention. For one thing, it was dangerous. Any gathering of more than a dozen people could draw fire from the gooks in the hills around us. Chaplain Stubbe often held church services with small groups of Marines spread out around him in the prone position or in holes.

One day we heard a small commotion on the road outside the company area. A few of us went out to see what was going on and saw a small crowd surrounding a black guy dressed in clean utilities. He wore no other equipment and really looked out of place. As he got closer, I recognized Floyd Patterson, the boxer. I think he was still the reigning heavyweight champion at the time. He was obviously touring the area with a small party and had just come from the helo pad. I got to shake his hand. He was the only celebrity with the stones to come out to our little bit of paradise. While he was there, there were a few bangs and a boom or two from some distance away. We gave them little thought because by that time, our subconscious was tuned to certain sounds and these noises did not fit into the threat category. Patterson didn't seem to notice but his "people" did and they hustled him back toward the helo pad.

On another occasion, the 3d Marine Division band came to Khe Sanh. They marched smartly down the road and stopped to play a few Sousa tunes. They were wearing jungle utilities but their boots were clean and their instruments gleamed like the sun. After about the fourth number, we heard the unmistakable whistle of artillery coming in. We had gotten to a point where we could tell pretty accurately how near an incoming round would hit by the sound it made. The band dropped their instruments and dove for the ditches along the road. Most of the rest of us just stood there watching them. After half a dozen rounds came over and exploded on the other side of the base, some of the bandsmen looked up from their ditch at us. A scruffy looking Leatherneck standing nearby spat a stream of Copenhagen and calmly said, "When *we* run, *you* run."

About a week or ten days after the misbegotten patrol of 1 August, came the Fizzie Incident. One of the sergeants, probably Cargroves, had obtained a bottle of local booze. The label was all in Vietnamese so we couldn't read it but there was a picture of a tiger or something on it. We dubbed it Panther Pee. I've never been much of a drinker so I don't know what kind of liquor it was. My guess was something in the gin family. It was after dark and we were just sitting around in the hooch gabbing,

Self-portrait at Khe Sanh. At right is the 6-holer from the Fizzie Incident.

Playing horseshoes in front of the sergeants' hooch at Khe Sanh.

reading, cleaning rifles and so on. The bottle was produced and it was decided we should all have a wee dram. Okay, what the heck? I'm a big, tough Sergeant of Marines. We gargle with rotgut each morning before breakfast. Everybody got out their canteen cup and held it out. Cargroves poured a couple of fingers into each one and we toasted The Corps. A couple of the guys tossed it down in two or three gulps but most of us couldn't get past the smell. Its bouquet actually resembled our bug juice and I don't mean the kind they serve at the mess tent. I took a tiny sip and had trouble swallowing it. It was vile. It was suggested that we cut it with some water. This idea was met with hearty shouts of approval, so water (full of chlorine) was added to the mix. If anything, it was worse!

Then I remembered my fizzies. I dug around in my homemade nightstand until I found them. I think they were grape. A fizzie dropped into each canteen cup produced quite a lot of purple foam. A few took sips and declared it fit for human consumption, and all declared what a fine fellow I was. After my first sip or two, it was at least tolerable. Over the next fifteen minutes or so, I might have drunk about an ounce. Then somebody asked me if I was all right. I said, "Why?"

"Because you're leaning over at a 45 degree angle."

It was only then that I realized I was slowly tipping over to my left as I sat on my cot. I said I felt fine but found that I had a lot of trouble sitting up straight.

Del Weidler said, "Are you sure-ure-ure-ure you're all right-ight-ight-ight? You look-ook-ook-ook a little pale-ale-ale-ale." There was a weird echo to everything I heard.

As soon as he said that, I felt nauseated. I knew I had to get outside quick. I managed to stand up and with my feet about a yard apart for balance, headed for the door. I opened it and stepped out into abyssal darkness! I could not see a thing! My right hand came down on the washstand so I knew where I was. I took about two steps and tossed my waffles. Then came an overpowering need to water the flowers, which I did right there. That was followed, not by any sense of relief, but by the rumblings of internal turmoil if you know what I mean. What villainy was this?

By then I had the vaguest sense of sight and got myself pointed in the direction of the six-holer. I knew I would have to navigate a row of tents before I got there. There are clotheslines strung between tents and I garroted myself on every one of them. I tripped over some sandbags and very nearly went headfirst into a trench around one of the tents. I finally reached the head and felt my way inside. I had barely sat down when the floodgates opened! It was painful! It burned! It would not stop! I felt like I was being eviscerated! I don't know how long I was there. When you're in that kind of agony, the brain mercifully shuts down to give its pain receptors a break.

Then I heard it. The siren! Incoming! I didn't care. I prayed to receive a clean, quick demise. I think it was mortars and they were hitting haphazardly around the area. I heard a couple of fragments zing through the screen as I sat there. After a few minutes, it got quiet and then the all-clear siren sounded. Of course, base S.O.P. required a nose count after an attack and soon I could hear people calling my name. I was feeling slightly better by then but was too weak to shout out where I was. Finally, someone came to the door in the darkness and said, "Johnson, are you in here?"

"Yeah," I said, weakly.

"Are you hurt?"

"No."

"You gonna be okay?"

"Yesh." I had always been an optimist.

"Okay, I'll come back in a few minutes if I don't see you soon."

"Okay, thang goo."

I eventually found my way back to the hooch, several pounds lighter and a few shades whiter. No one else seemed to have been affected at all. The other guys were very concerned as to my well-being and helped me flop down on my cot.

That was on a Saturday night. Most organizations in the Marines have what's called holiday routine (no reveille) on Sundays unless you have duty or some other required activity. I did not wake up until after noon on Sunday and the other guys said I never moved the whole time.

Even though we had hooches and tents that were relatively dry during the monsoon, you couldn't stay inside forever. If you weren't on patrol, there was constant maintenance of the bunkers and trenches so we were wet and muddy a lot. Almost everything we owned took on a permanent reddish stain from the red mud of Khe Sanh.

Lt. Pfeltz, four other team leaders, and I were informed that we would go to Da Nang to attend a one-day training session on calling in artillery. We already knew how to do it but a little refresher wouldn't hurt. Besides, it got us out of Khe Sanh for a while. Due to the vagaries of weather, the only air transport leaving Khe Sanh was an Air Force C-123. The C-123 is essentially a smaller two-engine version of the C-130.

It wasn't going to Da Nang, however, so we had to go where it took us and then catch a hop to Da Nang.

Where it took us was a huge Navy and Air Force base at Nha Trang, which is quite a distance south of Da Nang. We couldn't believe our eyes when we got off the plane. We had left Khe Sanh in gloom, rain, and cold. We emerged at Nha Trang to a warm, sunny day. It was like two different worlds. The differences didn't stop there. We quickly noted that there were paved streets with curbs and streetlights on poles. There were two story wood frame barracks and offices. There was grass that had obviously been trimmed so that the rows of rocks painted white stood out where they bordered the sidewalks. People were strolling around in civilian clothes and there was not a helmet or weapon in sight. There were no sandbag bunkers or shelters of any kind.

We stood gawking like Amish farmers in a Victoria's Secret shop.

Nearby, someone spotted what looked like a snack bar. It had to be a mirage. As we shuffled over to check it out, people were giving us a wide berth and looking at us as if we were from Mars. We had gotten accustomed to how we looked because we looked like everyone else at Khe Sanh. We were wearing helmets, flak jackets, web gear and had rifles slung over our shoulders. We hadn't shaved in a few days, we were still soggy, all of our web gear was tattered, our uniforms were grubby, and we stunk! Even though all of South Vietnam was considered a war zone, the people we encountered had never seen anything like us before. We might as well have been plunked down on a large stateside base. As we dried out in the sun, clods of red mud fell off our boots as we walked. We looked like the *Peanuts* character Pig Pen.

The snack bar was not a mirage. We went inside and stood staring almost tearfully at the menu on the wall. Hamburgers, hot dogs, french fries, milk shakes, and cold soft drinks. It had been months since any of us had seen such things. We piled our gear except for rifles on an empty table and placed our orders. Some of the guys ordered four hamburgers and double fries to go with two milk shakes. We sat down with our M-16s between our knees and ate like starving dogs. I noticed other people sitting agog, frozen with forks in mid air watching us feed.

The feeding frenzy lasted for about twenty minutes during which time no words were spoken. There is a time for talk and a time for chow. This was chow time! Bloated, we finally reached capacity and picked up our gear to leave. The table we had piled our stuff on had chunks of dirt left on it and the table we ate at looked like a pack of raccoons had tipped over a garbage can.

Lt. Pfeltz said we should get over to the terminal to arrange for a hop to Da Nang so we headed that way. The full stomachs and warm sun began having an effect and all we wanted to do was lie down and go to sleep. The terminal was a huge building and there were hundreds of people waiting for flights. As we moved toward the check-in counter, we became the center of attention. We really were an unbelievable sight to these people.

We found out that the next available flight was not until about 0600 the next morning so we would spend the night in the terminal. The terminal was so crowded that we went outside and sat on the curb. We were at a sort of cul-de-sac where the asphalt met the curb. Behind us were some benches against the wall of the terminal, all of them full of sailors and Air Force types. A Navy corpsman sitting there asked if we were Marines and somebody said, "Yes."

"Where are you from?"

"Khe Sanh."

His response was "Holy shit!" He explained that he had a buddy who was a corpsman at Khe Sanh and had written him about what it was like there. He went on to relate a couple of hair-raising stories from his buddy and quickly had the attention of everyone around him. Occasional glances of awe were turned toward us as the spectators realized they were in the presence of The Fiercest of Warriors! We just wanted to go to sleep.

It was getting dark by this time and one of our guys stretched out on his back on the asphalt with his head on the curb. In seconds, he was snoring on the warm asphalt. The rest of us followed suit and, laying our rifles across our chests and pulling our helmets down over our eyes, we floated swiftly into the arms of Morpheus. A couple of times during the night I woke up enough to hear our self-appointed protectors hushing people as they walked by. "These Marines are trying to sleep," they said, and the offenders actually made a point of being quiet. It was one of the most comfortable nights of sleep I had in Vietnam.

There was only one thing that really bothered me while I was on patrol. Just after dusk, when the rock apes had quieted down from their evening hooting, I would look out at the mountainous horizon. The darkening sky was still distinct from the black of the hills and it seemed terribly, silently, desolate. It hit me how far I was from, not only home, but also just the relative security of the base. The jungle looked like it had for probably eons and sometimes I wished I was the skinny little Swedish kid back in Jamestown. Then I would look at the grubby, smelly Leathernecks in the harborsite who depended on me and I would shake it off. When it got totally dark, I did not have that feeling. Maybe it was because it was so black my visual senses were completely cut off. Strange.

19. Puff, and Hill 950

We went by truck east over Route 9 to a Marine outpost named Camp Carroll. It was mainly a Marine firebase and I did not know there was a battery of army 175mm guns there, too. One-seven-fives are huge. They fire a round almost eight inches in diameter and they can go something like eighteen miles. We got to Camp Carroll at about dusk and were scheduled to walk into our RZ at daybreak. We were directed to an empty squad tent that even had cots in it so we settled in for the night.

At about 1:30 A.M. we discovered something. The 175 battery was only about 100 meters away. When one of those guns goes off, 100 meters is right next door. The first round raised us right up off the cots. They continued to fire two to three rounds an hour for the rest of the night for H&I fires. I don't know how anyone on that base ever got any sleep. At dawn the next morning, we were happy to head into the jungle where it was peaceful.

"Puff the Magic Dragon" was not just a song extolling the virtues of sidewalk pharmaceuticals by Peter, Paul and Mary. It was a real, flying, fire breathing dragon that saved many a Marine's sorry butt. Puff was a newer version of the venerable C-47 aircraft. The AC-47 was equipped with three side-firing 7.62mm miniguns. These miniguns resembled high tech Gatling guns and were capable of firing thousands of rounds per minute. They fired so fast that you could not hear individual rounds going off. It just made an earsplitting BRRRRRRRR! Following the success of the AC-47s as a gun platform, C-130s were equipped with miniguns as well as 40mm Bofors and then a 105mm howitzer for use along the Ho Chi Minh trail for supply interdiction. The Bofors 40 mm gun is a famous anti-aircraft auto cannon designed by the Swedish firm of Bofors. Crewmembers allegedly reported that when the Bofors was fired, the ship briefly flew sideways.

I never had the occasion to call for support from Puff but I saw it in action once. We were set into our harborsite on top of a hill one night and everything was quiet. We were several klicks west of 881S and everyone but the radio watch was trying to go to sleep when the guy on watch said, "I hear an airplane." Usually the only thing flying at night was a medevac chopper but we hadn't heard anything that sounded like a firefight anywhere around us. This was not a chopper, however, because it sounded like a propeller driven plane, and a large one, at that.

It was coming from the general direction of Khe Sanh but I didn't remember seeing anything that sounded that big in the airstrip revetments. It continued to get closer and by now all of the team was awake and paying attention. The first thing that went through my mind was the mysterious aerial flare that went off above the base a while back. Was this another flyover by an NVA plane? Distance was difficult to gauge but I figured it must be near 881S by now.

Without any warning, what appeared to be a solid column of luminous orange paint flowed down from the blackness spreading out as it neared the ground. A couple of seconds later, that visual shock was followed by a deafening roar. It had to be Puff! The lava flow stopped but it was many seconds before the bellow of the miniguns stopped echoing off the hills around us. Puff continued to circle that area and let go with several more lashings of the ground below. It is said that a three second burst from the miniguns will distribute one round in each square foot of an acre. I don't see how anything could live under that.

Puff finally droned away to its lair (Puff did indeed "live by the sea" in Da Nang) and the night regained its composure. I had the radioman call Rainbelt Bravo to see what was going on. The area Puff fired on was well outside our RZ but it was between 881S, Khe Sanh, and us. The radioman was silent for a few minutes and then whispered, "Roger, out" into the handset. I couldn't see him but I could sense him turning in my direction and he whispered, "They said the grunts heard something." That was it! The grunts on 881S had heard something! Whether it was a clumsy tree rat or a careless noise by an NVA unit, they were very quiet now. Well, better safe than sorry, and it was a terrific light show.

We were scheduled for a patrol that was going to be on the north side of the 950/1015 ridgeline. The master plan was to take a chopper up to the radio relay site on 950, climb down the north side of the ridge to our RZ and then see what we could see. Why not just take us direct to the RZ instead of hill 950? Ours is not to reason why...

Due to iffy weather, I had not been able to arrange an overflight this time, so I didn't know what the terrain looked like in the RZ. Since the initial insertion point was going to be the pinnacle of hill 950, and pretty much overlooking the RZ, I figured I could just look down and get a look as we landed. I may have indicated once or nine times that I did not especially like flying in the CH-34s. You can imagine how happy I was to see one sitting on the helo pad as we neared the airstrip. The crew chief was watching for us and when I gave him the high sign, the blades laboriously began to turn.

We climbed in, and after a couple of hang-fires and a rim shot or two, we got off the ground. In a matter of seconds, we were hammering our way across the north perimeter of the base. It was at that moment when I noticed some wisps of black smoke curling out from behind a panel on the firewall at the forward end of the troop compartment. I pounded the door gunner on the back and pointed at the panel. He immediately spoke into his helmet microphone and we spun around and hauled freight for the airstrip. As we passed over the edge of the runway, the pilot flared the bird up to land and it was at that moment that the chopper seemed to lose power. The chopper hit hard and bounced a couple of times but we were down in one piece and that was all I cared about.

The crew chief hustled us off the bird and the base crash truck hurried up to the side of it. My guess was that some wiring burned out. As the airdales say, "Any landing you can walk away from is a good one."

We climbed out of the 34 and headed across the airstrip to the helo pad a hundred meters away. I checked in with the "control tower" (a sandbag bunker about twelve feet high) and was told that it was my lucky day, as there just happened to be another 34 available in about fifteen minutes.

I should back up here and explain a little about helicopter assignments for insertions and extractions. The insertion birds were either 34s or 46s and there were always two of them. The team would be in one and the other would be empty. The empty one was a backup chopper in case the troop carrier went down. In addition, there were always two Huey gunships along as escorts in case there was trouble going in or coming out. Sometimes the Hueys would shoot up the LZ immediately before we landed and other times they would blast another possible LZ while we landed in a different one. It was meant to confuse anyone with evil intentions who might be lurking about. I was always impressed that four very expensive helicopters and eight commissioned officers plus enlisted crew did all that for little old me.

This particular insertion, however, involved no gunships and only one 34, probably to disguise the event as a resupply flight to 950. Sometimes we would walk out of a friendly position with a platoon of grunts and then at the first break, we'd stay there as they moved on and then we'd continue our patrol. Sneaky, yes?

At any rate, about a half hour later, I saw a 34 taxiing toward us from the helicopter revetments across the runway. Fixed wing craft, when taxiing, look like they can't wait to get off the ground. Helicopters taxiing just look tired. This 34 looked like a pelican waddling across a beach. We climbed aboard and took off one more time.

As we rattled and shook our way higher, I now noticed that the top of 950 was beginning to cloud over. By the time we were within a couple of hundred meters, it was not visible anymore. Once in the cloud, I could not judge our movement, and I was straining to see the LZ and then, *there it was!* I guess the pilot had a better view than I did, and I suppose it's possible he had done this a few hundred times before. The LZ was just big enough for one helicopter and the rotor blades seemed to overhang the LZ by a few feet on all sides. If one of the big CH-46s could fit in the LZ I'll bet they needed a giant shoehorn to do it. We were met by a couple of Marines who were tossing boxes into the chopper as we got out. Then a couple of others climbed in and the chopper lifted and just sort of fell away down the hill and was out of sight in the clouds. That whole exchange took place in about 90 seconds.

The radio relay position on 950 was quite small. It consisted of a few bunkers around the top of the hill in the center of which was the radio bunker. I don't think the whole position was much more than about 75 meters in diameter. Barbed wire and concertina liberally studded with Claymore mines ringed the outpost. This was the place where, back on the night of 6 June 1967, a sizeable force of NVA attempted to take the hill, and did, in fact, overrun the position briefly. The battle continued until dawn and of the platoon-sized unit of Marine grunts and radio operators on the hill, many were killed or wounded, but they held. I found out later that a radio operator whom I went to boot camp with was badly wounded but survived and earned a Bronze Star.

We went out through the sally port on the east side of the position and onto the trail that traced the spine of the ridge heading toward Hill 1015. The trail dropped somewhat to a saddle on the ridge top where we turned left and started down the north side of 950. It was steep and covered in thick jungle. We hadn't gone 20 meters when it became clear that we had better rope down. We always carried a couple hundred feet of ⅜-inch nylon climbing line and everyone had a carabiner. That's a heavy-duty oval aluminum or steel ring about 3½ inches across with a spring-loaded gate along one side. It is used with ropes for climbing and rappelling. The slope was probably 60 degrees and was much too steep to descend safely with all the weight we carried. Looping the rope around tree trunks, we used a modified rappel to get down the hill. This took about three hours and that was with gravity on our side. Arriving at the bottom, our thighs felt like jelly so we took 10. I didn't have to worry about comm with Rainbelt Bravo because it was right up there in the clouds above us.

On our maps there were dozens, if not scores, of place-names where villages once stood. Most of them probably consisted of no more than 4 to 8 grass huts and the inhabitants subsisted on farming. These village names were on the map but under each one, in parentheses, was the word *destroyed*. The villagers had been relocated in the early 1960s to larger centers of population because that way it was easier to give them at least some protection from communist incursions.

The villages had been destroyed so long ago that no trace remained of them. The second morning out, it was sunny but a bit chilly, and I noticed that according to the map we were very near a former village site. There was no evidence that there had ever been anything there, but then I saw three grapefruit trees. They must have been survivors of a small orchard. Better than that, there were grapefruit hanging from the branches. I called a brief halt and picked one. It was quite large, about eight inches in diameter. I cut it in half anticipating a real treat of chilled grapefruit. Well, the skin was nearly two inches thick covering a fruit the size of a baseball. It looked a little underdeveloped but I figured it was just another strange thing in a strange land. I cut out a chunk and bit into it. It was the absolutely bitterest thing I had ever put in my mouth. I spit it out but my mouth was so puckered up, I couldn't talk. My loyal minions all thought this was quite droll.

Not far away we came across a couple of banana palms with clusters of fruit on them. The bananas were not more than five inches long and obviously not anywhere near being ripe, so we did not molest them. I never saw any other wild fruit growing, ripe or otherwise, in this tropical and fertile country.

The RZ we patrolled took us west near where hill 950 drops like a wall to the plateau floor. Although it was a bit of a hike, we were scheduled to hump back to the base rather than be picked up by helicopters. Between Khe Sanh and us was the Rao Quan River, a good-sized river that flowed into the Rao Quan valley. This valley was more like a gorge and it coursed roughly east and west between Khe Sanh and the 950/1015 ridge. This patrol was in mid November, the monsoon had started, and although it was still sporadic, rainstorms had begun to hamper chopper activity. It began raining heavily our last night out and when we reached the river the next morning, it was a torrent! It had swollen to about thirty meters across and was really rolling and bucking. The water was brown with mud and small trees, and other debris was shooting past. We have to cross water all the time and we have a couple of methods that work pretty well but this was rougher than anything I had experienced and we couldn't go around it.

My best swimmer on that patrol was PFC Greg Popowitz, who volunteered to swim the safety line across to the other side. The vegetation here was scrubby bush and elephant grass and we could see across the river and around us for some distance. We set up security and Popowitz stripped down to just his trousers. He tied the line around his chest and waded in. The current snatched him so fast that it caught the rope handlers by surprise. They recovered quickly, though, and reeled Popowitz in like a big fish. He was choking and coughing but otherwise all right. He said after the first couple of steps his feet never touched bottom and getting across was out of the question.

I radioed back that we had attempted to cross the river and had nearly lost a man. Rainbelt Bravo relayed that message and then after some time went by, called to tell me to locate an LZ and expect an extraction within an hour. Outstanding! I could not help but marvel at this unexpected generosity.

Almost more or less on time, two 34s and two Hueys came whomping out of the mist to get us. I popped a smoke and the lead 34 landed, thoroughly lashing us with water and debris. After what amounted to hardly more than an aerial hop, skip, and jump, we were deposited at the helo pad and headed for the company area. When I came dripping into the warmth of the sergeants' hooch I could not help but notice that things were quieter than usual. I didn't say anything but shed my gear to organize myself for the walk up to C.O.C. for debriefing. Finally, Sergeant Dennis Herb said, "Did anybody tell you about Meggs?" PFC Marion Meggs was a member of my platoon and a happy-go-lucky kind of guy.

That kind of a question is always a bad one and I answered, "No."

Herb went on to tell me that three days before, Team Frostburg was out to the west of my patrol and were attempting to cross the same river. They had gotten their safety line across and while Meggs was crossing, he lost his footing, or got hit with a surge in the current, and went under. With all that gear on he was gone in a flash. The team tried looking for him from both sides of the river until it started getting dark and they had to give up. A medevac chopper was standing by on the helo pad in case he was found but instead just wound up bringing the team in.

> Dear Dad,
> Three days ago we lost another man. Because of the monsoon rains now, even the little streams are twice as wide and deep as normal. One of our teams was trying to get across a river and one of them got pulled under and never came up again. This morning they found his body and the memorial services will be held this afternoon.[1]

That was probably why the base sent out our chopper instead of making us keep trying to cross the river and walk in.

Early in December, mail call began to include more packages from home for a lot of the guys. And yet, there were some who never seemed to get any mail at any time. Those of us who did get occasional care packages always shared with our buddies and tried to "just happen" to have an extra brownie or candy bar when one of those unfortunates wandered by. Many people back home took to packing fragile edibles in popped popcorn. We ate that, too. I got a fruitcake from someone back home but since fruitcake is just about my least favorite confection, I gave the whole thing to my team. Some people will eat anything.

One of the corporal team leaders came into the sergeants' hooch with a package upon which the customs label indicated that it contained "bore cleaner." Bore cleaner is any solvent used to clean the carbon and lead deposits out of your rifle barrel, or bore. Upon opening the package, it was found to contain a large jar of what appeared to be soggy, brown cotton balls. As soon as the lid was removed, however, it became instantly apparent what they were. They were homemade rum balls and they were drenched in rum! The recipient quickly became the most popular guy in the hooch.

Remember, I've never been much of a drinker so rum didn't hold that much fascination for me, and the memory of the Fizzie Incident was still fresh in my mind. I took one of the rum balls and I must admit that it was potent but tasty. I had one more and within a few minutes was feeling a slight buzz. Whether it was real or psychosomatic, I don't know but I realized I had hit my rum ball limit and didn't have any more. Some of the guys got more than a little happy on the rum balls. I think it would be a fair assumption that that guy's mom used real rum and not just rum flavoring. She was instantly proclaimed Best Mom of the Week.

The worst part about mail call was the Dear John letters. Sometimes they were more or less expected because the relationship hadn't been all that strong. In fact, the recipient sometimes expressed relief that now he no longer had anything to worry about except keeping his own butt safe. Others, though, and there were more than you might think, were devastated. Some of the guys had practically no family back home so their girlfriend was their sole source of morale boosting.

It was, of course, none of my business as a Marine, and I certainly was no chaplain, but maybe being a sergeant and just a little older than most of them caused a few to unburden themselves to me. Anyone that ever sought my advice (as if I had a clue about females of the double-X-chromosome persuasion) freely showed me the letter announcing the breakup. In addition, every single one of them was, if not childishly cavalier, downright cold.

The Dear Johns from wives were the worst. They were full of the standard clichés: "I've met another and he's my soul mate," "I have to find myself," "You'll forget me in time," and my favorite kick in the head, "I'm doing this for the children. They deserve to have a father at home." There were even cases where instead of a Dear John, the Marine just got a copy of the divorce papers in the mail from the wife's lawyer requiring the Marine's signature. Surprise!

Unless you've seen the effect this has on someone who is halfway around the globe in a world that holds the distinct possibility of disaster at any moment, you can't imagine what it does to a person both mentally and physically. Generally, though, after a day or so of moping around, they gradually snapped out of it. After all, they were sharp enough to know that they had more immediate responsibilities. Some occupied themselves with elaborate plots on what they would do with Jody when they got home. Jody was the quintessential longhaired maggot civilian non-hacker who moves in on your girl while you are serving in the Marine Corps.

However, some, especially the married ones, took it extremely hard. That usually resulted in a visit or several to the chaplain. We were so close that we all suffered to some extent right along with the poor jerk who got blown off by Suzy back home.

PART FOUR

IN WHICH THE ELEPHANT
TAKES A SHORT VACATION

20. A New Company

By early December of 1967, things around Khe Sanh were beginning to heat up despite the cold drenching rain of the monsoon. One morning in mid December, the company pogue came to the sergeants' hooch and said that two other sergeants and I were to report to the company office. On the way, we caught up with two or three corporals who had also been summoned. All of us were team leaders and we figured something was in the wind.

At the company office, Capt. Phil Reynolds informed us that the Third Marine Division was going to form an additional Recon company, designated Echo. It would be composed entirely of volunteers from throughout the 3d MarDiv. He had been ordered to provide half a dozen experienced team leaders to join similar groups from the other existing Recon companies to form a nucleus around which to train the new company back on Okinawa. He said that probably none of the volunteers for Echo Company would have been to Recon school but that some of them may have some trigger time as grunts.

We were expected to report to the new company headquarters in Phu Bai by the next day so we needed to get packing. None of us was happy about this but orders are orders. We packed up our meager possessions and said our goodbyes. The next morning, orders in hand, we boarded a C-130 and headed south.

We found the temporary HQ for Echo and reported in. People drifted in all day and, that evening, the new company fell in for the first time. Except for the "press ganged" team leaders, the entire company was made up of volunteers from just about every MOS in the Corps. Marines who were tired of what they were doing or just craved a little adventure with the legendary Recon lunatics had stepped forward.

To my total surprise, our new company commander was none other than Capt. John Raymond; he of shaved head, handlebar mustache, and dislike of people tossing ammo off to the side of a trail. To my further surprise, he remembered me.

It was apparently at that formation that Capt. Raymond realized that none of us had any 782 gear or weapons. When we left our former commands, we had to turn all of that stuff in. He was not pleased because that meant a delay of at least a day while we were given a complete new issue. Apparently, he was able to pull a few strings because we were eventually told we'd be issued everything when we got to Okinawa, which, even though it was now the rear echelon, was the home of the Third Marine Division.

There was no Recon school on Okinawa. At the northern end of the island is a jungle warfare training area called, oddly enough, the Northern Training Area, or NTA. To supplement the NTA course, we team leaders were expected to organize some extracurricular training in Recon tactics.

We flew to Okinawa and trucked to Camp Hansen. Camp Hansen was named after Private Dale M. Hansen, who received the Medal of Honor posthumously for heroic action during the battle for Okinawa in World War II. Our convoy wended its way through many small towns and villages. Most of the towns were rather ramshackle places with nondescript businesses and residential areas. One stretch of the road skirted the east coastline. This "highway" was barely wide enough to accommodate the big six-by trucks we were loaded into. In fact, I have some movie film looking out the back and down to the edge of the road. The truck wheels were within about two feet of the edge of a sheer drop of a couple hundred feet to the crashing waves of the Pacific Ocean!

At Hansen, we were ensconced in what were, to us, very posh concrete barracks with real mattresses on the bunks and flushing toilets. There was even a real mess hall nearby that served gourmet meals (again, to us) three times a day. There was an Enlisted Men's [EM] club, a real nice PX, and a chapel. In short, civilization. The company staff was as new to us as we were to them. The company first sergeant was 1stSgt. Tom Cone. He seemed to be many years older than he probably was and didn't really say much. The Company Gunnery Sergeant was an affable, easygoing guy named Jim Larsen, who knew his stuff. The Company Gunny is the ramrod of a company. The C.O. tells him what is needed and, as it shall be ordered, so shall it be done.

Taken while on Okinawa, January 1968.

I was the platoon sergeant of the first platoon. We met our new platoon commander about the second day on Okinawa and did not get off to a good start. He was a brand new 2nd lieutenant who I will call Lt. Hardhead. He may have been a year older than me. He called the platoon's NCOs together and informed us, "In all the John Wayne movies, the old timer NCOs always take the new young officer under their wing and show them how things work. Well, I am a graduate of TBS and a commissioned officer in the Marine Corps. There is nothing any of you can tell me." We could not believe what we had just heard! That little speech set the tone for the rest of the time he was in the company, which, unfortunately for me, was the remainder of my tour in Vietnam.

We got issued our 782 gear and drew weapons. It was back to M-14s again. There didn't seem to be a training schedule waiting for us when we got to Camp Hansen and for the first day or so we did a lot of sitting around. There were some impromptu classes on land navigation and a few other subjects but we weren't really doing Recon stuff. Right behind the barracks was an undeveloped piece of land that contained several small ridges, gullies, and a variety of vegetation from tall grasses to forested areas.

I suggested to Lt. Hardhead that we break up into our teams and just run practice patrols the way Recon, not grunts, do. We had a number of experienced Recon team leaders who were perfectly capable and qualified to do this. You can drone on all day in a classroom about how to move through the bush but going out and doing it is the only way to learn in a fraction of the time. We needed to get used to moving quietly and using camouflage techniques. We needed to practice setting up harborsites, and most of all we needed to go through immediate action drills.

In mid January, after arriving on Okinawa, we heard about the "siege" that was commencing at Khe Sanh and heard that the Marines there were taking a lot of casualties. Even though I was now a member of Echo Company, I was still drawn to Bravo because I knew those guys and had yet to really establish a bond with my new team. I requested mast to see the company commander. Requesting mast is every Marine's right to be heard. At every step up the chain of command, any Marine may request to see the next person in authority all the way to the Commandant of the Marine Corps. When a "request mast" is asked for, the Marine does not have to explain why, but he or she must make the request at every step up the ladder.

Mast was granted, and I reported to Capt. Raymond. I explained that we knew Khe Sanh was getting pasted and I requested a transfer back to Bravo Company because I felt I was letting my buddies down by being on Okinawa. Capt. Raymond said, "I appreciate how you feel but you're in Echo now and we need you here."

Khe Sanh Bravo Company area shortly after the siege began in January 1968. It got worse (courtesy Cpl. Dave Doehrman).

I expected to be denied but I had to try. I said, "Aye aye, sir," and started to do an about face when the captain stopped me.

"If it makes you feel any better," he said, "I put in for a transfer back to my company yesterday but I got the same answer I just gave you."

I said, "Thank you, sir," and left. I really felt like a shirker.

21. Okinawa; Training

We eventually spent a week or so up at NTA. There was a mock up of a typical Vietnamese village and we went through a course of simulated booby traps, tactics in a developed area, etc, but the training was all geared for infantry, not Recon. Recon teams do not expose themselves by strolling through villages unless they are close to the base like the Ville or the Bru hamlets that straddled the roads to and from the base at Khe Sanh. We did get a chance to run some patrols, though, and that was beneficial from a team-work aspect.

On one outing, I had my team set up an ambush where a trail emerged at the edge of a tree line. Lt. Hardhead was in charge of another team that was supposed to come looking for us. As his team broke out of the bushes into our kill zone, we shot them to pieces and they pulled back. We could hear them thrashing around in the thick undergrowth about 50 meters away and then they came toward us again. They walked into the ambush in the same place they had before and received the same welcome. Later, in a critique of the day, Lt. Hardhead accused me of moving my team to intercept them the second time. We had not moved an inch. One of the guys in Hardhead's team told me later that Hardhead had gotten turned around after the first encounter and, against the advice of the normal team leader, went up the same trail again, all the while insisting that it was a different trail.

I never did figure out Lt. Hardhead's problem. Maybe he was a rich person's kid who was used to getting his own way every time. It seems like that would have been knocked out of him at Officer Candidate School or The Basic School, though. Almost all their instructors are sergeants and staff NCOs. While they do not lay hands on student officers, they can and do make life miserable for them. Maybe his behavior was his childish and dangerous way of getting even with us enlisted swine.

A few of us were shooting the breeze one day outside the barracks back at Camp Hansen when a sergeant who I did not know and who had wandered up casually asked how many of us either already had a Recon MOS or were

SCUBA qualified. Three or four of us raised a hand. He was a black Marine who appeared to be a little older than the average sergeant. I didn't think anything of it at the time. He then asked those of us who had raised our hands if we would be interested in some specialized training. I guess we all indicated that we might like to know more of what he had in mind.

He said that it wasn't exactly secret but he didn't want it noised around so he would meet us later at the EM Club, say, around 1900. He then left and we looked at each other as if to say, "What was that all about?"

At the appointed hour, we went to the EM Club and he was at a table waiting for us with a pitcher of beer and some glasses. He said that he was recruiting for a special unit to operate within Recon to conduct classified missions that would likely involve water insertions. He would not tell us his name nor would he acknowledge that he was a member of Echo Company. It was starting to sound a little fishy to me but he seemed sincere enough. Two of our group decided that they weren't interested anymore and left. That left me and one other Marine whose name I can't recall but who was very intrigued by what the sergeant had said so far.

The sergeant said that he needed to find out how well we worked in the water and wanted us to meet him the following Saturday morning at a beach area near the barracks. We said okay and he left. The other Marine, I'll call him Smith, and I, sat there for a while talking about what little the sergeant had said. We conjectured about how he might be from Force Recon, or even the C.I.A., because neither of us could remember having seen him at any time during training. Smith said that he wasn't a very strong swimmer, and for that matter, neither was I. With virtually none of our questions answered, we headed back to the barracks.

The following Saturday we went to the beach and were shortly joined by the sergeant. In the mean time, I had decided I didn't want to follow up on this but Smith asked me to come along even if all we got out of it was a swim in the ocean. I told the sergeant that I was out and he said that was okay. Then he told Smith to wade out about 100 feet to where the water was chest deep and swim back in as quietly as possible. Smith started into the water and when he got about ankle deep, he looked down and stopped. There was very smooth, flat rock and coral right up to the waterline and there were tiny critters that lived in little holes in the coral. I could see them bobbing in and out of their holes as they fed on whatever they feed on. Smith noticed them too and began backing out of the water.

The sergeant asked, "What's the matter?"

Smith said, "I've never been in water that had little shit living in it!"

I started laughing and said, "Where do you think fish and stuff lives?"

The sergeant seemed amused, too, but said, "If marine life bothers you that much, I don't know if you'll be able to qualify for the program. Listen, I have to get going but I'll be in touch with you."

We never saw him again. The original four of us talked about the incident later and each of us independently commented that the sergeant's demeanor was somewhat unusual. We had all noticed that he seemed a few years older than the average sergeant and yet too squared away to be either a slow promotion or busted back from a higher rank. We concluded that he was actually an officer, but whom was he recruiting for?

One night on a practice patrol at the NTA, it had gotten quite late but we were still on the move. L/Cpl. Bruce Tuthill was walking point. Tuthill was a very cocky guy who didn't seem to have a lot of respect for authority. I never had a problem with him although I sometimes had the impression he was just humoring me. I think I heard somewhere that his father was a senator or congressman from Rhode Island but I don't know that for a fact.

There was enough moon in a clear sky that night to allow some visibility as we moved through waist high elephant grass. Suddenly Tuthill disappeared. I mean, one second he was there, and the next second he was gone. I could see L/Cpl. Robert Sargent, ahead of me, looking down to his front. Then we heard Tuthill. "Wow, WOW, wow!" His voice seemed to be coming from the bowels of the earth. A few of us edged closer and then could see that Tuthill had stepped off the edge of a vertical drop-off of several feet. He hadn't seen it because the elephant grass had grown so tall that it completely filled the little gully. To all appearances, the elephant grass made it look like the ground was level ahead when, in fact, there was a crevasse.

We threw a rope down and hauled Tuthill up. He said he went down so fast he didn't know what happened until he hit bottom. When he looked up all he could see was a forest of elephant grass and stars.

I decided to hole up for the night so we went through our nightly procedure of setting out, in this case, simulated Claymores, calling in artillery registrations and assigning radio watches. That only took about 20 minutes and then we were just lying there looking at the galaxy above us. The NTA is like Vietnam in one respect and that is when it's dark, it's very dark, and stargazing achieved a new level.

We had a "base" to radio back to for calling in SALUTE reports and so forth, so there was some occasional radio traffic. Around midnight we began to hear call signs we weren't familiar with. Finally, my radioman, L/Cpl. Ernie Cooke, tried calling one of the call signs. Compared to the rest of us, Cooke was built like a linebacker. He carried the 25-pound radio like I carry my lunch.

He was answered immediately and in the course of a brief conversation, we discovered that he was talking to a grunt unit in Vietnam! The transmissions were coming in as clear as a bell and we and they were very surprised. There is an atmospheric phenomenon commonly called "skip" where normally short-range radio transmissions bounce off the atmosphere, or Uranus, or something and can be picked up hundreds of miles, or more, away. The normal flat terrain range of the AN/PRC25 radio is three to five miles on a good day.

Those of us who were already Recon qualified either had called in artillery for real or at least knew how to do it. The rest of the company hadn't a clue so we spent the better part of a day in a classroom going over the various parts of a "call for fire." You don't have to be a forward observer to call in artillery and, in fact, because Recon teams were so small, they didn't rate a forward observer or a forward air controller so we enlisted mortals had to do it ourselves.

Close air support was another matter. CAS was developed by the Marines as far back as the 1920s in Nicaragua during the period known to Marines as the Banana Wars when we were still flying biplanes. The tactic was perfected in World War II and used extensively in Korea. The Air Force and Army can fly CAS but the Marines have turned it into an art form and I say that because it's true. The Marine Corps Air-Ground team is second to none.

However, unless you were a forward air controller it was difficult to speak the language of pilots. In an air strike there were such things as a variety of control points ... usually prominent geographical positions which, when reached, mark such things as rendezvous point, en route point, contact point, initial point, egress control point, and penetration point. Pilots are also concerned with visibility, ceiling, contour of the ground below, attack angle for different ordnance, and in which direction were the nearest friendlies in case they are hit during an attack run and have to bail out or ditch. That's not to mention knowing exactly which 30 square feet of Vietnam my team occupied on the ground far, far below. In other words, an air strike is very complicated and involves many more people than just the pilots. It would not be inconceivable that once we holler for CAS as many as 100 ground crew, technical, and command personnel might be involved at one point or another.

At any rate, one overcast and cool morning (it was monsoon conditions most of the time while we were on Okinawa) we hiked up to a promontory that afforded a view over much of the island and out over the Pacific. We were there to put into practice what we had learned about CAS in the classroom on a chalkboard. We actually had four A-4 Skyhawks on station overhead who we could give information to and who would run a bombing mission on the area below us. The A-4 was a small, nimble fighter-bomber that was used in large numbers in Vietnam. Senator John McCain was a Navy A-4 pilot. My favorite, though, was still the F-4 Phantom.

This was not a live fire range so no bombs or other ordnance was dropped, but a number of new team leaders got a chance to call them in. It actually got a little boring for me after a while. Due to airspace restrictions and airtime limits on the jets, they just ran the same swooping runs past our mountain repeatedly. A couple of times the pilots got a little frisky and flew by lower than our vantage point so we were actually looking down at them. We figured they were the unmarried pilots.

There was a sizable obstacle course at NTA. One of the most notable parts of it was called the "Slide for Life." While it wasn't necessarily life threatening, it was nonetheless challenging and made a few people a bit apprehensive. It consisted of a cable stretched between a rocky outcrop 40 or more feet above the terrain and it ended secured to a very large tree about six feet up the trunk. I think it was about 250 feet in length. The expanse beneath the cable was a swampy bog with about four feet of stagnant muddy water and muck. The object was to hang on to a rope handle hung over a hook on the bottom side of a large pulley wheel. The participant would get a running start on the high end and hang on for dear life as it sped down the cable going faster and faster. You had to keep your eyes on an instructor at the bottom end who, at the precise moment, would raise a stick with a red flag attached to it. That was the signal to let go of the rope handle and plunge, hopefully feet first, into the water. If you hesitated, you would smack into the very large tree trunk! Upon hitting the water, you submerged with a mighty splash and your feet would plow into the muddy bottom. Fortunately, you didn't stick there because the thousands of Little Green Amphibious Monsters who had preceded you had kept the bottom loosened up. You then sloshed your way out of the swamp to dry land. The purpose was to build confidence and some became so confident that they went back for seconds and even thirds. It actually was fun (once you made it down) but I had mud caked in places where mud shouldn't be and declined a return to the top.

We also did some rappelling work. Sometimes due to the lack of an LZ, it might become necessary to rappel into the patrol zone from a helicopter so those who had never been through Recon School needed to learn how to do that. In those days, rappelling was not taught at boot camp as it is now, so many of the Marines had never done it. They were shown the basics of how to go off a vertical terrain feature and as long as you follow directions and tie into your Swiss Seat correctly there was little to fear. However, going out of a chopper is a different story because once you leave the helicopter there is nothing to brace your feet against. The rope runs through a carabiner secured to the front of the Swiss Seat just below your waistline, which is fine under normal circumstances. However, with a pack and other gear on, you can become top heavy if you're not careful. It's very easy to wind up upside down and then your pack swings down to bash you smartly on the back of your head. If things aren't secured correctly, you will rain equipment onto the ground and people below.

To make it even more difficult we rappelled out through the "Hell Hole." That is a square hatch in the floor of a CH-46 and it's only about 36 inches on a side. That might not seem small but when you are sitting on the edge with your feet dangling out the hatch 100 feet in the air it makes you feel as if you will smash your face on the opposite side as you drop down through it. The technique is to reel in several feet of rope so that you free fall until the slack runs out. Then you descend the rope in the normal fashion. Once on the ground, you run backwards to allow the loose end of the rope to run out through the carabiner and then the next man ties in above you in the helicopter.

On the day that we practiced this technique it was very windy and the 46, though hovering, was still moving up and down as much as several feet. One of the guys, after dropping through the Hell Hole was descending nicely but just seconds before he reached the ground the chopper swooped up and he ran out of rope. He dropped about six feet and wasn't hurt, but it must have been rather unnerving when he was suddenly as free as a bird.

Near the end of training on a Sunday afternoon, my platoon decided it would be fun if we had a football game. There was a nearby athletic field so someone procured a football and off we went. It had already been decided that since we had no other football equipment that we would play touch football, green T-shirts against white T-shirts. Sides were chosen but even with eleven on a side, that still left another ten or so who wanted to play. What the heck! Let's have half the platoon play the other half.

We wound up with about fifteen on a side so there were multiple ends and running backs. By the same token, there were an equal number of defenders. Just a few minutes into the game, it went from touch to full body contact tackle football. It was just more fun that way. With that many players it soon became apparent that we needed a referee, so Lt. Hardhead, in a flash of good sense, volunteered to officiate thereby assuring himself safe from bodily injury.

The game progressed with each side being slowly whittled down by casualties. Finally, the quarterback of the green T-shirts threw a Hail Mary pass that went wide toward the sidelines. Lt. Hardhead was in that area and since no one else was near the ball, he adroitly intercepted the pass and ran it in for the score. That was the one and only time I saw Hardhead do anything that could resemble loosening up and having fun. The final score of the game went into sports annals as unrecorded and we all marched, or in some cases limped, back to the barracks in high spirits.

The monsoon was affecting Okinawa but we didn't seem to have quite as much rain as in Vietnam. It could still get sloppy, though. On a training patrol at NTA one of the radiomen in the company slipped and fell into a bog that was deep enough that with the weight of his pack and radio, he drowned before anyone could get to him.

The E.M. club had a couple of slot machines in it and one afternoon I was playing one of them and hit a jackpot of $63.00. I thought about what to do with this windfall. I rarely had much money on me because, of my monthly pay of $325.00, I usually kept only about ten or twenty dollars and sent the rest home to my dad to put in a savings account. The $325 included base pay as a sergeant, overseas pay, and combat pay. Who says the military isn't handsomely paid? In country, there was very little to spend anything on anyway.

Camp Hansen had a small tailor shop run by a Chinese tailor. He made handmade suits for very reasonable prices. I decided I would get myself a suit so I picked out a gray sharkskin material. Sharkskin was all the rage then. I think it cost $65.00, so with my slot machine winnings it was almost free. Toward the end of our training on Okinawa, a couple friends and I went off base to a dinner theater in Kin Village, a little ramshackle town just outside the gate at Hansen. You stayed off the side streets at night.

I didn't recognize some of what we ate because it was Japanese cuisine. After that, there was a Kabuki theater performance with much clanging of cymbals and gongs that I found interesting even if I didn't understand the plot. I wore my new suit and I don't think I ever wore it again after that. I mailed it home the next day.

Near the end of our time on Okinawa, a brigadier general assembled the company in the mess hall for a speech of some kind. I don't know who he was, possibly the base commander. All I remember is that after his speech he stayed around shaking hands as we all drifted away. Then the word went out to fall in our barracks and stand by for a search because the general's cover was missing. Marines call the things we wear on our heads covers or caps, regardless of what the headgear actually is ... except for helmets ... they're called helmets. Everybody else in the world wears hats. A Marine's cover is always removed when indoors unless that Marine is armed.

The general had set his overseas cap down somewhere and a person or persons unknown apparently thought it would make a grand souvenir. The search commenced and after about fifteen minutes, his cover was found in a G.I. can ... minus his one-star rank emblem. The general was not pleased. No, not at all. Buncha damn Recon pirates!

A couple of days before we were due to head back to Vietnam, I went to the PX for one last look around. I spotted a big Sony reel-to-reel tape recorder that could handle the big six-inch reels. A lot of the guys had gotten tapes from home but had nothing to play them on. I could even record the music that Hanoi Hannah played on the radio. I wish I had those tapes now.

I picked one out that was still in the box and was lugging it toward the checkout, and it struck me that maybe a movie camera might be fun. I had a few bucks in my pocket because, instead of sending my pay home as I usually did, I kept my last pay while on Okinawa. There was not much of anything to spend money on in Vietnam ... at least nowhere that I had been.

The small Super-8mm cameras were just becoming popular and weren't terribly expensive. We were in Japan, after all. I never thought about how I would carry it with all the gear we were already saddled with. After a little experimenting, though, I found it would fit inside my gas mask while the gas mask was inside its pouch, which we wore on our left hip. It would stay protected there but if I needed that gas mask I could dump the camera on the ground as I pulled out the mask. I weighed the possible loss of the camera against the advantage of being able to get at the gas mask and the camera came up on the expendable side of the equation.

I took a total of about 400 feet of color film on Okinawa and in Vietnam after we got back to Quang Tri. It's too bad the cheaper cameras didn't have sound then, but I got some interesting footage.

One of the last nights we were at Camp Hansen, some of the team went out for a last toot. They came back to the barracks quite late and, my bunk being near the shower end of the squad bay, I heard a commotion, a lot of giggling, and water running. Then the pitter-patter of little feet went scurrying by my cubicle.

The water continued to run so I got up to see what was going on. I looked in the shower room and there sat, or sprawled, L/Cpl. Don Schleman. Schleman was an average looking guy but as soon as he started talking, he had "good ole boy" written all over his face. He was a good Marine and followed orders. I don't know how he came by it, but his nickname was Meatball.

Meatball had apparently tried to singlehandedly eliminate all the beer from Okinawa. His "friends" had carried him back to the barracks and dumped him under a shower. He was still dressed in his civvies and was, by now, soaked. I sloshed over to the corner he was propped up in and shook him. At first, I got no response but he finally opened his eyes and looked at me. I asked him if he was okay and he said something like, "Gablub flubba."

I took that to mean that he would live and told him I'd help him to his bunk. I made him take his sodden clothes off and wring them out. With his laundry under one arm and me under the other, we weaved our way to his bunk and I dropped him onto it. I covered him up and I think he was asleep before I got ten feet away. The next morning he looked like he'd gone ten rounds with Jack Dempsey, but he was in formation and responding to verbal stimuli. As I said, he was a good Marine.

22. Back In Country; Quang Tri

Training was over, Echo Company was pronounced Recon qualified, and we flew back to Da Nang. Third Division HQ was now in Quang Tri, a very large base north of Da Nang. Our new company area was right on the western perimeter. It was an odd setup because even though there were rows of barbed wire and concertina just outside the company living area, there did not appear to be any bunkers or other defensive positions at or beyond the wire. In fact, it looked like the gooks could just waltz right up to the back door of some of the tents.

Immediately outside the wire was an LZ. At least that meant that over-flights and patrol insertions were only about a one-minute walk from your cot. Squad tents had already been erected for us but there were no sandbag bunkers, so correcting that deficiency became the order of the day. Most of the officers willingly pitched in to fill sandbags for their bunker. There were only four officers in the company so each platoon usually assigned a couple of snuffies to help them out. A typical bunker required a few hundred sandbags. It was tedious work with one man holding open the sandbag and another shoveling in sand, dirt, rocks, whatever was available. The sandbags were then put into place as needed and someone else would hammer them flat with a piece of board or a shovel. This made them into a solid and dense wall which was, in some cases, four to five sandbags thick.

Where Khe Sanh had been red clay, Quang Tri was almost entirely sand. Most of the company had previously been in country long enough to know how to construct a bunker so little time was lost. Small foraging parties were sent out to "find" planks, beams, or Marston matting to use as support for the bunker roofs. Overhead protection was just as vital as protection from a round impacting on the ground. The NVA artillery, as did ours, possessed artillery rounds called VT, or variable time fuses. That meant that they could be adjusted to detonate at a specific distance above the ground, usually about 100 feet. This airburst was deadly and we used it on them whenever there was no canopy above the target.

CH-34 at a maintenance facility(courtesy 1st Lt. Fisher).

The Quang Tri area was relatively flat compared to Khe Sanh. That didn't mean there weren't hills, but many of them were just bumps beside Khe Sanh's craggy massifs. Since Quang Tri was only a couple of miles or so from the east coast of Vietnam, the vast majority of our patrols were to the northwest, west, and southwest of the base. Much of that area was covered with two to five foot elephant grass. In the story about the NVA Elk, I mentioned that we called this area the back yard.

Patrols commenced within days of our arrival at Quang Tri. S-2 briefings concerning known enemy activity were a little thin but that, of course, is why we were there. Many of the patrols were inserted by truck because the area was so open that helicopters stuck out like big, noisy sore thumbs. There were no grunt units manning outposts like the hills west of Khe Sanh, so Recon patrols were really the only thing out there. Being near the coast also meant that there were a number of roads leading from Route 1 into the countryside. Route 1 is the national highway that runs north and south on the east coast. These roads were hardly more that unpaved dirt tracks, and where the roads petered out, well-used trails took up.

One of the first things we had to do as a company was to go to the rifle range for familiarization fire. When being issued a new type of weapon it was common to fam-fire it, not for marksmanship, but for just getting used to handling and shooting it. We were being treated as if the whole company had just come from stateside with no previous time in country. I guess some genius decided we needed to get acquainted with them there new-fangled M-16s (that we had been carrying for months).

Gunny Larsen had an M-3 "grease gun" with him. I was pretty sure it was not current issue and was, in fact, a World War II/Korean War vintage weapon. I don't know where he got it and didn't ask. Mainly because sergeants do not interrogate gunnery sergeants about how they procured an unauthorized weapon.

The M-3 was a stubby little thing made from stamped sheet metal rather than precision machining. It fired the same round as the .45 caliber pistol and was just about as accurate. They were designed for tank crewmembers as a personal defense weapon that would fit in the confines of a tank better than a rifle would. I asked the Gunny if I could fire a few rounds and he said, "Go ahead." There wasn't much recoil and it went futt-futt-futt-futt, and you could see the barrel wobble as it fired. I don't know who would be in more peril, the shooter or the shootee. It was still fun, though.

The whole team was sent on a working party to fill sandbags for somebody who was apparently much too busy to make their own. Normally, all we had for digging were entrenching tools. These are small, folding shovels about 18 inches long and are meant to dig foxholes with. At the dig site, however, we were also provided with a couple of longer shovels of the type that you see strapped to jeeps and trucks. In overall charge of this project was a staff sergeant from combat engineers. This staff sergeant spoke incredibly broken English. I don't know where he was from but it sounded like somewhere in South America.

He came to inspect our progress just moments after I had given the team a break. It was very nearly 100 degrees and we were sweating like horses. Most of our shirts and covers were draped over some nearby bushes to dry out.

Staff Sergeant Honduras said, "Wha are joo doin' layn aroun'?"

L/Cpl. Sargent was nearest so he spoke up and said that their team leader (me) had told them to take a break. Sargent was a tall, thin, rather serious sort who alternated at the point with Tuthill. The SSgt. apparently took offense at being spoken to in articulate, concise English and he said, "Hoo are joo?"

Sargent said, "Sargent."

"I din axe joo wha joor rank. I axe joo hoo joo are!"

"Sargent."

"Hokay wise guy, wha joor rank?"

Lance Corporal."

"Are joo a lanz corpal or are joo a sarjen?" Now he was getting irritated.

Sargent, leaning on a shovel and with a totally straight face answered calmly, "Well I guess you could say I'm both."

Staff Sergeant Honduras was beginning to foam at the mouth. "Hoo de squa' leader here?"

I introduced myself.

"Hoo iss dese wiseass?" he demanded, pointing at Sargent.

I said, "Lance Corporal Sargent."

That was too much. He glared at me and shouted, "I gonna show joo hoo funny!" and stomped away.

Everybody was turning purple not to laugh out loud until he marched out of sight and then we just screamed, knowing we, or at least I, would soon be in hot water. Sure enough, about fifteen minutes later, a lieutenant could be seen walking toward us. When he got within saluting distance, I came to attention and greeted him.

"Was SSgt. Honduras just here?" he asked.

"Yes, Sir."

"Was there a problem of some sort?"

I then explained as clearly as I could what had transpired and the obvious language barrier. The lieutenant listened and then said, "There's just one thing I need to know. Which of you is Sargent?"

Sargent put his heels together and said, "Me, Sir."

"Let me see your dog tags."

"Aye, aye, Sir."

Sargent complied; the lieutenant looked them over, verified Sargent's name, and then broke up. "Okay," he said, laughing. "I believe you. I wish I could have been here to see that. Don't worry about it."

He was wiping his eyes as I saluted and he left. We finished filling sand-bags and then we group gaggled our way back to the company area.

Part Five

In Which I Finally See the Elephant

23. More Patrols
and Agent Orange

A number of patrols had gone out with no contact of any kind. We were even doing some short-range patrols near the base that were only two days long. These were security patrols because there just weren't any grunt units around the perimeter as there had been at Khe Sanh. We carried only about half the ordnance on these patrols as we usually would. Our proximity to the base was a major safety factor. One such patrol I took out went a little north and west of the base. We walked out of our own perimeter before daybreak and never got more than about 1000 meters from the base. This was a luxury for us because we carried no packs. We had a small pack fastened to the cartridge belt in the back called an ass pack, and there was enough room in it for a few cans of C-rats and a pair of socks. The poncho was rolled up and tied underneath it. The only ones stuck with a pack were the two radiomen but they still carried a much lighter load than normal.

We had been out for a few hours when Tuthill, on the point, indicated that there was some kind of noise up ahead. We stopped and listened for a minute and determined that whoever it was, they were speaking English and not being very quiet about it. We had already moved through a couple of flattened and deserted villages and there wasn't supposed to be anyone out here but us. We cautiously moved closer and finally could see a group of about 25 Marines sitting on a pile of debris, drinking beer and having a merry old time. Not a weapon was in sight.

We were painted up and wearing boonie hats as usual. On the odd chance that there was even one pistol among them, I didn't want them to mistake us for gooks, so I threw a rock into their midst to get their attention. Several of them looked our way so I stood up and hollered, "Marines. We're coming in!"

At first, our camouflaged appearance resulted in a few snickers. I asked who was in charge and one said that he was lieutenant so-and-so. I asked him what was going on and he said it was just a little beer party for his engineer platoon. Then I asked him if he knew where he was and he said, "Yeah, the wire is just over there a little bit."

I took out my map and showed him that he was almost 500 meters outside the lines and was in our RZ. The snickering came to a screeching halt and they started looking nervously around. The lieutenant said he had no idea they had gotten that far out. I said that I thought it would be a good idea if they took their party closer to the base and he agreed. I asked them to form into a column and then I parceled the team out as point, Tail End Charlie, and intermediate positions. I had the lieutenant stay right behind me.

We got within sight of the wire and I turned them loose. I thought about calling in a SALUTE report but it wouldn't have accomplished anything except to embarrass the engineers. Engineers work hard but I guess they don't spend a lot of time on land-nav.

Part of the patrol paralleled a river that was about 40 feet wide and had vertical banks several feet high. At one point, we saw a rectangular hole cut into the opposite bank. It was a couple feet below the top of the bank and appeared to be about eighteen inches wide and eight inches high. I called it in and asked if we should go across and check it out. To my surprise, I was told, "Negative," and to continue the patrol. Okie-dokie. We never did figure out what that hole was for.

Later in the day, we came to the ruins of a village. This place still had a few partially standing walls. We found the remains of what must have been a bakery but mostly it was just masonry walls and foundations. To my surprise, we found some flowers growing wild that I'm sure would be classified as orchids. They were very large, colorful, and ornate and probably would have cost $40.00 each back home.

Our proximity to the base on these short patrols meant that we had to be aware of the possibility of booby traps. After we had been in Quang Tri for a few weeks, the team leader of another patrol, Sergeant Bob Saylor, tripped a booby trap and lost one leg below the knee. Several weeks after that he sent us a photo of himself in a stateside hospital with his stump all taped up. In the photo he was laughing. Maybe he got into the medicinal brandy.

One of the guys in my team should never have been there. He would have looked right at home as a Remington Raider. He was small, bespectacled, and complained about everything. We were descending a leaf-covered embankment and he slipped and fell onto his right hip. He continued to slide down the bank for a few feet and was brought to a stop when a thick vine ran up between his legs to his crotch.

It didn't look like it should have hurt as much as he indicated that it did.

He started wailing out loud and a couple guys jumped on him to shut him up. He calmed down but continued to whimper and moan about the horrible pain. I told the team we'd take a fifteen-minute break to let him recover and I even had the corpsman check him out. He kept pleading to be medevacked but the Doc said he couldn't justify it and I agreed with him.

It finally took threats of further bodily distress from other team members to get him moving, but he still whined every time someone looked at him. When we got back off that patrol I went to Captain Raymond and asked that this guy be removed from my team in particular and, if possible, Recon altogether. Captain Raymond was one who felt that if a man couldn't pull his weight he was gone, and the "non-hacker" was quickly that.

One of the sergeants in the platoon, named Singer, had been sent to the Vietnamese language school in, probably, Da Nang. He was not fluent but could carry on a fair conversation in Vietnamese. After he had come back from the school, his platoon acquired a Chieu Hoi. The Chieu Hoi program (pronounced "Choo Hoy," literally translated as "Open Arms") was an initiative by the South Vietnamese to encourage defection by the Viet Cong and their supporters to the side of the government during the Vietnam War. Defection was urged by means of a propaganda campaign, usually leaflets delivered by artillery shell or dropped over enemy-controlled areas by aircraft, or messages broadcast over areas of South Vietnam, and a number of incentives were offered to those who chose to cooperate.

The only name I knew for him was Minh, which is as common as John in English. Minh was a former V.C. who had been forced to join them under the threat that his family would be killed if he didn't. This was common practice among the V.C. Minh was permanently assigned to Singer's team as one of the "Kit Carson Scouts." Kit Carson Scouts, *Hoi Chanh Vien* in Vietnamese,

TƯỞNG THƯỞNG ĐẶC BIỆT

Kêu gọi mọi công dân Việt-Nam Cộng Hoà (dân chúng - quân nhân - công chức, cán bộ) tham gia chương trình thi đua kêu gọi cán binh Cộng Sản về hồi chánh và tưởng thưởng tiền mặt cho những ai có thành tích. Tiền thưởng sẽ được trao cho người hữu công tại Tỉnh hoặc Quận chậm nhứt là 3 ngày sau khi ban hành Quyết định tưởng thưởng. Tên họ người có công kêu gọi cán binh Cộng Sản về hồi chánh sẽ được giữ kín.   2903

HÃY THAM GIA CHIẾN DỊCH THI ĐUA CHIÊU HỒI

Chieu Hoi leaflet.

loosely translated as "members who have returned." They belonged to a special program created by the U.S. Marine Corps during the Viet Nam conflict and involving the use of former Viet Cong enemy combatants.

Minh and Singer would spend hours teaching each other English and Vietnamese. I even taught Minh a few phrases in Swedish. There was naturally a certain amount of mistrust toward the Kit Carson Scouts but as far as I know, Minh turned out to be a good troop.

One day as I wandered by Singer's tent, I saw him sitting on his cot with his elbows on his knees and his face in his hands. Something just didn't look right so I asked him if he was okay. He looked up at me and the look on his face startled me. He looked scared, sad, and worried all at the same time. He was clearly very distressed. I sat on the cot opposite him and waited for him to say something. He just looked at me for a moment and then, almost tearfully, said, "Steve, I don't know if I can take this anymore."

I didn't know what to say so I just made soothing comments like, "It'll be okay," and, "Keep your chin up." Lame stuff, but I didn't know what else to do. I don't recall that he ever specified what was bothering him. Maybe a "Dear John" letter or a death in the family? None of our teams at that point had had any enemy contact to speak of, certainly not Singer's, so it didn't seem as if it would have been a combat related problem. No one else was in the tent so I couldn't even ask around.

After a bit he calmed down and changed the subject entirely so I eventually moved on. I stopped at the company office, took the duty corpsman aside, and told him about Singer. He said he'd see what he could do. I don't know what transpired after that. Singer was with the company until I rotated home a few months later and in that time, he seemed to be the same old Singer. To quote Yul Brynner as the King of Siam in *The King and I*, "Is a puzzlement!"

Lt. Hardhead was assigned to one of my patrols as an observer. I don't recall that he had been on any patrols yet and he needed some OJT. Technically, an observer is not part of the chain of command but since he was an officer, the lieutenant would be third in line if something happened to me *and* my APL, Cpl. Rudd. Remember, his experience level at that time was nearly zero. I took him around with me to C.O.C. and did all the preparations for the patrol. We were inserted into our RZ and everything was going well. On the morning of the second day out, however, Lt. Hardhead came to me and announced that he would now take command of the patrol.

I said, "Pardon, Sir?"

He then went on to explain that he had observed enough and was going to take his rightful place as patrol leader. I told him that wasn't the way it worked. This was my team, my patrol, and that's about all there was to it.

He insisted that he was going to give the orders from now on and it was about then that I really got steamed. I told the lieutenant that I was the unit leader of record and if he were going to relieve me it would have to be for cause. I suggested that he have the corpsman examine me to see if there was a physical or psychological reason why I was no longer competent. Of course, if that were the case, I should probably be medevacked, which would cause many questions to be asked.

He thought about it for a few seconds and then told me that he would allow me to continue to lead the patrol but that if I needed any help, he would be right there for me. Under my camouflage face paint, my face must have been beet red! Upon returning from that patrol, I had an informal chat with Captain Raymond about this. I didn't really want to make a formal complaint because I just didn't need the heartburn. I also knew I could talk to Captain Raymond and he would take what I had to say seriously. Being enlisted swine, it was not my place to inquire further as to what would be done about this jackass, but I didn't hear of him ever trying that stunt again.

One afternoon I was slogging along in the sand of the company street and Lt. Hardhead fell in beside me as he was headed in the same direction. One of the troops needed to speak to him about something and from about 40 feet away called out, "Hey lieutenant, can I come and talk to you in a few minutes?" Hardhead said something like, "I'll catch you later."

As we took a few more steps, Hardhead muttered, more to himself than me, "It's, 'Hey, lieutenant,' *Sir!* Not just hey, lieutenant! Where does he think he is?" That was my very thought but it wasn't in reference to the Marine in question.

I have no idea what the other company officers thought of Hardhead. Again, it was not my place to even broach the subject with any of them and it's possible that as peers, they just didn't see him the same way we did. I hope he has done well in life and has risen at least to assistant manager at some small town Taco Bell.

In Khe Sanh and Quang Tri, we occasionally had to move through areas that had been defoliated. We didn't really know what Agent Orange was then. We certainly were never told that it was dangerous so we didn't really give it much thought. If Dow Chemical knew, they weren't saying. In later years, I read the results of studies conducted in regard to Agent Orange contamination. The study compared Vietnam veterans, military veterans who had not been to Vietnam, and civilians who never had military service between the ages of say, 18 and 30 and all during the same time span ... let's say 1964 to 1971. The studies showed beyond doubt that the veterans who had served in Vietnam had a dramatically higher incident rate of various cancers and also stillborns and birth defects in their kids than did the other two groups.

The evidence shows that Agent Orange was dispensed in Vietnam in amounts far in excess of previous use; thus, the exposure of U.S. soldiers and the Vietnamese was *not* [italics by author] as directed. Soldiers [those handling Agent Orange, mostly U.S. Air Force] in Vietnam sprayed one another with Agent Orange in spray fights as they were told the chemical was harmless.[1]

As for Agent Orange, [Secretary of Defense] McNamara knew about its potential deadly effects even as it was being used in Vietnam, and long before veterans came home to die or waste away from the herbicide's after effects.

McNamara remained silent for years as the government stonewalled Vietnam veterans who claimed Agent Orange caused their cancer or nausea or violent rages or numbness in limbs or birth defects in their children. Veterans' pleas for testing, treatment, and compensation continued to be ignored.[2]

The reports show a list of several kinds of cancer and the Veterans Affairs now recognizes the following illnesses as being associated with exposure to Agent Orange.[3] They are Parkinson's disease, B cell leukemias, ischemic heart disease, acute and sub acute transient peripheral neuropathy, AL amyloidosis, chloracne, chronic lymphocytic leukemia, diabetes mellitus (Type 2), Hodgkin's disease, multiple myeloma, non–Hodgkin's lymphoma, porphyria cutanea tarda, prostate cancer, respiratory cancers, and soft tissue sarcoma.

Most of the cancers have virtually no time limit as to when they might strike.

For many years, Dow denied any connection between Agent Orange exposure and the horrible cancers and birth defects that manifested themselves exclusively among Vietnam veterans. We just knew that the Air Force had a miracle chemical that stripped the trees of their leaves, giving the gooks no place to hide. However, it didn't leave much for Recon to hide in either. We never knew that there would be long term effects from Agent Orange as we slept on the ground, inhaled the dust we kicked up and drank the water that flowed through those dioxin-laced areas. Thank you Dow and Monsanto chemical corporations. Thank you very much.

The word went out one day that there were several openings for jump school and anyone interested should get their name on a list at the company office. Battalion Recon, unlike Force Recon, was not required to be parachute qualified. However, any Marine that wanted to go to jump school, and there was an opening available, could apply whether they were in Recon or not. Wearing those silver jump wings on your uniform certainly looked good, and at the very least was worth some bragging rights. I wasn't too sure though because I knew that the only jump school was at Fort Benning, Georgia, at the army base there. It was a tough school and no consideration was given to rank. Privates and generals were treated with equal contempt. I just didn't know if I wanted jump wings that badly.

Then I found out that the jump school would be conducted a bit differently in this case. Jump school is normally two weeks long with the first week being ground school and the second involving five actual jumps. Qualified Marine instructors would hold the ground school there at Quang Tri. The jump week would then take place in either Okinawa or the Philippines, I don't remember which.

Well, I hemmed and hawed long enough that by the time I decided to do it, it was too late, as the quota had been filled. Just a few days later, while in the back of a six-by going somewhere, we went past the area where the ground school was being held. I saw all the candidates doing pushups and mountain climbers while wearing a full parachute and reserve chute. In that heat, they looked like they were dying. I decided that not going to jump school was a good thing.

GySgt. Jim Larsen, the Echo Company Gunny, was strolling around the company area one day wearing a utility cover made from the herringbone material that was issued up through the late 1950s. He had been in the Corps for a number of years and would have been previously issued herringbones. At any rate, the herringbone utilities were long out of the system and to have any part of the uniform was considered very "salty" and "Old Corps" to be sure. Salty refers to someone or something with a lot of experience, particularly at sea. A salty Marine is one who has been around a while. A salty utility uniform is one that is more faded and obviously used but still serviceable. To be "Old Corps" is even saltier than salty. To us, Marines like the Gunny were both.

One of our corpsmen was admiring the Gunny's cover but felt that even though it was faded and a bit worn, it could stand to be a tad saltier. The Gunny asked him how he felt that could be accomplished. The corpsman thought for a moment, then pulled out his Ka-bar, and held it point upward in his hand. "Jam your cover down so the Ka-bar makes a gash in the center of the top. That'll really make it saltier," he said. For whatever reason, Gunny Larsen hesitated only a second before doing just that! There he stood with his prized Herringbone cover now rendered useless and a look on his face as if he'd lost his faithful old beagle. I don't think that corpsman remained on the Gunny's Christmas card list after that.

Another patrol in more mountainous terrain several miles west of Quang Tri had one rather scary moment. We had stopped on the side of a good-sized hill in thick cover for a break. When we stop or, for that matter, do anything, we use the brevity code to indicate our status. We also send our position using the shackle code. On this occasion, I had Cooke try to contact Airminded Bravo, our radio relay, but could not get out over the hills around us. Suddenly Cooke whispered seriously, "Hey, listen to this!"

He handed the handset to me and I heard a voice in unmistakably Vietnamese accented English say, *"Northtide, Northtide, Northtide,"* on our frequency. A gook was calling our call sign! The call was repeated, so we hadn't been hearing things. In that hilly terrain if we could hear him that clearly, he was close! Worse, we couldn't raise Airminded Bravo! This was very bad! We immediately went on high alert and got ready to move out.

We headed for high ground as quickly and quietly as possible. For all I knew we were moving right toward the gooks but we had to get enough elevation to reach Airminded Bravo. I think it was L/Cpl. Jim McAfee who was carrying the secondary radio and, as we climbed, Mac constantly attempted to contact them on the secondary frequency, which was always monitored. Totally the opposite of Cooke, Mac was a skinny, quiet guy. I always had the feeling he was thinking about a lot of serious stuff.

The AN/PRC25 radio had two antennae. One was the tape, which looked like a three-foot strip of metal cut from a carpenter's tape measure and it had a short range. The other was the whip antenna, which was fiberglass; it was about eight feet long and fit together like a fishing rod and had somewhat greater range. The whip antenna was impossible to move through overhead cover with. Either antenna made a target of the radioman. I didn't want any more transmissions to go out on the erstwhile primary freq and we finally gained enough elevation for the tape antenna to make contact.

When Mac finally passed the word up that he had made contact with Airminded, I stopped the team, and we set up a hasty 360 degree defensive position. On the secondary frequency, I told Airminded Bravo what we had heard and requested permission to immediately begin using the secondary freq as our primary. This was quickly granted and we were then sent a shackle-coded new secondary frequency for Mac's radio. Knowing the bad guys had the equipment to scan for an in-use frequency was scary. To know that they were relatively close was even scarier!

24. Ambush

I had some free time on my hands one afternoon so I wandered out to the gook shop outside the main gate. This was a ramshackle affair of bamboo, canvass, plywood, and assorted sheets of tin, housing four or five small shops. They sold everything from cheap jewelry, shower shoes made from old tires (we called them Ho Chi Minh sandals. They were very popular among civilians and Viet Cong alike), and, unbelievably, U.S. issue camouflage utilities. I bought a set of cammies there that were originally Air Force issue. They were obviously stolen at some point but they were being sold openly so I guess nobody cared. There was even a Mama San there with an ancient treadle powered Singer sewing machine so any alterations could be made on the spot. Mama San was a common term of relative respect for older Asian women. Papa San is the male equivalent.

Why the Air Force had cammies and Marines didn't was beyond me. Some of the guys bought Vietnamese manufactured Tiger Stripe utilities. They weren't as well made but the camouflage pattern was surprisingly effective.

I had gotten a little shaggy so, as long as I was there, I figured I'd get a haircut. The barbershop was equipped with a folding chair and a Papa San with a set of manual hair clippers. They looked like something you would shear sheep with. I knew it wouldn't be pretty but there was no one to look pretty for. I got in the line for haircuts and after standing there for a few minutes, I took note of the Marine in front of me. The back of his head looked strangely familiar. Even the way his ears stuck out reminded me of someone. He was a few inches shorter than I was so I risked a peek over his shoulder. I couldn't see his collar rank clearly but it was the partial profile that put it all together.

I said, "Sergeant Cowan?" (his rank the last time I had seen him).

Gunnery Sergeant Arthur Cowan turned, looked me up and down and said, "Johnson ... ya hahg, drop and give me ten!" When Gunny Cowan called his recruits "Hog," it came out sounding more like "hahg." From him, as a D.I., it was a term of endearment.

One of the gook shops (courtesy L/Cpl Standiford).

It was my senior drill instructor from Parris Island! I did exactly as I was told and dropped in the haircut line to execute ten perfect pushups. When I got done, he shook my hand and said, "How the hell are you, Johnson?"

Bear in mind that it had been nearly three years and hundreds of shave-headed Little Green Amphibious Monsters since he saw me last, but he remembered me. I was tickled pink. We chatted for several minutes and he mentioned that he had just come down from Con Thien where his company (I presume he was the Company Gunny) took something of a beating.

As a drill instructor, two things (among many things) that the then Sergeant Cowan said that stuck in my gourd were, "If you see extra ammo lying around, scarf it up. You can never have enough." The other pearl of wisdom was, "Learning by the book is fine. You have to know the fundamentals. But once the first shot is fired, all the book is good for is toilet paper!" Years later, I found out from one of his drill instructor colleagues that his nickname among the D.I.s was Igor! Perfect!

He got his haircut, we shot the breeze a little more, and then he was gone. It's often said that with the relatively small size of the Marine Corps, no matter where you are, you keep running into people you know.

On a patrol that actually took us into the southeast TAOR of Khe Sanh, in other words, considerably northwest of Quang Tri, we were in some very thick, heavy bush with numerous waterways. While crossing a swiftly running rock and boulder-strewn river that was quite wide, but only two or three feet deep, one of the team slipped and fell. He went under and came right up again but without his rifle. In floundering around, he managed to move a few feet from where he fell and he couldn't locate it. The river was making enough noise so that it covered up his splashing around but it still wasn't a good spot to be in. Part of the team was still on the other side and at least two others were in midstream.

My APL was Corporal Steve Rudd. The Marine Corps likes to say that a Marine is a Marine ... there are no black Marines, nor any white Marines ... just green Marines. As it happens, Rudd was a dark green Marine. He was rather quiet but as solid as a rock and I could count on him without question. Rudd was with the remainder of the team on the other side. He immediately sized up the situation and put the men with him in security positions to watch our backs. I did the same on my side of the river. The three in the middle took turns holding their breath while ducking under the water to search for the rifle on their hands and knees. After a few anxious minutes, one of them triumphantly surfaced with the M-16.

A day or so later on the same patrol, the point man turned and indicated that he needed me up front. When I got to him, he pointed at the ground a few feet ahead. Sticking out of the ground at the edge of some tall elephant grass was the tail fin assembly of some sort of projectile. We were in the middle of nowhere and there were no trails nearby so it wasn't likely that this was a booby trap. I moved closer and could then see that it was an unexploded U.S. issue 4.2-inch mortar round. In other words, a dud, and therefore highly unstable. The 4.2 was commonly called a Four Deuce and was usually a regimental level weapon.

I passed the word for the team to drop their gear, set up security, and have chow. I told everybody not to touch the round and I went back to the radioman, L/Cpl. Ernie Cooke, and advised C.O.C. what we had and further suggested that we bury it. It was too dangerous to handle and, if left to be found by the gooks, they could turn it into a booby trap somewhere else. Apparently, after several minutes of high-level consultation in the rear by some captains and majors, they agreed with me.

When I went back to where the round was, I couldn't believe my eyes. Standing there, hefting the mortar round as if it was a football was my corpsman! The same one who had convinced Gunny Larsen to put a hole in his HBT cover. This guy had been a bit of a maverick since he joined the platoon. He tended to be a bit of a hot dog ... frequently relating his alleged deeds of derring-do while with his former unit. He also had a little trouble taking orders. I told him to stand very still. I had my Kodak Instamatic in my shirt pocket so I took it out and told him I wanted to have something to remember

Corpsman waiting for a dud 4.2 round to explode.

him by if it went off, and took his picture. Then I told him to continue to stand very still while a hole was quickly dug at his feet. The round was gingerly buried and camouflaged.

It was while he was holding the round that I noticed something else. This corpsman was wearing a pistol. Recon corpsmen are not issued pistols. Upon closer inspection I could see that it was not even a government issue .45 automatic but a nickel-plated stag handled six-shooter. He had it wrapped in a plastic bag to keep it dry, although I have no idea how he thought he would draw and fire it in an emergency. Furthermore, it was in an Old West type cowboy holster and belt. He had kept it in his pack until we got out in the bush and then put it on.

I ordered him to put it back in his pack and not to get it out again unless he was going to use it on himself. When we returned from that patrol, he was given the option of turning it in to our armory to be returned when he left the unit, or losing it altogether. I assume he chose the former.

A short distance away from the company on the Quang Tri perimeter was a sandbag bunker that doubled as temporary living quarters and full time .50 caliber machine gun position. Teams from Recon rotated two or three

Most of Team Northtide, left to right, kneeling, Rodriguez behind the rifle?, Christie, 2nd row, Sargent, Schleman, Cooke, 3rd row, Tuthill, me (courtesy L/Cpl. Christie).

days at a time in this and other bunkers on either side of it, to augment the few grunts on that part of the perimeter. The .50 caliber stayed there and we were responsible for keeping it oiled and clean. The area to the front of this bunker was a hundred yards of rice paddy and then a tree line. I don't remember ever getting any directions on what to do if we were attacked except to cut loose with the .50. One night it rained very hard and part of the bunker roof collapsed. We spent most of the next day taking it apart and rebuilding it. Hey, at least it was something to do.

At night, we maintained 50 percent watches on the perimeter, so every other man was awake. On one night, a pop flare went up from somewhere farther down the line. Within seconds, the mortars a little ways behind us started launching illumination rounds. They are meant to light up an area like daylight and consist of a bright flare that descends by parachute. They stay lit for about 20 seconds before burning out. The trees on the other side of the rice paddies were festooned with those little parachutes.

The dangerous thing about illumination rounds was that the canister they are launched in falls free after the flare is ejected. As they fall they go, "Wooo, wooo, woo," like when you blow across the open neck of a bottle. They also land with a thunk because they're made of metal or possibly a ceramic material. If one of them hits you, it could cause serious damage.

Echo Company had been in Quang Tri for at least a month and had sent out many patrols. There were a few sightings made but aside from that, we were beginning to think the gooks had all moved away. On March 11, 1968, I got my patrol warning order for a patrol that would go out the next day and made my rounds of the various C.O.C. liaisons.

The mission paragraph of every Recon patrol op-order states, "Determine the nature of enemy activity developing along the natural infiltration routes that could be used by VC/NVA and also check area for use as VC base camp area. Pay particular attention to size and direction of enemy movement. Act as a forward observer for artillery on targets of opportunity. Make every attempt to capture a prisoner."

This patrol area was the legendary back yard, and vegetation big enough to hide in was scarce here in places, for many, many square acres. Due to the openness of the terrain, I decided that we would break with custom and carry an M-60 machine gun. We don't ordinarily carry one because we usually move through the thickest of vegetation and the big M-60 is incredibly awkward to move within that stuff.

Tuthill volunteered to carry the twenty-six pound gun. I asked him if he knew what to do with it and he said something like, "How hard could it be?" Tuthill, as gunner, carried 300 rounds of machine gun ammo in 100 round belts. Seven additional 100-round belts were spread loaded through the team. A belt of 100 rounds, if rolled up tightly, would just fit into a canteen pouch. The clips on the pouch made it easy to attach to the outside of your pack for quick access.

Except in Hollywood and other fantasy worlds, infantry troops do not routinely run around in the jungle festooned with long criss-crossed belts of machine gun ammunition. Here's why. The bright brass casings show up nicely against the green foliage and your green uniform. The exposed bullets will snag every vine and leaf and collect dirt and muck every time you sit down or hit the deck. When the belts are clogged with debris, they don't work in a machine gun. To use them in the gun, the loop of ammo has to be broken. That takes precious seconds and you can lose rounds doing it. About the only legitimate exception is if you are in the middle of a gunfight and you are running ammo to the gun because they need it right now. Even then, the belts are not made into loops ... they are just slung over the shoulders or carried in the ammo boxes they come in.

We were going to travel by six-by up Route 1 and then west on Route 559 to a point where 559 turned straight north to eventually connect with Route 9. Remember, the interior roads like 559 were nothing more than oxcart tracks and within a mile of turning off Route 1 there were no signs of habitation. The truck we were on was alone, no gunships or other escort, and I think the driver was scared spitless. He was driving like a maniac. With the whole team in the back, it was standing room only and there was very little to hang on to as he bucketed down the road. Team members made several threats to the driver but he didn't seem to hear them. Finally, when he almost threw a couple of people out of the truck, Cpl. Rudd climbed out of the box onto the running board by the driver's door, stuck his rifle barrel in the kid's face and told him he'd be dead if he didn't slow down. This finally got through to the driver and he drove a bit more carefully.

On my map, I saw the insertion point coming up, so I hollered to the driver to stop at just short of a bend in the road. He slammed on the brakes, which catapulted everybody forward, and when we got off the truck, I had to restrain a few of my little monsters from introducing their rifle butt-plates to his teeth. He tore off as quickly as he could and we were left to the relative tranquility of the back yard. It was in this same general area that a previous patrol had received one sniper round that did no damage.

That team leader, an NCO, felt that the team was so exposed that he refused to move the team any further until dark. C.O.C. told him to continue the patrol and he still refused. After a bit more back and forth, the matter was dropped and he finished the patrol by moving at night and observing by day. A logical way to do a Recon when there is nowhere to hide.

If it had been me, and I felt that strongly about moving when a sniper was obviously watching you, I might have moved rapidly to a place I could hide, and then waited till dark. Besides, this wasn't a grunt combat patrol; it was sneaking and peeking, or at least supposed to be. When the patrol got back to the base, the team leader was written up for disobedience to an order and lost a stripe. Another example of people making ignorant decisions from miles away.

We moved very slowly from tree line to tree line being careful to observe the area ahead of us for any movement. After having moved not more than a half a klick, I heard a muffled expletive behind me. I turned around and saw McAfee backing away from our line of march and watching the ground intently. I stopped the team and went back to see what the problem was. McAfee said that he felt a solid tap against his right boot top and looked down to see a snake, probably a viper, recoiling to strike again. He quickly backed away and the snake slithered off in the opposite direction. Everybody ahead of Mac had just walked through that spot but the snake apparently thought Mac looked tastier than the rest of us. He was also very lucky that the snake hit his boot instead of being an inch or so higher. All of Vietnam is snake country but we all decided to keep a closer look out after that.

About midday, we came to a small hump that overlooked quite a large expanse of elephant grass and clumps of trees to the west with some large forested areas beyond and south of that. I figured this was as good as any spot for an O.P. for a few hours so we set out Claymores, established a 360 degree perimeter and began taking turns with the binoculars. As long as we stayed down in the brush, we were not visible from the surrounding area.

A little over 1000 meters northwest of our O.P. there was a long stretch of trail, about 1200 meters worth, running north-south from the heavy forest that I was particularly interested in. It was over 1000 meters away but could easily be watched with binoculars.

121520H (YD 162540)[1] PATROL OBSERVED FOUR VC/NVA MOVING NORTH ON TRAIL AT (YD 155547). TWO ENEMY WORE BLACK PJ'S AND THE OTHER TWO WORE KHAKIS. ALL WORE BUSH COVERS, HEAVY PACKS AND CARRIED RIFLES OF UNKNOWN TYPE. ALL WERE HEAVILY CAMOUFLAGED. ENEMY MOVED OUT OF SIGHT. PATROL KEPT THE AREA UNDER OBSERVATION AND CONTINUED MISSION.

121540H (YD 162540) PATROL OBSERVED TWELVE VC/NVA MOVING NORTH ON TRAIL AT (YD 155547). ALL ENEMY WORE KHAKIS, BUSH COVERS, HEAVY PACKS, RIFLES OF UNKNOWN TYPE AND WERE HEAVILY CAMOUFLAGED WITH BRUSH. PATROL CALLED AN ARTILLERY MISSION OF 10 ROUNDS WITH EXCELLENT COVERAGE OF TARGET AND UNKNOWN RESULTS. THE ENEMY MOVED OUT TO THE NORTH. PATROL CONTINUED ITS MISSION.

With only a dozen NVA as a target, I didn't have all day so rather than write the information on my Plexiglas map case and then hand it to Cooke, I took a quick compass azimuth to the target and called it in myself.

"Airminded Bravo, Airminded Bravo, this is Northtide, over."

"Northtide, this is Airminded Bravo, over."

"Airminded Bravo, Northtide, call for fire, will adjust, over." That meant that the artillery battery would fire only two rounds to see if the figures I gave them put the hits on target. If I determined that an adjustment was necessary I would give corrections in meters either left, right, add, or drop depending on where I wanted the next two rounds to impact. Once I had a bracket on the target, I then asked for a "fire for effect."

"Northtide, Airminded. Send your traffic, over."

"Roger, Airminded. Mils 5420, distance 1000 [meters], grid 154547, infantry in the open. Observer-target line from 162540 [our location], over."

"Northtide, Airminded, roger, over." Airminded then repeated the info to the artillery. The azimuth is given in mils instead of degrees because it is more accurate.

121630H (YD 162540) PATROL OBSERVED THREE VC/NVA MOVING NORTH ON TRAIL AT (YD 155547). ENEMY WORE BLACK PJ'S, HEAVY PACKS, ONE CARRIED A WEAPON AND ALL WERE HEAVILY CAMOUFLAGED WITH BRUSH. ENEMY MOVED OUT OF SIGHT. PATROL CONTINUED MISSION.

121640 (YD 162540) PATROL OBSERVED FOUR VC/NVA MOVING NORTH ON A TRAIL AT (YD 155547). ENEMY WORE BLACK PJ'S, HEAVY PACKS, RIFLES OF UNKNOWN TYPE AND ALL WORE HEAVY NATURAL CAMO. ENEMY WENT INTO THE BRUSH AND REAPPEARED ABOUT 30 SECONDS LATER. ENEMY WORE LIGHT SHIRTS AND DARK TROUSERS AND RAN UP THE TRAIL TO THE NORTH. IT APPEARED AS THOUGH THE ENEMY HAD HIDDEN THE GEAR THEY HAD BEEN WEARING. THE PATROL CONTINUED MISSION. PATROL CHECKED OUT THE AREA AT 130845 [THE NEXT DAY] WITH NEGATIVE RESULTS.

121715H (YD 162540) PATROL OBSERVED 28 VC/NVA MOVING NORTH ON A TRAIL IN THE VICINITY OF (YD 155547). THE ENEMY WORE KHAKIS, BUSH COVERS, HEAVY PACKS, AND CARRIED RIFLES OF UNKNOWN TYPE AND ALL WORE NATURAL CAMOUFLAGE. PATROL CALLED AN ARTILLERY MISSION OF 24 ROUNDS WITH EXCELLENT COVERAGE OF TARGET AND UNK RESULTS. PATROL FIRED V.T. WITH OUTSTANDING COVERAGE OF AREA. PATROL COULD NOT OBSERVE ANY MOVEMENT AFTER FOURTH FIRE FOR EFFECT. PATROL KEPT AREA UNDER SURVEILLANCE.

The earlier fire mission had been inconclusive but the target of a platoon of NVA moving up the trail looked much more promising. The fact that there were so many gave me a little more time to ask for another call for fire.

121915H (YD 162540) PATROL OBSERVED (7) VC/NVA RUNNING SOUTH BACK DOWN THE TRAIL FROM THE IMPACT AREA. THE PATROL COULD NOT OBSERVE UNIFORMS, WEAPONS OR EQUIPMENT BECAUSE OF DARKNESS. ALL ENEMY WORE HEAVY NATURAL CAMOUFLAGE. THE PATROL KEPT THE AREA UNDER SURVEILLANCE. THE PATROL HEARD MOANS FROM THE ARTILLERY IMPACT AREA DURING THE NIGHT.[2]

Now that it was dusk, and having no better place to move to for a harborsite, I decided to stay put. This was taking something of a risk because we had been there for several hours. If we had been spotted, we would be easy to find at night. I had to weigh that against the distinct possibility that survivors of the artillery attack down on the trail could very well be watching likely O.P. positions to see where the fire had been directed from. As I've said before, they know what Recon is and does.

Then the armchair tacticians got into the act again. A message relayed from C.O.C. indicated that we should just run down to the impact zone and do a little body count, up close and personal, like. I didn't think I'd heard it right and asked Airminded Bravo to repeat the message. I heard it right. I sent a message back pointing out that the impact zone was over a klick away in the dark and the people down there were probably a bit cross right now. When I said we'd check it out first thing in the morning they allowed as how that might be acceptable.

I could just imagine the conversation that had taken place back at REMFland: "Major, have the captain tell the lieutenant to instruct the sergeant to thrash around in the dark looking for bodies. And whilst he's there, pick up a few souvenirs for the General's office."

That night it was quiet. The cannon cockers launched a few H&I fires into the target area for good measure. From first light the next morning, I watched the target area for a while to see if there was any movement. Everything looked very still. Tuthill mentioned something about since there was so much activity, maybe we should go down there and set up an ambush. During the night, I had been mulling over similar thoughts. We certainly couldn't stay where we were any longer. By Recon standards, we had outstayed our welcome. I pulled the guys in a little closer so I could talk to all of them without raising my voice above a whisper.

"We will definitely go to the impact zone to see if there are any bodies or gear left lying around and if there are, we will search for any intelligence related material because that's part of our mission. However, when we get there I will assess the terrain to see if an ambush can be safely conducted. If it looks okay, you must bear in mind two things. One, there is not much to hide in down there, and as we've seen, it's regularly used by units much bigger than we are. And two, if it doesn't look promising, we'll move on and set up another O.P. We are not here to engage the enemy in a slugfest the way the grunts do. Does everybody understand?"

There were serious-faced nods of assent all around and we got ready to move. Cooke sent the brevity code for *moving* and we headed a little north and then west, taking advantage of a tree line that brought us to a point about 100 meters north of the impact zone. We stopped and watched the area for a little while because we were going to leave the cover of the trees and move to a rather exposed area.

THE PATROL CHECKED OUT THE AREA AT 130845H AND FOUND A BLOODY CHICOM GRENADE POUCH, A PIECE OF BLOODY ROPE, ONE CARRYING POLE, WRAPPING FROM [RUSSIAN MANUFACTURE] BANDAGES, AND BLOODY WALKING STICKS AND NATURAL CAMOUFLAGE. THE AREA IN THE IMPACT AREA WAS MATTED DOWN AND BLOODY. THE PATROL FOUND SEVERAL DRAG MARKS.[3]

It was obvious we had hurt them the night before. I was counting on the fact that the NVA did not have the kind of communications networks we had so it was doubtful that the word had gotten out to other units to avoid this area. I didn't want anyone coming through there alert with revenge in mind.

Just a few meters south of the impact zone was a small rise about 50 feet to the west of the trail. On top of it was a natural row of shrubbery and stunted growth no more than four feet high. It wasn't much but if we stayed prone and well cammied up, we could, in effect, hide in plain sight. Obvious ambush terrain made the potential victim more alert if he had any experience at all. If an area looked like it shouldn't be used as an ambush, it sometimes made a better one. The biggest risk here was if a larger unit than I cared to tackle came through, we would have to be invisible. If we were detected, we would be in a bad spot, indeed.

We could see more than 1000 meters of the trail as it went south into a large tree line. Looking north, we could see only about 100 meters. All of the traffic we saw yesterday was going north and I was hoping that trend would continue. I positioned each man where I wanted him, with Tuthill and the gun on the right flank. He, Sargent, and Meatball with the M-79 grenade launcher were there as right flank security as well as having the longest field of fire for the M-60. Corporal Rudd and another man were left flank security. I placed my new corpsman, HM3 Sid Rosser, near the middle of the line with Cooke and L/Cpl. Wayne Standiford. Standiford was Tuthill's buddy and definitely the more cerebral of the two. His nickname, presumably bestowed upon him by Tuthill, was Elmer Fudd. I had McAfee position a Claymore mine right next to the trail in the middle of the kill zone. If things started turning sour, touching off a Claymore usually threw water on that fire.

Cooke had possibly the worst assignment you can have when you know there's probably going to be a shootout. As radioman, his responsibility is communications. Almost everything else has a lower priority for him. At the first shot, he must call in with the brevity code for enemy contact, which at that time was *collision*. He then had to give a lengthy and detailed report called a Zulu report consisting of sixteen different elements that, although important, were difficult to concentrate on when bullets are flying. Some of that information was our location, approximate number of enemy, are we receiving fire at this time, number of killed and wounded, direction and approximate distance to a suitable LZ, and method to signal aircraft, just to name a few. I don't know who came up with the Zulu report format but I'll bet it was somebody with (a) lots of time on their hands, or (b) not currently being shot at.

On top of that, a properly set ambush requires rear security. Sometimes ambushers get ambushed. Remember my counter-ambush patrol at Recon School? Cooke was my rear security, which meant that he had to lay prone facing away from the kill zone watching our backs. Can you imagine how much discipline that takes? In this case, since we would be initiating the fight, I could determine most of the elements of the Zulu report in advance. I wrote them out and gave them to Cooke. All he would have to do is fill in a couple of blanks about enemy numbers and so forth.

To initiate an ambush, you do not do as Hollywood does. There, the flint-eyed hero bellows, "Fire." By doing so, you give the enemy a split second to react and that can mean the difference between success and disaster. An ambush is sprung by fire, not verbal command (contrary to the aforementioned Recon School caper), either by shooting what appears to be a leader or radioman, or squeezing off a Claymore.

130915H (YD 153547) PATROL ESTABLISHED AMBUSH ALONG THE TRAIL. 131029H (YD 153547) PATROL OBSERVED SIX CIVILIANS, THREE CHILDREN, TWO WOMEN, AND ONE MAN MOVING SOUTH AT (YD 159547). CIVILIANS REACHED A TRAIL JUNCTION AT (YD 155544), OBSERVED THE AREA WHERE THE ARTILLERY HAD BEEN FIRED AND MOVED BACK TO THE NORTH UP THE TRAIL. PATROL LOST SIGHT OF THE CIVILIANS. PATROL CONTINUED MISSION.[4]

The day wore on and it was hot. We lay behind our meager cover and baked. A little after noon I told the team to eat chow two at a time and keep movement to the absolute minimum. A short time later, I heard a commotion to my left and was surprised to see Standiford scuttling rapidly backward. I crawled over to see what the problem was and Standiford pointed into the bush that he had been peering through for the previous three hours or so. Curled up on a small branch about a foot off the ground was the coolest looking, bright green bamboo pit viper. It was looking right at us and flicking its tongue in and out. Standiford had been concentrating on the trail so hard that he didn't focus on the snake right in front of his face. This one wasn't very big and may have been a baby, but vipers are known as "two-steppers." It is said that if you are bitten, you take two steps and drop. Whatever the number of steps, they are very deadly.

Somebody poked at it with a stick until it dropped to the ground and slithered away. After that, we all paid closer attention to the shrubbery in front of us.

Just after 4:00 P.M., Tuthill passed the word that there was movement at the south end of the trail.

131610H (YD 153547) Patrol observed three VC moving north up a trail at (YD 155535). Enemy wore civilian clothing and one wore black PJ's and one wore a khaki shirt.[5]

I crawled over and watched them for a while with binoculars. They were far enough away that it would take them possibly 30 minutes to reach us. I decided they were fair game for us but I wanted to make sure they weren't just the point unit for an entire company of gooks. After they had progressed a couple hundred meters, it was apparent that they were alone.

I had Cooke call in a SALUTE report as we had done on the earlier sightings but this time I had him add that we were probably going to ambush them. Each time they got 100 meters closer, I called in their distance from us. By the time they were about 400 meters away, I could only see one visible weapon. They were wearing a lot of natural camouflage of leaves and branches so details of their equipment were hard to see. I passed the word that I would initiate the ambush by shooting the one with the weapon. He was number two of the four. I emphasized that I wanted prisoners but if there was resistance of any kind, shoot to kill.

When they were within 75 meters, I told Cooke to radio that contact was imminent. They were trudging along with their heads down and paying no attention to the innocent looking bushes to their left. I had my rifle sights right on the left side of the gook with the weapon. I tracked him along until he was directly in front of me and then I shot him once in the left rib area. He dropped immediately. Cooke yelled, "Collision!" into the handset.

131610H (YD 153547) Patrol initiated small arms fire as enemy moved into killing zone. Enemy returned small arms fire. All enemy carried weapons, (three of the enemy had their rifles hidden in the camouflage which they wore.) The enemy was approximately 50 feet from the patrol when the ambush was initiated.[6]

When the ambush was sprung, the NVA point man went down quickly and the third and fourth turned to run. I stood up and emptied my magazine at number three as he ran and Tuthill opened up with the M-60. He only fired a half dozen rounds and the gun jammed! Meatball was also firing at number three who went tumbling and lay still. After number three dropped, I yelled, "Cease fire!"

Number four actually made it to a small fold in the ground that had some scrubby bushes growing out of it. Tuthill turned to me and I hollered for him, Sargent, and Meatball to chase him down. Meatball had the M-79 and he put a round right into the spot where the gook disappeared. As I was focused on that, I heard a long string of automatic fire to my left followed instantly by another long burst. I turned to see Cpl. Rudd emptying a magazine at the point man on the ground. It turned out that when I shot number two, the point man dropped and played dead. Then when he heard the firing stop, he rolled over and got a full 30 round magazine off at us. Fortunately, he shot high. He was just about opposite Rudd when that happened and Rudd stitched a circle around the gook, hitting him in both hands and both feet. Later, Rudd stoutly maintained that was exactly where he meant to hit him.

I moved down across the little knob we were on toward the point man, who was lying on his back but painfully trying to sit up to reach his AK-47 which Rudd had shot out of his hands. I had to give this guy credit for chutz-pah. The only Vietnamese that came to mind right then was the words for *halt.* I shouted, "Dung lai, or I'll blow you away." I was advancing on him with my rifle pointed right at his head. He looked at me as I was about 30 feet away and, deciding that discretion was the better part of valor, slowly raised his hands over his head. I relieved him of a pair of binoculars that he had around his neck on a strap. A fair amount of blood was sloshed on them that had probably come from one of his hands. Somebody else grabbed his AK-47.

Several things now happened all at once as we went on "auto pilot." Doc Rosser went to the one I had shot, lifted up the front of his shirt, and shook his head. He then came over to the point man and determined that his wounds were not life threatening. Cooke called in the extraction coordinates, which were right on top of our ambush position. Tuthill and party returned saying that the gook that ran into the little depression must have taken a nearly direct hit from the M-79 because there wasn't much left. I returned to the top of the rise and called in a fire mission on the trail where it came out of the tree line to the south. This was to discourage anyone who might be down that way from getting too curious. I also called in a fire mission on our present position, to be fired after we had been extracted. That, too, was to discourage curiosity seekers.

The wounded gook that had been shot down as he ran was carried, along with his colleague, to the LZ. Doc Rosser immediately gave him an I.V. This was a strange one. The only visible wound was a bullet wound to the back of his right thigh. It went through and left a large exit wound on the front. The exit wound was not really bleeding and it was so clean I could see the various layers of fat and muscle right down to the bone. He was conscious but appeared to be in shock. Neither of the two prisoners said a word to each other or us.

Doc was tending his patient, McAfee was busy rolling up the Claymore

March 13, 1968, immediately after the ambush, with two wounded NVA Prisoners of War. At left, McAfee rolls up Claymore wire. I'm in the center. At right, Doc Sid Rosser gives an albumin I.V. to a wounded prisoner. We were hiding right there (courtesy L/Cpl. Standiford).

wire, and everyone else was in a 360 around the LZ as we awaited extraction. Standiford, from his position on the perimeter, was taking some pictures so I asked him to get one of me. I was going to put my foot on the chest of the wounded point man (like with a trophy tiger) but I didn't. At the last second, it occurred to me that this guy had done his duty and was now out of the fight. Putting my foot on his chest would only add unnecessary insult to injury. I liked to think, and still do, that we are better than that. Instead, I knelt down beside him.

Tuthill was still cursing his nonfunctioning M-60 when we could hear the choppers coming. The artillery I called on the south end of the trail was also landing with a sharp CRUMP! CRUMP! CAAARUMP! Sorry, Hollywood, artillery doesn't result in enormous fireballs unless it hits something like fuel or other types of explosives. In reality, there is usually a brief flash and then a cloud of dirty gray smoke and debris.

Cooke was on the horn with one of the chopper pilots. We never really knew which of the four birds we were talking to but I think it was usually the lead gun ship because they always arrived on scene first. However, he would eventually turn us over to the lead troop ship because he would be the only one actually landing on the LZ. Any need for noise discipline was gone due to the increasing din from artillery exploding and the rapidly growing population of helicopters in the neighborhood, so Cooke was no longer attempting to whisper into the radio handset. Although I could not hear the helicopter side of the conversation, I knew from many past patrols what the exchange sounded like.

Chopper pilot, "Northtide, Northtide, this is Top Hat lead, over."

Cooke (loudly now), "This is Northtide, over."

"Northtide, Top Hat lead. What is your latest enemy situation? Over."

"Top Hat, we ambushed four NVA and have two wounded prisoners. No other known enemy in the area. We are not, repeat not in contact at this time, over."

"Northtide, we are about three klicks out." (As if we didn't know. On a bright clear day, you are bound to take note of two Hueys angrily buzzing around overhead and two Marine Green flying school buses boring in on us from three quarters of a mile away.) "What does the LZ look like? Over."

"Top Hat lead, it's flat and almost bare of vegetation for about 75 meters in all directions, over."

"Roger that, Northtide. Pop your smoke, over."

Cooke yelled to me to throw the smoke grenade. We cleared off to the edges of the LZ and kept our eyes peeled outboard for any enemy movement. I had already chosen an attractive saffron hue from my palette of smoke grenades so I pulled the pin and tossed the canister into the middle of the LZ. There were a few seconds of delay as the incendiary element got hot enough to ignite the solid color element and burn through tape that covered the emission holes on the can. The yellow cloud quickly boiled out of the grenade and expanded to completely obscure the LZ for a moment.

Cooke radioed, "Top Hat lead, Northtide. Smoke is out. What color do you see? Over."

"Northtide, I have a yellow, over."

"Roger, Top Hat, come and get us. Northtide out."

The Huey gunbirds had arrived ahead of the 46s and were aggressively orbiting the immediate area looking for bad guys approaching the ambush site/LZ.

I had one more ritual to perform before we left the ambush site. We had been told that the Vietnamese abhorred the symbol of the spade as is found on a deck of playing cards. The most prominent one was on the ace of spades. Apparently, if someone dies with the mark of the spade upon them their soul would forever wander in some kind of limbo and never achieve Nirvana. Most of the team leaders carried a couple of aces of spades with them. Of course that meant that all our decks of cards were missing the ace of spades and had a hand made one in its place in the deck. Everybody knew if you had that card when playing rummy or old maid or whatever.

At any rate, one of the guys had written a letter to the U.S. Playing Card Company asking if they had any rejects or misprints of the ace of spades. He also explained why we wanted them. A couple of weeks later, that patriotic American company sent him two or three brand new decks of all aces of spades.

I have no idea if the wandering soul thing had any basis in fact but we bought it and left aces of spades on or near enemy bodies if for no other reason than to piss them off. Often we would write our name or Recon on the card.

Huey gunship (courtesy 1st Lt. Fisher).

A CH-46 descending on top of you is an inspiring sight. From about 100 feet up the rotor wash whips the remnant of the smoke cloud into nothingness. Then all vegetation in the LZ gets hammered flat. Any loose ground cover, dirt, or loose equipment gets blown away in a stinging whirlwind. However, for its size, a 46 is almost graceful as it settles the last few feet to the ground. The crew chief inside lowered the rear ramp as soon as the chopper touched down and my guys double-timed inside. The prisoners were scooped up and carried by two Marines each onto the chopper. The rest of us scurried on board through the oven-hot blast of turbine exhaust and we lifted off. I imagine my ace of spades was blown into oblivion.

At about 100 feet off the ground the chopper shook with heavy machine gun fire and my heart almost stopped! Had some gooks snuck up on the LZ and now we were taking fire? Then I saw the source. The door gunner on the right side of the bird had chopped up the LZ with his .50 caliber machine gun. He probably used the body we left behind as a target.

Even though it was laced with the reek of JP-4 exhaust and hydraulic fluid fumes, the wind blowing through the chopper was like fresh air after the alternating tedium and tenseness of the day. We had completed a textbook

CH-46 landing to take us home. Note the remnant of yellow smoke at lower left (courtesy L/Cpl. Standiford).

In the air after the ambush, looking out the rear of the CH-46. Left to right, sitting, Rudd, standing, Tuthill, Cooke, Me, Sargent, sitting Doc Rosser. Everybody is smoking but me (courtesy L/Cpl. Standiford).

Recon patrol, taken prisoners, and except for Standiford's scare, none of my Marines got a scratch. There were grins and thumbs up all around.

The chopper landed at Dong Ha to offload the wounded prisoners at Delta Med. We heard later on that the gook with the leg wound died. He didn't look that bad to me but maybe it was shock. He was carrying a thick wad of North Vietnamese currency and a lot of typed documents in his shirt pockets. My guess is that he was a paymaster-courier. I suppose it's even possible that if he was some kind of big wheel, he took cyanide so he wouldn't talk, but who knows? One other odd thing was that he definitely did not look Vietnamese. He was much chunkier and had a round; almost ... dare I say it, Chinese face.

The team stayed on the chopper as corpsmen from Delta Med removed the prisoners and then we were whisked down to Quang Tri. We landed at the LZ right outside the company area and most of the company was there to greet us. I guess I didn't realize it right then but we had taken first combat blood for the company. Echo Company was no longer a virgin! As we moved off the LZ, I glanced up to see Captain Raymond running like a maniac down the company street toward us. My first thought was, "Did I do something stupid again?"

The captain skidded to a stop in front of me with an ear-to-ear grin on his face. He started pounding me on the back and pumping my hand and, well, he beat the crap out of me! Then he proceeded to hammer on everybody in the team. It was good, albeit painful, when the captain was happy.

We were finally able to drop our gear and open up the poncho full of weapons and equipment we had taken from the gooks. The stuff was laid out on a bunker for everyone to gawk at. I was told that when we called in that we were going to spring an ambush soon, someone from C.O.C. notified the company office and a radio was tuned to our frequency. One of the guys in the platoon said that most of the company gathered around the radio at the company office and listened to the play by play of the whole thing.

Shortly after returning to Quang Tri, however, I and Cpl. Rudd were summoned back to Dong Ha. It seems that in the flurry of activity of unloading the wounded prisoners we had neglected to report to S-2 for debriefing and to turn in the captured weapons and equipment. The S-2 people are funny about that stuff. We bundled up our booty, hitched a ride north and went through debriefing. It was then that we learned the prisoner with the leg wound had died. The S-2 officer, in an incredible act of generosity, gave me some of the North Vietnamese currency ... one bill for each member of the team. He didn't know that we had already liberated a few belts, belt buckles, and ChiCom web gear. I managed to get away with the binoculars the point man was carrying. After debriefing, Rudd and I went out to the main gate and got lucky enough to catch a jeep ride with a chaplain who was going to Quang Tri.

Lieutenant Hardhead had been with a patrol a few klicks from ours and when they got back a couple of days later, he had the nerve to say, "We heard the firing from your ambush. You didn't need to fire that many rounds." I felt that trying to explain the purpose for every round fired was a total waste of my time so I just said that maybe there was an echo and found a reason to leave and go count my toes or something. What do you say to that kind of ignorance?

I had the binoculars I had taken off the wounded point man after the ambush and, again, my sense of complying with the rules compelled me to go to the G-2 shop to declare them as a war trophy. I really didn't think anyone would have a problem with me keeping them, but I figured better to do it right than risk brig time for something so trivial.

On March 15, I got permission to leave the company area and went to G-2 at 3d Marine Division Headquarters. I filled out a short form and the officer I talked to said they were now mine but that when I rotated home, I should go to G-2 on Okinawa and show them the copy of the war trophy registration form to make sure I had obtained them according to regulations.

A brief word about the Marines of the air wing. The pilots and aircrew are beyond belief when it comes to flying big targets into very dangerous places. That being said, I have always found wingers to be just a little out of touch with the rest of the Corps. Over the years, I have read many memoirs, all written by pilots, about their experiences in Vietnam. Maybe it's all that vibration and noise or the constant exposure to hydraulic and JP-4 fumes but I found many of their uses of basic Marine Corps terminology to be uniformly off the mark.

For instance, the Marine field uniforms are called utilities. The writers consistently called them fatigues. That's Army talk. They would, when nature called, use a latrine, not the head. More Army stuff. Chopper pilots routinely insert Recon teams into their zones but they did not seem to understand the difference between Force Recon and Battalion Recon. In their books, they often bemoaned the occasional lack of ice and beer but frequently availed themselves of the ability to fly to the Royal Thai Air Force Base at Udorn, Thailand, to replenish said items. (Must be nice.) Many squadrons even had their own clubs in addition to the officers' club on their base. I read of several pilots who plotted to meet up with German nurses who worked on a German hospital ship, the SS *Helgoland*. However, the most egregious gaff in my opinion was the labeling, more often than not, of Marines as soldiers. These guys know better but maybe it was to clarify their stories for civilians who might read them. Yeah, that must be it.

Like I said ... brave as the day is long, so it must have been the fumes. Just be quiet and eat your gruel, Marine.

25. China Beach and Malaria

The Third Marine Division had a policy that granted an extra out of country R&R to anyone who took a prisoner. The team had taken two, so Cpl. Rudd, my APL, and I were called to the company office. Captain Raymond asked us where we wanted to go. I actually didn't know about this policy so I was a little surprised. I thought for a second and then I looked at Rudd and said, "The whole team took those prisoners. It isn't fair if we go on R&R and they continue to run patrols." Rudd nodded in agreement and I asked the captain if it was possible to give the whole team some kind of reward.

He pondered for a moment and then said, "I'll see if I can get authorization for you all to take three days in country R&R at China Beach." Rudd and I thought that was an excellent idea. While we were talking about R&R I pointed out to the captain that I had not yet chosen my own personal R&R location.

I had thought about where to go and had talked to several others who had already been to some of those places. I said, "I'd like Sydney, Australia." I mostly wanted to go someplace where the people had round eyes. Most of the R&R locations were in Asia: Tokyo, Bangkok, etc. The captain said he'd put me in for it but it was the most popular R&R so be prepared to make another choice.

I asked Rudd not to tell the team about China Beach because if my request was denied I didn't want them to be too disappointed. Just a few days later I got the word that China Beach had been approved and we were leaving the next day. I informed the team and they were happy, to say the least. Three days of decent food, cold drinks, white sand beaches, and no patrols or filling sandbags. Outstanding!

China Beach is part of the huge Da Nang base so it wasn't like we weren't still in the Marines. But there was no reveille, no taps, and not much else in the way of rules beyond those of civil behavior. When we arrived, the first thing we did was turn in weapons at the armory. The second thing we did was hit the geedunk and scarf down a few dozen hamburgers and fries. Then we found our barracks and everybody crapped out for a couple of hours.

Each night at China Beach there was a live band on an outdoor stage and it was a huge disappointment. While we were there, it was a very bad Filipino rock band composed of what appeared to be 15-year-old kids. They were crude and lewd and what they didn't sing in incredibly bad English, they sang in Tagolog. The last thing any of us wanted to see or hear was a bad Asian band singing in a foreign language. Other than that, though, we had a pretty relaxing three days.

During the day, besides the beach, there were movies to see, all the sack time you wanted, and a means by which to call home (if you don't mind standing in line for two hours).

When I say call home, that is an oversimplification. In reality it was a combination telephone/Ham radio operation that, to me, was more trouble than it was worth. It was called the MARS system — Military Amateur Radio System. Basically, as I understood it, it was a system whereby contact was made through volunteer military Ham operators in Vietnam to any one of hundreds of Ham radio volunteers in the States. They would then establish a network of Ham operators across the country to one that was close to the person you wanted to talk to — let's say your mother. Final contact was made by telephone. Starting in Vietnam, the radio traffic would sound something like:

"ABC123 to anyone on this band, over."

(In Hawaii for example). "ABC123, this is DEF456, go ahead, over."

"DEF456, ABC123, I am calling from Da Nang and I want to contact Mrs. Honoria Frothingslosh in Bugtussle, Pennsylvania. Her phone number is Davenport Oh, Oh, Two Short, over."

"Roger, ABC123. Break. HIG789, this is DEF456, you awake over there Bill? Over." In this representative account Bill was a regular contact of DEF456 in California or maybe even farther east.

"DEF456 this is HIG789, that's affirmative Dave, what do you have? Over."

Dave would then pass the information about Mrs. Frothingslosh to Bill who would make contact through a chain of Ham operators across the country until they got to an operator as close as possible to Bugtussle. Many of these Ham operators knew each other well but had never met. Let's say the chain of operators has reached Jim in Ludlow, Pennsylvania, but he can't raise anyone closer to Bugtussle. Jim then calls Mrs. Frothingslosh on his own telephone and tells her that her son Obediah is calling her and to just stay on the line until he gives her further instructions. Jim then radios back to Bob who calls Bubba who calls Shirley who calls Henry and the chain of operators ripples all the way back to ABC123 in Da Nang. The reason why transmissions need to end with the word *over* is because certain two-way radios, such as military and Ham operators use, have only one-way transmission capability. In other words, you are either receiving (listening) or transmitting (talking).There is a switch on each radio set that the operator moves to *transmit* when talking, and *receive* when listening. When A is through talking to B, he says, "over." That means "over to you," and moves his switch to *receive*. B, who had his switch set on *receive* so he could hear A now moves his switch to *transmit* so he can reply to A. After speaking to A, if B does not say "over," A will not switch to *receive* because he thinks B has more to say. Military field radios work the same way but the handset is always in the receive mode. A button on the handset will key the transmit mode so there isn't as much switching back and forth. However, it still does not work like a telephone where the parties can both listen and talk simultaneously. See how it works? Now the fun starts.

Remember ... Mrs. Frothingslosh knows zero about radio procedure. However, procedure must be followed — it's FCC rules. Here's how it would sound;

Private Obediah Frothingslosh, "Hi mom. Just listen to me for a minute. We will be talking over a Ham radio net so when I am through saying something and I want you to answer, I will say *over*. Then all the radio operators will throw a switch so you can answer back. When you are through saying something, you have to say *over* so they can throw a switch so I can answer back. Okay? Over."

Mrs. Frothingslosh, "Oh Obie it's so good to hear your voice. How are you?"

Silence.

"Obie, are you there?"

Silence.

"I think we've been cut off."

Ham operator on the phone in Ludlow, "Ma'am, you have to say over."

"What?"

"You have to say over so your son can answer you."

"But he just called. I don't want it to be over!"

"No, I mean you have to say over so all of us Ham operators can throw a switch so your son can answer you."

"That doesn't make any sense at all!"

"Ma'am..."

"Oh all right! Obie how are you ... uh, over?"

"I'm fine mom. How are dad and Cindy Lou? Over."

"They're both great and missing you."

Silence.

"I said, they're both great and missing you."

Silence.

Ham operator. "Ma'am..."

"Oh, I forgot, Obie. Over..." — This is ridiculous!"

"I miss you too, mom. Did you get the silk blouse I sent you from Okinawa last month? Over."

"Yes, and it's beautiful. Cindy Lou says she'd like one, too."

Silence.

"She's a size small but you probably know that."

Silence.

"Obie?"

Silence.

Ham operator. "Mrs...."

"OVER, DAMMIT!"

By this time, the "siege" at Khe Sanh had lifted. The U.S. Army likes to say that they rescued the Marines in a heavily reinforced drive over Route 9 to the base. The Marines naturally take great exception to that claim. They didn't, after all, need rescuing. The truth is that the two divisions of NVA around Khe Sanh finally tired of having their asses handed to them for the previous 2½ months and just went away.

Most of the nearly 40 percent casualties (22 killed in action) Bravo Company took during that battle were not sustained facing the enemy. It was often due to the company's geographical position on the base. Any incoming that was fired at Charlie Med or the ammo dump that went wide either way landed on Bravo. Any incoming fired at the regimental command post or the airstrip that went short or long landed on Bravo. The company area became known as the V ring (as in the center of the target). After the siege had begun, and patrols outside the base were terminated, I don't think a Recon Marine ever fired a round at the enemy. However, that was when they took the majority of casualties. All they could do was dig their holes deeper.

What was left of Bravo was transported down to Quang Tri to an area not too far from Echo Company. They were no longer effective as a Recon company and were taken "out of the line" for re-manning, re-equipping and licking their wounds. Those of us who had originally come from Bravo went over to pay a visit and see who we knew that was still standing. Most of my old team had either been killed or medevaced. We saw Sgt. Dennis Herb and talked with him for a while as he tried to sort through his gear to see what was salvageable. He was noticeably thinner and pale. He was also very distant and only spoke when someone asked him a direct question. It was as if he was in shock and didn't really know who we were. We stayed for a few minutes but soon ran out of things to say. Herb never smiled once. We briefly saw a couple of other old friends but we began to feel out of place. None of us had ever faced anything remotely as harrowing as what the survivors of the siege had been through. I, at least, felt almost unworthy to bother them. We finally headed back to Echo Company in a very despondent mood. I think hardly a word was spoken among us.

One afternoon at Quang Tri, I was sitting on my cot getting ready for a patrol. It was a very hot day and we had the sides of the tent rolled up to capture any breeze that wandered our way. I suddenly began to feel chilly so I put my shirt on. A little while later, I rolled down my sleeves because I had goose bumps on my arms. My head was aching some and I got the feeling something wasn't quite right. Within an hour, I was lying on my cot and shivering. Somebody went to find Doc Rosser. I vaguely remember him taking my temperature and then putting at least two wool G.I. blankets on me. I was still freezing and now my whole body was shaking. The last thing I remember him saying was, "I think you have malaria. You're being medevacked."

I don't remember the trip to the Naval Hospital at Da Nang but I became aware that I was in a hospital ward feeling as if I had been kicked by a horse.

Hi there,

I guess you can tell by the heading on this paper [American National Red Cross stationery] that I'm in the hospital. Don't get all rattled, now, because nobody dropped a bomb on me or stabbed me or anything. All it is is some kind of bug. The doctors said it may be malaria [or] some kind of parasite in my blood stream. I'd had a bad headache since the 22nd and then about noon on the 23rd I came down with a fever of almost 103°. Right now I think a 3 year old girl could drop kick me all over the place and I wouldn't be able to put up much of a fight. Sometimes I feel so weak I can hardly sit up. Well I guess that's all for now. Just wanted you to know what's going on.

Steve[1]

After several days in the hospital, I was allowed to get out of bed and wobble around a little. I was still very weak and my weight was down to about 145 pounds. One day I went outside to a sort of courtyard where there was a large cage. In the cage was some kind of snake, probably a type of constrictor that must have been at least twelve feet long. I wondered who caught it. More than that, I wondered, why?

Malaria is not a fun time. Each episode begins with chills that last for hours. There is no way to get warm. After the chills pass, there is a brief time where you just feel wrung out. Then the fever hits and you burn to a crisp. In extreme cases, the victim is literally packed in ice or they fry their brain and die. After the fever passes, you go through several hours of the worst muscle pain you can imagine. The severe tensing of the muscles when you have the chills and the beating your body takes during the fever probably bring that on. All of that is accompanied by vomiting and diarrhea. In the later stages, your urine and stool are black. One of the doctors said it was from the internal bleeding of, I think, the liver. That all takes two to three days. Then you have a day of feeling not too bad and it starts all over again. To add insult to injury, I had faithfully taken my anti-malarial pills. They were big orange things we called horse pills. A lot of guys didn't or wouldn't take them and I don't know of any of them getting malaria. I finally got discharged from the hospital and went back to Quang Tri. In my absence, Cpl. Rudd had taken the patrols and did a good job.

Right after I got back to Quang Tri, the word was passed for me to report to the company office. I was met by Lt. Youngstrom who told me that a correspondent from the *Sea Tiger* was there to see me. The *Sea Tiger* was a small tabloid sized newspaper that was published weekly by III Marine Amphibious Force and was similar in nature to the *Stars and Stripes* that has been published under authorization of the Department of Defense since before World War I. The *Sea Tiger*, however, was published only for the Marines.

A staff sergeant introduced himself to me and said he wanted to write an account of the ambush patrol. Wow! Little Stevie's going to be in the papers! He quizzed me for about a half hour, all the while taking notes as well as using a tape recorder. When he was done, he thanked me and that was it. Just a few days later, my team was lounging around in the company LZ along with at least three other teams. We were all waiting our turn to load up on the choppers and head out on another patrol.

The birds that were making the insertions returned for the next team and one of the guys who had been reading a newspaper to pass the time came over to us and handed it to one of my guys. He then hurried away to join his team and the choppers hammered their way into the sky while we lay there being sandblasted by the rotor wash and choking on hot exhaust fumes. After a few minutes, whoever had the paper suddenly whooped and said, "Hey look at this! We're in the paper!" Sure enough, there was the article about our patrol. We all quickly read it and then I folded it up and shoved it in my pack. That *Sea Tiger* is now yellow and crumbling but I still have it. Oddly enough, that issue of *Sea Tiger* was the one and only issue I ever actually saw while I was in Vietnam. Kismet!

I had been using my tape recorder to record messages home and I had gotten a few in return. That gave everything a real personal touch and I let some of the other guys use it for that purpose.

Dear group,
    I'm having to write this instead of taping because we got hit by rockets last night and the generator took a direct hit.
    My orders and my flight date [home] came in today. I will be leaving here on the 2nd of June. I will be transferred to Camp Lejeune. It's not what I wanted but at least it's on the east coast.

I sold my tape recorder because it is full of dust and dirt [and a few holes]. When I go back thru Okinawa I am going to buy another one so it will be brand new.

I was signed up for R&R in Australia for the end of this month but I think I may cancel it because I can't see going down there and spending a couple hundred bucks and then coming home a few days later.

I have one more patrol left. I hope we don't see anything at all. It'd be a real kick in the head to get greased this late in the game. I wonder why there was such a high duty on the suit I sent home. I never thought it would be anything like that. Well that's all I can think of for now.

Steve[2]

My R&R to Sydney, Australia, had been approved but then I found out that the date of the return flight to Viet Nam was going to be only one day before my flight back to The World. I wanted to take no chance that I would miss the Freedom Bird even by one day so I canceled it. Cpl. Rudd had applied for R&R when I did, so I asked if he could have my Sydney because I knew he wanted that one, too. I don't know if he got it but I hope he did. He was a steady and capable NCO.

Being at Quang Tri did have a few perks. We were allowed to have a local Mama San come and pick up our dirty laundry. She would then take it home with her, or to a real laundry shop. (More likely a flat rock down by the river.) She would bring it back in a couple of days folded and tied in a bundle with string. It cost only a dollar or two for a couple sets of utilities, socks and skivvies. Then the word went out that the Mama Sans were no longer allowed to do laundry. It seems that every now and then a tent or hooch would blow up. CID figured out that VC were sneaking into the homes or laundries of the Mama Sans at night and putting a grenade with the pin pulled into the finished laundry bundle. The string tied around it was enough pressure to keep the spoon in place until the bundle was untied and then, BOOM! The sense I got was that the Mama Sans were being as victimized as much as we were. They were just trying to make a living.

The electricity was hit and miss. Sometimes we had it and sometimes we didn't. When we didn't, we used candles. The gook shops outside the base sold big candles about a foot long and probably two inches in diameter. They came in red, white, or blue. As with the laundry, every now and again a tent went up. This time, the problem was the candles. Somewhere along the line, an explosive charge was being molded into the candle so that after several hours of use, the wick would burn down and ignite the charge. It was found that if you held the loaded candles up to a strong light, a dark blob could be detected in the white candles but not the red or blue. The gook shops were only allowed to sell white candles after that. I think the MP's checked them but we did our own inspections, too.

Echo Company did not have a sergeants' hooch like Bravo did. I guess nobody gave it a thought. All the accommodations, including the officers,' were squad tents. At any rate, sergeants lived in the same tent as their team. Late one night we heard the whistles of incoming artillery. Everybody scrambled out of their cots, grabbed their boots, helmet, and rifle and ran for the bunker next to the tent. Inside, it was dark as pitch so I had everybody sound off by name so I knew if we were all there. One was missing. It was Tuthill.

Standiford had the cot next to Tuthill so I asked him where Tuthill was.

Standiford said, "I poked him and told him we had incoming and to get in the bunker. He just grunted and told me to go away."

We had only received a half dozen incoming and they had landed some distance away so I went back in the tent and hollered for Tuthill. From the darkness, there was a muffled reply and I said, "Get out in the bunker."

He said, "I'm too tired. If any more come in I'll get up." There is actually no law that says you must seek shelter when someone is shooting large projectiles at you. It's just a common sense kind of thing. The incoming had stopped and continuing to try to convince Tuthill of the error of his ways seemed pointless right then. The rest of the team drifted back into the tent yawning and scratching and peace soon reigned.

Just a few days before I was scheduled to rotate home, there was a very large formation held in the regimental headquarters area. To my surprise, the

3rd Reconnaissance Battalion logo.

Gunny told me to fall in with a group who were to receive awards. I figured maybe it was the Good Conduct medal that I had qualified for a few months earlier. The Good Conduct Medal is an individual award given to enlisted Marines for three consecutive years of undetected crime, I mean, exemplary conduct while on active duty.

Upon arrival at the designated place at the designated time, an officious staff sergeant shuffled us awardees into the proper order. A sergeant major, a colonel, and a couple of medal carriers worked their way down the line handing out medals and shaking hands. Then they stepped in front of me and it was then that I learned I was being awarded the Vietnamese Cross of Gallantry w/bronze device. It was actually a Vietnamese decoration for meritorious achievement and the bronze device (a tiny bronze colored star attached to the suspension ribbon) made it the approximate equivalent of the U.S. Bronze Star. This was for the ambush patrol and came as a total surprise!

COMPANY E
3d Reconnaissance Battalion
3d Marine Division (Rein), FMF
FPO San Francisco, 96602

JWR:ram
1650
20 Mar 1968

From: Commanding Officer

To: Commanding Officer, 3d Reconnaissance Battalion

Subj: Vietnamese Cross of Gallantry, recommendation for; case of Sgt Steven A. JOHNSON 2112659/0311/8651, U.S. Marine Corps

Ref: (a) Verbal request of Executive Officer, 3dReconBn of 17Mar68

Encl: (1) Proposed citation

1. Pursuant to the direction of reference (a),it is strongly recommended that Sgt Steven A. JOHNSON 2112659/0311/8651, U.S. Marine Corps attached to and serving with Company E, 3d Reconnaissance Battalion be awarded the Vietnamese Cross of Gallantry for meritorious achievement.

2. Sgt JOHNSON serving in the capacity as a Reconnaissance squad leader during 10 to 15 March 1968 aptly demonstrated his professional skill and exemplary initiative in the performance of his Reconnaissance mission by observing, ambushing and capturing members of a Vietnamese enemy element. While observing his Reconnaissance zone located southwest of Dong Ha Combat Base, he keenly sighted a small enemy element and hastily positioned his squad in ambush. Springing the ambush with devastating effect, he totally ineffectuated the enemy element by killing and capturing two NVA/VC respectively without casualties to his squad. Smoothly executing a successful helicopter extraction, Sgt JOHNSON returned with his two prisoners who proved to be of especially intelligence value.

3. The facts contained in the proposed citation are personally known to me.

4. The estimated date of detachment from present assignment is 8 June 1968.

J.W. Raymond

PART SIX

IN WHICH I RELEASE THE ELEPHANT BACK INTO THE JUNGLE

26. Going Home

On May 24, 1968, I was notified that my orders had come through and that I was leaving Vietnam in two days. My 13-month combat tour was over. I have been asked why the Marines did a 13-month tour when the other branches of the military did a shorter 12-month tour. The only answer to that question that I have ever been able to come up with was that Marines did 13 months *just because* the others did 12.

Now I had to go through the exact reverse of the first day that I reported in to Bravo Company. I made the rounds of the battalion aid station, battalion supply, armory, and personnel, where I returned the equipment and weapon I had been issued over a year ago. When I went to disbursing, I was told that this was the last chance I would have to exchange the MPC we were paid with for U.S. American style greenbacks. I decided to keep a few of the notes as souvenirs and cash the rest. I think it came to about fifteen dollars and change. I had gotten so used to the MPC "monopoly money" that the Yankee dollars looked like foreign money. Now I had no weapon or ammunition, nor was I even allowed to hang on to my helmet and flak jacket until at least the next day. This wasn't a real big deal because our current home was relatively safe but I still felt almost naked. Except for a file that was to be kept somewhere, my physical presence was being erased from 3d Recon.

There was no big emotional farewell because under the individual rotation system in effect, people came and people went, literally, on a daily basis. Sometimes you would go looking for so and so only to find out he had gone home two weeks before. The fact that our patrols were in and out on such a flexible schedule also hindered keeping track of other people.

After I got checked out of the battalion, I had nothing to do and virtually no responsibilities other that just being a Sergeant of Marines. Cpl. Rudd had assumed the mantle of team leader and I felt that the guys were in good hands.

Then I did, in retrospect, one of the most ill conceived acts, among many, in my life up to that point. Recon activities were not exactly in the James Bond realm of the intelligence field but I always took the safeguarding of our codes and tactics seriously. Each patrol leader maintains a notebook of the daily events of his patrols. On a milk run — a patrol that resulted in virtually nothing happening — they are very basic, consisting mostly of date, time, and location of stops, starts, observations if any, harborsite coordinates, and often little else. There were a lot more of those than there were involving shooting and blowing things up.

Other patrols almost cause writer's cramp as detailed notes are made of sightings, actions, etc. If contact is made, the notes are brought up to date as soon as possible after contact is broken or the team is extracted. These notes were important at the time because it was my reference material for the S-2 debriefings that followed each patrol.

At any rate, I had a small book's worth of patrol notes from about 30 patrols, and for some misguided reason I thought there should be no chance of them falling into the wrong hands. *So I burned them!* At that time, of course, I had no thought or intention of writing about any of my experience. It was just another day at the office. In fact, I did not really regret my decision until many years later when I realized that it might have been fun to read the notes again. Throughout this manuscript, I have made frequent references to, "Then one day," or, "On another patrol." That's because the event was clear in my memory but I could only give an approximation of a time frame. I was able to extrapolate many chronological events through my letters home and some official documents but imagine how much more detail I could have given if I had the original notes. Stupid! Stupid! Oh, well.

I had one more task to accomplish and that was to reclaim the sea bag of stateside uniforms I had stored when I first got here. I went to the Butler building where I had left it but honestly did not expect to see it. However, the sea bags were stacked in an organized manner and, surprise of surprises; I found mine in about fifteen minutes. I dragged it back to my tent and took a quick inventory. Everything seemed to be there. I saved out one set of tropicals to wear once I got to the States and then crammed everything except the clothes I was wearing and my shave kit into the sea bag. I placed the incredibly wrinkled tropicals and a pair of dress shoes in the top of the sea bag. My intention was to have the uniform dry cleaned and spit shine the shoes on Okinawa because I was pretty sure I'd be there for at least a couple of days.

The next morning I went around shaking hands with as many of the guys as I could find and then went to the company office. Captain Raymond handed me my orders and wished me good luck. As happy as I was to be going home, it was still a little tough to just walk away from the home I had gotten used to. The duty driver took me over to the airstrip where I was put on a manifest for the next chopper to Da Nang.

Arriving in Da Nang, there was little to do but check in with flight ops and, since my flight wasn't until the next morning, go find a bunk in the transient barracks. That was just a large hooch full of bunk beds. I went to the linen locker and signed out a pillow and a blanket, made up an empty upper bunk and tossed my sea bag on top of it. My sea bag was padlocked shut and further padlocked to the iron frame of the bunk. By now, it was around lunchtime so I found the mess hall and had yet another unremarkable meal.

I didn't sleep much that night partly because it was very warm in the barracks but also because I was thinking about all I had seen and done for the past year or so. I hadn't gone through the horrendous combat situations that a lot of Marines had endured but I had truly seen the elephant. The morning couldn't come soon enough.

After breakfast, I wandered back through the transient barracks and suddenly spotted a familiar face. It was now Sergeant Forrest Darcus, who was in the Marine Detachment on the *Albany* with me. He was the same old Darcus. He rarely smiled as he chain smoked cigarettes and always had a slight but perpetually cynical viewpoint of the world. I was only able to shoot the breeze with him for a few minutes because he was on the way to the terminal to catch his flight home. I already knew that Huggard and the *Albany* dog handler had gone from the ship to Vietnam but their circumstances were then unknown to me. I was glad to see that at least Darcus and I had made it through.

It was now May 27, 1968. I checked in at flight ops to make sure I was on the manifest and then went outside and sat down against the wall of the building along with 150 or so other Marines going home. It wasn't much later that a civilian airliner landed and rolled up to the terminal. Without being told, we all got up and shuffled into a line. The stairs were rolled up to the door of the plane and when it opened there was a real genuine Yankee American stewardess standing there smiling at us. We just gaped at her. She was beautiful! She could have had a face like a horse but the fact that her hair was not black, and she had round eyes, was all we needed.

The planeload of newcomers filed off the plane in their stateside utilities and some of our group couldn't help themselves calling out, "You'll be so-o-o-ory." Other than that, we were fairly subdued. We looked just like the guys I had seen waiting to get on the plane when I first arrived, including several who were sporting casts and bandages. We all just looked very tired. We got the word to board and when I got to the top of the stairway, I had to walk close by the stewardess. She smelled so good I almost got dizzy. We all found seats and got the usual safety lecture from the rest of the stewardesses and then the plane began to taxi toward the runway. As we picked up speed the thought went through my head that this would be an awful time to get shot down. We knew that airliners occasionally took some small arms ground fire as they lifted off.

As soon as the plane left the ground there was an ear splitting roar from all of us. A few were crying from relief and joy. We had made it!

The flight to Okinawa was a few hours long and eventually everybody settled down and most went to sleep. After we landed at Kadena Air Force Base on Okinawa, we were trucked to Camp Hansen for processing. We were told that this would take two to three days. We were granted liberty but we could only go as far as Kin Village, which was right outside the gate. This was the same place Echo Company had been back in January. The first thing I did was take a set of tropicals to the base dry cleaners. Then I went to the PX and bought shoe polish, the ribbons that I knew for sure that I rated, a ditty bag, and pockets full of pogey bait.

I remembered that I had to take my binoculars to G-2 so I went there that afternoon. I showed the binoculars and my registration form to a young and officious second lieutenant. He gave me another form to fill out and then said that they would have to keep them for an undetermined period to see if they had any Intel value. I thought, "What?" That made no sense at all. I asked the lieutenant what possible Intel value a beat up pair of 6.8 × 30 binoculars could have and he hemmed, hawed, and then told me he couldn't discuss it with me. I told him I was headed home in just a couple of days but that didn't seem to make any difference. The light bulbs were going on in my head and I got a little steamed. I just knew if I surrendered them I'd never see them again.

I didn't say that out loud because that would be insubordination. Since I was there as a transient, I had no 1st sergeant or company commander to go to for help. I still didn't like what was going on so I asked the lieutenant for a signed receipt for the binoculars. He really didn't like that but by then I didn't much care. He glared at me for a moment and then told me he'd be right back. He went into an office and was gone for a few minutes. When he came out, he handed the binoculars to me and said that they were probably okay after all. I seriously doubt he conferred with anyone in that office and just did his little act to save face.

My next encounter was when I went to personnel to begin the out-processing. Now I was being erased from the 3d Marine Division. I was standing right up close to the desk of yet another second lieutenant who began looking over my orders. The desk happened to come just exactly to the knuckles of my hands as I stood there at ease. He suddenly looked me up and down and yelled, "Don't lean on my Marine Corps desk!" I could not believe my ears but I stepped back about two inches so my filthy paws were no longer in the immediate proximity of his apparently sterile furniture. Now that I think about it, I don't think I ever met a butter bar who didn't have a personality disorder.

At the PX, I also bought a short-sleeved civilian shirt and a pair of trousers so I could go on liberty and just to wear something that wasn't green. Then I went to the barbershop and got a regulation haircut. It wasn't one of those high and tight jobs.... I never did like those. It was just a regular Marine Corps haircut. I was feeling more civilized by the moment. I went to Kin Village and bought a lightweight jacket and had a 3d Recon logo patch sewn on the back. All you do is pick one from the artwork on the walls of the shop. The patch was actually embroidered for me while I waited. Talk about fast service, and it cost just a few dollars including the jacket. Later, I went to the Enlisted Men's club on the base and had a cold coke. It tasted like ambrosia!

The dry cleaner had one-hour service so I picked up my uniform before chow and that evening set to work squaring away. I spit shined my shoes and the visor of my barracks cover. The barracks, or frame, cover is a cap with a leather visor and a metal hoop frame that supports the cloth covering. There is a white cover for the dress blues, a tan cover for the tropicals and a green cover for the green uniform. It has a chinstrap that is worn setting above the visor and the cover is adorned with a large black eagle, globe and anchor above the chinstrap. It can be dismantled into four parts for transport purposes.

I pinned my ribbons and Expert Rifle badge on the shirt and put the uniform back into the plastic bag from the cleaners. Then I took apart my barracks cover so it could go in my ditty bag. I pulled a pair of dress socks over the front half of my shoes to protect the shine and put them in my ditty bag, too. I was ready to go home. Most of the others planned to travel in civvies once we hit the States but having gotten accustomed to the spit and polish requirements of Sea Duty, I wanted to get back into a proper uniform for a change. Marines are never allowed to wear utilities off base unless they are in a vehicle going straight home. Technically, they are not even allowed to get out of the vehicle to get gas or stop at a convenience store. Army personnel, on the other hand, are frequently seen strolling around in public in rumpled fatigues with hands in pockets and hats on the back of their head.

The next day went by quickly and the following morning we got the word that our flight to the States would be that evening, the 30th of May. Late that afternoon we were trucked back to Kadena. I wandered around in the huge PX for at least an hour just soaking up civilization. I was still acclimating to clean floors and streets, sheets and showers, and a total absence of sandbagged bunkers and hooches. About an hour before flight time, I found my way to the terminal and after checking in with flight ops, I found a group of Marines outside who had the same flight. It was now dark and we were lounging on the warm asphalt under a streetlight. I was sitting with my back against a chain link fence. The weather was very mild and I was going home. Everything was right.

Among this group were a handful of civilian dependents of military personnel. One young mother was nearby and she had a toddler with her. The baby was well behaved and was wobbling around a few feet away. Suddenly he (or she) took off at a good clip in a straight line towards one of the Marines. I'm guessing he looked like dad to the baby. Anyway, one of the Marines quickly began calling cadence with the baby's footsteps. "LeftRightLeft-RightLeftRight." The whole little scene hit everyone's funny bone and we all just roared. The baby stopped abruptly, turned a shocked face to us and then hustled back to mom as fast as its chubby little legs would carry it. Even mom was laughing.

27. Welcome Back?

Our flight was announced and this time when the plane left the ground there were only a few cheers. I think we had become used to the idea that we were officially out of Vietnam. This flight went straight to Travis Air Force Base in San Francisco and landed late in the afternoon of the 29th. That's right; we left Okinawa on the 30th and arrived in the States on the 29th. We went back a day due to crossing the International Date Line.

Several hours out from California, I began to feel a little chilly. That progressed to shaking to the point that the Marines in the seats on either side of me noticed and asked if I was okay. I knew by then that it was malaria again and I asked the stewardess for a blanket. That was back when you actually got a blanket on an airplane instead of a tea towel. Not many minutes went by and I asked for another and then another. I was freezing! My seatmates were getting concerned that I had something catching but I assured them that it was malaria and that I would keep it to myself. After a couple of hours, the chills passed and then the fever came on. The stewardesses were pouring cold drinks into me and putting wet towels on my head but it didn't help much. By now, I was the center of attention and the stewardesses hovered around like mother hens. Of course the other guys nearby didn't mind that in the least.

The fever eventually subsided and the muscle pain set in. I guess we were about an hour or two away from landing when the pilot came back to talk to me. It turned out that he was a Marine veteran of World War II and he flew Corsairs in the Pacific. He also said that he had had malaria too, and knew how I felt. Then he asked if I wanted an ambulance to meet the plane at the airport.

Before I could answer, he added, "If an ambulance meets the plane, the authorities will place the entire crew and passengers in quarantine until they determine what is wrong with you."

When he said that, the looks of concern around me turned to frowns and scowls. However, he pointed out that if I could possibly postpone my death until I got inside the terminal there would be no problem. Aside from some pain, I was beginning to feel a little better so I told the pilot that I would get off the plane under my own steam, no matter what. By the time we landed after the twelve-hour flight, I felt considerably better and everybody was happy.

We had been warned that there might be protestors at the airport. We hadn't really heard much about the cowardly and disruptive carrying on by the hippies and other non-hackers back home. We had heard about "campus unrest" but isn't that what suddenly-possessed-with-all-the-wisdom-in-the-world college students do with their spare time? Anyway, we were instructed to ignore any catcalls, maintain discipline and, above all, please don't maim or kill any of the longhaired freaks!

We disembarked and were herded into a small hangar-like building where we had our orders and leave papers double-checked, cleared customs, and then we were on our own. In the main terminal, I went to the men's room with my sea bag, ditty bag, and uniform. I already had my air ticket to Buffalo, New York, and a Greyhound ticket to Jamestown because when we were on Okinawa, we were informed that it would be more efficient to buy the tickets there and we would spend less time in the terminal among all those patriotic American citizens. I don't know if that was for our benefit or theirs.

My flight was due to leave in about 45 minutes so I hurriedly jumped into a clean, pressed, squared away uniform. Man, did that feel civilized! I stuffed my semi grubby utilities and boots into my sea bag and ditty bag and headed for the gate. On the way, I went past a small group of the guys who had been on the plane. They were just standing there in their jungle utilities looking around and had a rather forlorn look about them. None of the civilians acknowledged them in any way. They weren't being threatened at all but it looked like they had herded up for a little safety in numbers. Remember that airports then were wide open and anybody and his cousin Cuthbert could stroll around at will. In addition to a lot of skuzzy looking, guitar carrying rejects of society, I saw the Hare Krishna whackos. There were fire teams of them in their orange robes scattered around the terminal bumming change and singing unintelligible songs whilst dancing in circles and clanging finger cymbals. What an incredible waste of oxygen!

The flight to Buffalo was an overnighter and we made a few stops along the way, which made for a long flight. I arrived early in the morning of the 30th. It struck me that it was Memorial Day. That was when Memorial Day was on the 30th of May and was dutifully observed on the 30th regardless of the day of the week. I found my bus ticket to Jamestown so I went out to wait at the airport's bus stop. I was, you will recall, wearing the summer tropical uniform. I had also, barely 24 hours before, been basting in 90-plus degree heat. Even though I was wearing long sleeves and a tie, it was typical western New York May weather. In other words, cold!

The bus pulled in and the driver opened the cargo door on the side so I could stuff my sea bag in. The bus was only about two thirds full but every seat was taken by someone sitting or that person's belongings piled on the seat next to them. No one looked at me and no one made any effort to clear off a seat. The driver never spoke. I moved toward the back of the bus, took hold of the luggage rack on either side, and stood all the way to Jamestown. Having spent many hours on the plane, standing for an hour and a half was not uncomfortable. I was a bit ticked off, though!

The bus arrived at the Jamestown Greyhound station at about 11:30 A.M. The city's traditional Memorial Day parade was always held at 10:00 on this day but was now long over and there was not a soul to be seen. The bus station itself was closed for the holiday so there was only drop off and pick up. It was cold and raining. I was really tired by now and beginning to feel somewhat miserable. I went to the phone booth by the station and called home. No answer. Well, I wasn't too surprised because my travel schedule for the past few days was always subject to change and I had been unable to tell my dad exactly when I would be getting home.

My next call was to the local cab company. By now, I was pretty damp and shivering. The cab arrived quickly and I was happy to bask in the warmth of the cab's heater. The cabbie was a guy I recognized as having been a cab driver in Jamestown for many years. At that time there was only one cab company in Jamestown and they drove those big old Checker cabs. He didn't know me from Adam, though, and I don't think he said anything except to ask where I wanted to go.

As we drove the familiar streets, I kept looking for things that had changed. It seemed odd to me that nothing had in the lifetime I felt I had been gone. On the other hand, a year and a half in a small town is only a tick on the cosmic clock.

When we stopped in front of 229 Curtis Street, the house looked exactly the same and the sensation, for a few seconds, was that I had never left. I paid the cab driver and then I climbed the familiar concrete steps from the sidewalk to the front yard. When I stepped onto the front porch, I had a small dilemma. It occurred to me suddenly that I didn't *really* live here anymore. It had been almost four years since I left for boot camp. I had been home on leave a couple of times but that was still a while ago. I was not sure if I should ring the doorbell or just walk in. Hardly anyone locked their doors then unless they were going away for a few days. I opened the front door and stuck my head in. "Hello?" There would only have been my dad and my younger twin brothers. Silence. No one was home.

I stood there in the living room for several minutes just soaking in the fact that I was home. It even smelled like home, but at the same time, it was an alien smell. I walked around in the house seeing all the same familiar objects, hearing the same stair creak as I stepped on it and looking out the back door seeing the big old snowberry bush that we used for ammunition in backyard snowberry fights. I loosened my tie and flopped on the couch. I don't even remember dozing off; I just went out like a light.

I don't know how long I slept but I was battered awake by both of the twins jumping on me. For a few seconds I wasn't sure where I was. I recognized the twins but my foggy brain was wondering what they were doing in Vietnam. My little brothers were gabbing like magpies wanting to know everything about everything and all at once.

My dad shook my hand and then he gave me a hug, something that I'm not sure I ever remember him doing before. I was finally home.

PART SEVEN

NO MORE ELEPHANTS

28. More Malaria

During the last couple of months in Vietnam, I had my dad send me brochures for different makes of cars. I wanted to buy a new car (my first car ever) when I got home so I could drive it to Camp Lejeune, which was the location of 2nd Recon Battalion, and my next duty station. The day after I got home, I went to the DMV, took the written test, and got my learner's permit. Almost at the same time, I sent in my application for my road test. I included a note that I was home on leave and had a limited amount of time available to me. I received my road test appointment only a few days later.

Even though I was going on 22, I still did not have a driver's license and my family had never had any spare cars sitting around waiting to be driven. I had taken driver's education in high school but with nothing to drive and no money to buy a car, it was purely academic. In addition, I was going into the Marines right after graduation so getting a license just wasn't a priority. However, now I was preparing to buy a brand new car and a license suddenly became a necessity.

After I had gotten over the jet lag and just being tired out, dad and I went to the local Chevy dealer. I still had not had a chance to get any civvies besides the shirt and trousers I had bought in Okinawa so I went in uniform. I had decided on a 1968 Camaro and there was a nice Teal Blue specimen on the lot with automatic transmission and a 327 motor. There were no power brakes or power steering, which was typical of on-the-lot cars then but that was okay with me. We talked with the salesman, took the car for a short ride, and arrived at a cash figure of $3800.00. I told him I needed to go to the bank and would be back in the afternoon to pick the car up.

For almost the whole of my tour, each payday I kept out about $20.00 of the princely sum of $325.00 (my pay for a month!) and sent the rest home for dad to put in a savings account. We went to the bank, withdrew the amount necessary, and then went someplace for lunch. Dad said the dealership would need some time to prep the car and get the paperwork in order. About 2:00 P.M., we went back to the dealership. We found the salesman and the look on his face spoke volumes. He had obviously thought we were just fishing and had not even begun to get the car ready to go. This was after having arrived at a figure and shaking hands on it. Maybe this civilian puke blew me off because I was in uniform; I don't know. Dad took a couple of strips of hide off this bozo and he fell all over himself getting things organized. We still had to wait for almost an hour but finally he came out and handed me the keys. He didn't even have the class to apologize for the delay.

On the day of my road test, my dad and I drove to the test site and my turn eventually came. My examiner got into the passenger side and rather sternly said, "Go to the intersection ahead and turn left." I had come to the test site in uniform in the off chance that it would help a bit. Just as we had arrived at the site, it struck me that maybe the examiner would be some kind of hippie but by then it was too late. This guy was not a hippie but he was probably in his 50s and didn't have a very happy look on his face. As I made the left turn I could see out of the corner of my eye that he was looking over at me.

"Marines?"

I said, "Yes, sir."

"Just back from Vietnam?"

"Yes, sir."

He didn't say another word except to give me brief instructions on where to go and turn. He made no notes on his exam form. Arriving back at the starting point he got out of the car. I asked him if I had passed. He said, "I'm not allowed to tell you right now. You'll be notified by mail." I slid over as my dad got behind the wheel.

"Did you pass?" he asked.

I told him the examiner couldn't say right then but that I didn't think I had done very well because he never wrote anything down. I figured I must have really messed up to get washed out right at the start. About four days later, an envelope from the DMV arrived. I opened it expecting the worst. Inside was my brand new New York State driver's license. Huzzah!

I still had about three weeks of leave and a couple days travel time left so I spent a good share of my time home just messing around. I tried to look up some high school friends but there was hardly anyone still in the area. Almost everyone I knew was away at college or in the service. A couple had already been killed in Vietnam. By the time my leave was up, I was more than ready to head for North Carolina. I figured it would take me at least two days to get to Lejeune because this was long before much of the interstate highway system existed, at least in this mostly rural section of New York and Pennsylvania. I planned on going along the southern tier of New York State on Route 17 and then head as straight south as possible from Elmira, New York.

I made my good-byes to dad and the twins and several aunts and uncles and headed east. It felt good to be on the road, my own boss, in my new car, and gas was 30 cents a gallon. We had no idea how good we had it then. About two hours into the trip, I began to feel queasy. I tried to shrug it off but I felt worse and worse as time went by. Then I realized what was going on ... my old friend malaria had come back to visit!

Dear Dad,
  Just thought I'd let you know what's going on. While I was on my way back I had gotten almost to Erwins, NY, when I felt a malaria spell coming on. I pulled off the road and sat it out for about 3 hours. When I felt a little better I went to a restaurant to get something to drink because I was all dried out.[1]

I was nauseated and burning up and needed something to drink so I stopped at a roadside restaurant near Erwins, New York, a few miles west of Painted Post, New York. I had taken off my shoes because it was a little more comfortable so it took me a few minutes, sitting in the car, to get them back on again. I got out, straightened my tie, put my cover on, and went inside. I was the only customer and a teenage girl behind the counter went into a back area as soon as I came in. An older lady came out and asked me what I wanted ... and not so friendly, either. I said I was not feeling well and would like a cold glass of ginger ale. She asked what was wrong with me and I said, "I got malaria in Vietnam and I'm having a relapse of it and I'm really thirsty."

She immediately became concerned and felt my forehead. She said, "You have a real fever going on!" She told me she thought a glass of cold milk would be better on my stomach and I agreed with her, being in no shape to debate the point. The girl had come back out by now and the lady explained that the girl was her daughter and when they noticed me taking a long time to get out of the car, they thought I was drunk.

I was feeling sicker by the minute and both of them were now genuinely concerned about me. Finally, the lady said she was going to call a friend who could help. A little while went by and two young men came in. I explained what was happening and one said he would drive me in my car to the hospital in Corning, New York, and his friend would follow us. I said that was okay with me. I don't remember if I thanked the lady for her help or not. I remember being helped to my car and a little bit about the short ride to Corning but not much else.

Two or three times over the past couple of years while traveling in that area, I tried to find that restaurant. Interstate 86 now bypasses Erwins but the old Route 17, now Route 417, is still there and largely undeveloped since then. I tried to picture the terrain at the time but about all I could remember was that the restaurant sat by itself on the south side of the highway. I just couldn't place it and the building might very well have been torn down sometime in the last 40 plus years.

At the hospital, the guys helped me to the emergency room, where I stood at a counter while being interrogated by a nurse whose demeanor was just short of being outright hostile. She was not happy with me or anything about me. One of the guys told her she was being very rude and that's the last I remember because I passed out right on the floor. I sure wish I knew who those people who helped me were.

A couple hours later I was awake and feeling considerably better but still weak. I was on a gurney in an alcove in a hall near the emergency room. I didn't see "Nurse Ratched"[2] again. Instead, a very nice nurse asked me if I was hungry. I wasn't sure if I was or not but she brought me a chicken dinner that actually looked pretty good for hospital chow. I could only manage a bite or two, though, because I just wasn't up to the physical demands of raising a fork to my mouth and chewing.

I guess it must have been toward evening when a doctor came to talk to me. He said they had taken blood from me but it might be a while before any results were back and that they would keep me overnight. In the meantime, he suggested that I would be better off in a Veteran's Administration hospital.

> They were going to transfer me to St. Alban's naval hospital in New York but they were having trouble getting government transportation. That was when I called home the first time because I thought you would have to come get my car. Then they said that since I was feeling better that I could drive myself to St. Alban's or to Lejeune. I said I figured I could make it before my next attack because they come every other day.[3]

I didn't even want to think about driving to New York City and told him so. I also told him I had to report to Camp Lejeune the day after next and if I stayed until tomorrow, I would almost certainly be A.W.O.L., or absent without leave. I asked him if he could call Lejeune, explain the situation, and see if I could get one extra travel day. He said he would so I gave him my leave orders so he'd know who to talk to. He came back later and said that I had been authorized an additional 24 hours and he had the name of the officer he talked to written on my leave papers.

I spent the night in the alcove but the nurses had rolled up a couple of curtains on wheels so I had at least a semblance of privacy. I remember having nightmares and sweating a lot but by morning I actually felt semi-human. Whoever had taken my uniform off me had hung it up and it didn't look any the worse for wear. I got dressed, collected my personal effects, and checked out. I had to wander around the parking lot for a few minutes to find my car but I was soon on my way.

I don't remember where I stopped that night but I think I was within a couple hours of the base. As I headed south through farm country the next morning on some North Carolina highway I suddenly got that old feeling again. It got bad enough that I couldn't drive so I pulled off the highway into a little dirt road that gave access to a tobacco field. I stayed there, sick to my stomach, for a couple hours but finally the heat was too much and I decided to start driving again. I wasn't far from Lejeune now so I stopped briefly for something to drink and kept going.

Arriving at the main gate at Camp Lejeune, I showed the MP my orders and he directed me to a small building nearby. There, I picked up a temporary pass to have my car on base and got directions to 2nd Recon. It was at an area called Onslow Beach, which is right on the ocean but several miles away. I still wasn't feeling very grand and all I wanted to do was check in and take a nap if I could. I arrived at the battalion HQ building and went inside to check in. I noticed many people standing around nervously and everybody was eyeballing me as an unfamiliar face. I reported to the Officer of the Day and he seemed a bit distracted, too. He said they were awaiting the arrival of an I.G. team and further pointed out that I didn't look so good. I.G. means inspector general, a type of investigator charged with examining the actions of a military organization to ensure they are operating in compliance with general established policies.

I quickly explained my current health status and he said I should go directly to the BAS. First, was because I was sick and, second, because they didn't have time to mess around getting me checked in and assigned a company and all the rest of it while the I.G. was there. They would rather that the BAS have me to deal with.

I walked over to the BAS and the duty corpsman took one look at my eyes and told me to sit down. One of the tell tales of malaria is that your skin and eyes acquire a yellowish tint due to jaundice. I sat down and the Doc was starting to take my blood pressure when the door opened and in came a veritable covey of majors and colonels. I did what every Marine is trained to do and that was leap to my feet assuming the position of attention along with the other medical people in the room. I had hardly straightened up when I heard roaring in my ears and I went right back down again in a heap on the deck. I heard one of the officers say, "What's the matter with him?"

The corpsman said, "He's just reporting in and he's having a malaria attack, Sir."

I heard the officer, bless him, say, "Well then get him in a rack and take care of him!"

The next few hours were a blur, but when I was more aware, the corpsman came and said, "Thanks for passing out like that." I thought he was being a wise guy until he explained that with the corpsmen and doctors having me to attend to, the I.G. team decided to stay out of the way. They took a quick look around, perused some records and left. He said it was the easiest I.G. they had ever stood. I always was a helper-outer.

It was determined that I should get checked in to the battalion and then go to the base hospital. I was feeling pretty wrung out so at battalion, a PFC was detailed to help me get organized and I was assigned to Alpha Company. I reported to the company 1st sergeant and he gave me to the Third Platoon whose platoon sergeant put me in a team and got me assigned a bunk in the NCO quarters. I lashed my sea bag to my rack, got my footlocker and wall locker squared away and went back to the company office. They had my name on the sick list already so I got directions to the hospital back at Mainside and left. It had been quite a chaotic introduction to my new unit.

At the hospital, I was thoroughly examined and admitted. I stayed there for a few weeks with two or three more episodes of chills, fevers, nausea, and pain. I wrote home, "As it stands right now I don't know what's going to happen because I don't know how long I'll be in the hospital. I guess that's all for now. Steve"[4]

Finally, after getting back to Alpha Company and meeting the C.O. and my platoon commander and teammates, I got into the training regimen. It was a lot of rubber boat work (we were right on the beach, remember?) because insertions by boat were one of our tactics. We were also called upon to act as opposing forces for the grunt units on base in training exercises.

29. Duty Done—A New Journey

Not long after I got out of the hospital, Larry Moyer, who had been in Echo Company with me, reported in to Alpha Company, having completed his tour. He told me about a four-man patrol that Lt. Hardhead had led that got shot up pretty badly. In fact, two of the four were killed when they walked into a fortified NVA bunker. Clark Christie, one of the platoon's radiomen, was seriously wounded three separate times but was still able to call for a medevac, air support, and a reaction force in addition to returning fire at the enemy. Christie had blond hair and glasses, and looked like a choirboy. He fought like a lion that day and aside from the Purple Heart, he was not, to my knowledge, otherwise decorated.[1]

Moyer also told me that Team Sky Merchant, led by one of our platoon lieutenants, got into a lethal scrap in the back yard. Four team members were killed, the lieutenant and one other Marine seriously wounded, and another Marine, L/Cpl. Dave Padilla (who had been on a couple of my patrols) was missing and was never found.

On 18 May, an entire Recon team was killed. At approximately 1100H, the patrol came under heavy small arms and mortar fire. A large explosion occurred where L/Cpl. Padilla was sitting, and a later search of the area revealed parts of his utility jacket and utility belt around a 12–15 inch hole caused by the explosion. There were no remains; his body had disintegrated. 1st Lt. Nels C. Youngstrom, CO of Echo Company, 3rd Reconnaissance Bn., stated that the men were killed at [map coordinates] XD885512 after they had run into the point of a supposed NVA platoon. They took evasive action, but ran into a squad of NVA. They finally reached their extraction LZ, and it was there that they were killed.[2]

I only had about three months left in my enlistment and was looking forward to getting discharged. The Marine Corps had been a singular experience but I felt I had done my duty. The word went around that a couple of Marines had been killed in a motor vehicle accident off base. Every time something like that happens, everyone, and I mean everyone on base, gets the safety lecture. We are even required to watch a couple of movies about fatal accidents. One was *Highway of Death* and the other had an equally blood-curdling title. The battalion was informed that we would see these movies in the mess hall at such and such a time on such and such a date. Oh well, at least it was a break from training.

We were assembled in the mess hall waiting for the battalion staff to arrive. Somebody called, "Attention on deck!" and we all leaped to our feet as the battalion officers made their entrance. Imagine my surprise when I thought I saw another familiar face. I only got a glimpse but I thought I knew the major in the group. When the movies were over (they were very graphic and had a lot of documentary footage of accidents with headless bodies and so on) we were called to attention again and the staff left. As soon as I could get outside, I saw the major walking toward battalion HQ. He was some distance ahead of me so I started running to catch up. As I got closer, I could tell for sure that it was former Captain Ed Butchart, who was the MarDet C.O. on the *Albany*. As I caught up to him, I slowed to a walk (one salutes only while standing still or moving at a walking pace ... never at the gallop) and said, "Major Butchart?" He turned as I saluted and exclaimed, "Johnson!" Forgetting all about returning my salute and, to my astonishment, he grabbed me in a bear hug and spun me around in a very un–officer-like manner. He was the newly assigned executive officer of the battalion and had reported in while I was in the hospital.

Major Butchart told me to go to admin, pick up my SRB (service record book), and report to his office after noon chow. I went to admin and they gave me the old fish eye when I said the XO told me to get my SRB and take it to him. Normally, SRBs are treated like the original copy of the Declaration of Independence. It is never allowed to be in the private hands of the person it refers to. It is just automatically assumed that you will add or delete information or otherwise falsify records. Handing it out to the person it actually belongs to just isn't done. It took a call to the major's office to verify that I was, indeed, given the sacred trust of carrying my SRB 100 feet to the battalion XO's office without committing extensive forgery or seditious acts.

After chow, I went to battalion HQ and was confronted by the battalion sergeant major, who looked at me as if I was an insect and just didn't believe I had been granted an audience with the XO without His knowledge. He stuck His head in the major's door and returned quickly to usher me in. There, Major Butchart had me sit down and wanted to know all about where I had been and what I had been doing. He was glad that I had seen or heard from the three former MarDet guys. I quickly found out that he had also just returned from Vietnam. His assignment was as an advisor to the ARVN public affairs office in Da Nang. The major was more or less a press officer for the ARVN, encouraging coverage by the free world press. He drove a jeep 15,000 miles taking news people around to cover different stories than they were used to covering. He said he got shot at a few times, but they missed him.

Major Butchart asked if I would like some coffee and, although I'm not much of a coffee drinker, I said yes. The major called to the sergeant major and asked Him to bring a couple coffees. When He brought the coffee in I got a look from Him that would have stunned several small mammals into immobility. It was clear that I was sliding rapidly down the sergeant major's maggot list into the very depths of His contempt. In fact, for the rest of my time in Alpha Company, I made a point of steering clear of this guy. Sergeant majors don't like surprises or serving coffee to little weasel sergeants.

Since I was due to be discharged soon, the company 1st sergeant gave me the obligatory "shipping over" lecture. Besides extolling the virtues of a career in the Corps, he said that if I re-enlisted I would get staff sergeant. Of course, I knew he couldn't just say that. I also knew that once you had been stateside for a minimum of six months you could be involuntarily ordered back to Vietnam. I had only just gotten home and the thought of going back over, even if it didn't happen right away, was not high on my list of things to do. Promotion to staff sergeant would be nice but I just didn't know right then if it was worth another four-year commitment.

The next couple of months came and went. I had heard about a federal program whereby police agencies at any level, due to mass retirements of police due mostly to the civil disorder of the times, could hire about-to-be discharged service members and that service member could get up to a 90 day early discharge. I had only about a month to go in my enlistment but I knew it was time to start thinking about a life after the Corps.

I had some leave time to use up before I got out so I went home for a few days and went to see the Jamestown police chief. He knew me because his son, also a Marine, and I had gone all the way through school together, and, as a kid, I had been to the chief's house many times for Cub Scout meetings. I asked him if he knew about the program and he said he did. I told him I was interested and he then asked me, "How do I know you won't just take the job for a little while to get out of the Marines and then quit?" I told him I could only promise to give it my best shot and he said that was good enough. Before hearing of this program, I had never even considered becoming a police officer. I had thought that I might become a firefighter like my dad.

The chief sent a letter of intent to hire to the battalion commander and on August 28, 1968, I took off my green uniform and drove out the main gate at Camp Lejeune for the last time. Two days later, I was getting measured for a blue uniform with a badge on it. Twenty years and one day after that, I retired as a lieutenant.

A word of retrospection. In 1982, realizing that I missed the Corps, but not enough to forfeit my 14 years on the police department (not to mention my wife, Judy's, opinion about that), I joined the Marine Corps Reserve unit, India Company, Third Battalion, 25th Marines, in Buffalo, New York. It was a rifle company and I felt at home there despite the number of years I had been "out of harness." In January of 1991, the 25th Marines was called to active duty in support of Operation Desert Storm.

We were mobilized for six months and spent part of that time deployed to northern Norway. There actually was a sound tactical reason for that but I won't bore anyone with it here. During our last couple of months of active duty when we were back at Camp Lejeune, we began seeing other 2nd Marine Division units returning from Kuwait. The highway approaches to the base were lined on both sides with billboard-sized signs and banners proudly welcoming these units back. They deserved all of it and I was moved by the support that the entire country was showering on the returning veterans.

At the same time, I could not help but remember the reception we received coming home from Vietnam. I will put it simply. It hurt!

Appendix A:
After Action Report

Besides telling my story, I want to show anyone who has read this account that Vietnam vets are not a bunch of psychotic drug users living in a box under a bridge as Hollywood and people who love to trash patriotism would have them believe. Of the men I mentioned in this account, aside from the deceased, three of them were impossible to locate despite strenuous effort. However, without exception, the men I have been able to actually contact have made successes of themselves and became contributing members of society.

- Butchart, Maj. Ed, USMC (ret) — Retired from the Marine Corps in 1978. Founded an organization that distributes refurbished wheelchairs and walkers free to people who need them. He is now an ordained Baptist minister and a published author living near Atlanta, Georgia.

- Christie, L/Cpl. Clark, USMC — Retired as a project engineer and technical advisor in the coal and natural gas industry and lives near Bluefield, West Virginia.

- Cooke, L/Cpl Ernie, USMC — Retired from the Norfolk Naval Shipyard and lives in Florida.

- Cowan, Sgt. Arthur A., USMC — Retired as the Sergeant Major of the 2nd Marine Division and is living near Lansing, Michigan.

- Fisher, Lt. Jeff, USMC — Works as an investor, advisor, and board of directors member for several technology companies and lives in the Atlanta, Georgia, area.

- Huggard, Sgt. John, USMC — Became a lawyer and retired from the U.S. Navy Reserve as a four stripe captain. He is a faculty member at North Carolina State University in Raleigh and is a published author.

- Larsen, GySgt. James R., USMC — Retired as a master sergeant and then had another career with an armored car company. He is living near San Diego, California.

- Macaulay, Cpl. Kevin, USMC — Retired from the Long Island, New York, school system and lives near Buffalo, New York.
- Mullaney, Sgt. Bob, USMC — Retired from the federal corrections system and is living near Fort Myers, Florida.
- Pfeltz, 1st Lt. Albert, USMC — A partner in, and works in sales of, microwave communications systems and lives near Escondido, California.
- Reynolds, Capt. Philip, USMC — Retired as a major and was an assistant professor at the Naval Academy. He is now retired from the banking business and lives near San Diego, California.
- Schlack, Lt. Carl, USMC — Retired after 29 years in the Corps. Now retired from the security division of California Edison and is living in the Carlsbad, California, area.
- Schleman, L/Cpl. Don (AKA Meatball), USMC — Retired as a firefighter and is living near Tampa, Florida.
- Standiford, L/Cpl. Wayne, USMC — An electrical contractor in Oregon, and is a published author.
- Stubbe, Lt. Ray, USN — Retired from the Navy as a lieutenant commander in 1984. Lutheran chaplain of 1st Battalion 26th Marines at Khe Sanh. He is a published author of many books about Vietnam and lives near Milwaukee, Wisconsin.
- Weidler, Sgt. Del, USMC — Retired from the National Guard as a sergeant 1st class and is living near Iowa City, Iowa.
- Williams, Capt. James L., USMC — Retired as a colonel and is now a community relations consultant living near the Marine base at Camp Pendleton, California.
- Youngstrom, Jr., Lt. Nels C., USMC — Retired as a computer analyst and is living near Syracuse, New York.

Awards

- Col. David Lownds was awarded the Navy Cross for his leadership at Khe Sanh from August 1967 to March 1968.
- Lt. Al Pfeltz was awarded the Silver Star for actions against the enemy on August 24–25, 1967.
- Tuthill was awarded not one but two Bronze Stars w/V device for actions against the enemy on August 14 and September 26, 1968, respectively, as well as the Vietnamese Cross of Gallantry w/bronze star device.
- Meatball, Tuthill, and Standiford went on to lead Recon teams of their own. I like to think that I had a hand in preparing them for that very responsible position.

Deaths

- Darcus, Sgt. Forrest W., USMC — Died of unknown cause December 13, 2010.
- Herb, Sgt. Dennis, USMC — Died of natural causes on November 27, 2001, in Lebanon, Pennsylvania.
- Hudson, Capt. Jerry, USMC — Retired as a major and died June 29, 2005.
- Lumpkin, Sgt. Albert, USMC — Died at home in Tyrone, Pennsylvania, from heart failure December 9, 2000.
- McAfee, L/Cpl. James, USMC — Died from unknown cause April 19, 2001.
- Meggs, PFC Marion, USMC — Drowned near Khe Sanh, November 16, 1967.
- Miller, HN Charles, USN — Killed in action at Khe Sanh, January 24, 1968.
- Padilla, L/Cpl. Dave, USMC — Killed in action, body not recovered, Quang Tri Province, May 18, 1968.
- Popowitz, L/Cpl. Greg, USMC — Killed in action at Khe Sanh, January 24, 1968.
- Raymond, Captain John, USMC — Retired as a colonel and about a month later, on August 26, 1987, died of a heart attack.
- Richards, Cpl. Larry, USMC — Died February 18, 2008.
- Rosa, L/Cpl. Juan, USMC — Killed in action at Khe Sanh, January 24, 1968.
- Rosser, HM2 Sid, USN — Died of an unknown cause June 12, 1992.
- Sargent, L/Cpl. Robert C., USMC — Died of a heart related problem on June 27, 2008.
- Scribner, L/Cpl. Gary, USMC — Killed in action at Khe Sanh, January 24, 1968.
- Tallent, L/Cpl. Garry, USMC — Killed in action at Khe Sanh, August 20, 1967.
- Tuthill, L/Cpl. Bruce, USMC — Died from complications following appendicitis surgery on March 15, 2010.
- Poilane, Mme. Madeleine, French citizen — Died of cancer January 6, 2007, in Paris.

Appendix B:
Myth Busters

Myth Buster

A favorite story among some Vietnam veterans and self-styled experts is that the round fired out of the M-16 was designed to tumble in flight to increase its effectiveness when it hits the target. HA! Anyone who has ever been on a rifle range and has seen the bullet holes in the target will remember that they are round. Not elliptical, not square, not anything but round. How could you possibly fire accurately and qualify for marksmanship awards at distances of up to 500 meters if the projectile is floundering all over the place? It is, however, a fact that if a projectile hits even the slightest obstruction (blade of grass, twig, someone else) before it hits the target, the ballistics of the round will be thrown off, causing it to become erratic. M-16 ammunition was not, nor is it now, designed to tumble.

Myth Buster

Ask any World War II veteran what he thinks of movies about World War II, especially if he was at the battle being depicted and he will, almost without exception, say, "It was an okay movie but it didn't really happen that way." Ask veterans of Korea and they say the same thing. I have yet to see a movie about Vietnam that wasn't just an excuse to blow things up and cause people to die in the most horrible and bloody fashion.

When the movie *Platoon* came out, *Newsweek* trumpeted on its front cover, "Vietnam the way it really was." The movie was a nonstop festival of psychotic behavior, racial bigotry, drug use, and atrocities. However, if *Newsweek* said that's the way it was, it must be true.

Apocalypse Now is my all-time favorite Hollywood joke. The movie was an "adaptation" of a Joseph Conrad novel (that means fiction) that was written in 1899 about an ivory procurer named Kurtz who had apparently gone native as well as insane. It had nothing to do with anyone's military or anyone's war, the setting was in Africa, not Vietnam, and it was written 75 years before Frances Fraud Coppola filmed his warped version of it. The idea of having what looked like a brilliantly lighted carnival every couple of miles in enemy territory, among other things, was surreal!

Clint Eastwood's *Hamburger Hill* was a farce. There were too many inaccuracies to even start to list. And it was about Recon, too!

John Wayne's *Green Berets* was laughable, as well. (Sorry Duke). What was supposed to be the jungles of Southeast Asia looked more like a training area at Fort Benning, Georgia. (It was.) The troops were constantly leaping nimbly from this bush to that tree and all they carried was a rifle, one ammo pouch, and a canteen. While sneaking up on bad guys, they talked loudly back and forth and made no effort to assume tactical positions, preferring the tried and true Hollywood Group Gaggle formation. That allowed the actors to more photogenically exchange steely-eyed grimaces while manfully clenching their jaw muscles.

In addition, don't you love it when Hollywood war heroes like George Clooney, Martin Sheen, Alec Baldwin, Sean Penn, and Matt Damon take home paychecks like you will never see in your life and then lead anti–American parades in Washington, or pop off about U.S. military strategy? Military and foreign policy experts, all.

My other favorite thing is when long, detailed chats take place in the middle of even a small firefight. The noise during an armed engagement becomes almost physical, making verbal communications all but impossible. Oh, and in Hollywood, the rifles never run out of ammunition, the marksmanship is incredible, and there are übermodels experiencing wardrobe malfunctions running around on the battlefield.

Myth Buster

A lot of "experts" who weren't there claim that racial conflict was everywhere in Vietnam. The number of blacks in the combat units was purported to be disproportionate. To begin with that's inaccurate, but I never worried about proportions. I only worried that we would all look after each other, and we did. Not saying there weren't problems here and there but we were too busy with things that were more important. The only problem I ever experienced was when I was in Echo Company and some of the black guys started wearing their utility covers (remember that Marines wear covers, other people wear hats), backwards and a few were sporting green T-shirts with "Black Power" or raised fists stenciled on them. One morning formation, the Echo company X.O., First Lieutenant Nels Youngstrom, stood in front of the company and said, "After this formation is dismissed, the next Marine I see with anything but USMC stenciled on their shirt will be in the brig on charges of being out of uniform and direct disobedience of an order. If I see a cover that isn't squared away on your gourd, you will suffer the same fate. Questions?" That ended that. Lt. Youngstrom was a nice guy, a good officer and he meant what he said, and he said what he meant. He handled that situation the way a Marine officer should.

Myth Buster

In Vietnam, there are bugs *everywhere*. In Hollywood war movies, mosquitoes never attacked Randolph Scott. Of course, they didn't dare even land on John Wayne, and the rest of those actors must have had some powerful repellant in the makeup and fake dirt on their faces. The only time a bug (probably a stunt bug) ever got squashed on film was in the 1957 Jack Webb move, *The D.I.* It was, and may still be, required viewing for recruits at Parris Island.

Myth Buster

"Never make any friends in a combat zone 'cuz that way, when they go and get themselves killed, you don't have to mourn them." They're just an expendable item. Nonsense!

I know guys who were closer to each other than their own real brother was. When you depend on the other guy to watch your back, you had better believe he's a good friend. If you're rude and aloof, how likely is it that someone else will risk death to protect your sorry butt? How can you care, especially as a supervisor, about your people if they are anonymous to you? A difference in rank sometimes requires some separation as far as fraternization goes, but your subordinates (or superiors) sure aren't the enemy. As a sergeant, it wasn't quite proper for me to pal around with the junior men like they do with each other, but that didn't mean I didn't care about them. I took it personally if any of them got hurt.

Myth Buster

Every now and then, I read a newspaper interview with a Vietnam "veteran" who claims to not be able to talk about his job when he was in country. He will fall back on the old "It's still classified" alibi. The best part is that these guys are almost all former PFCs or some other junior rank and I'm pretty sure people like that weren't given top secret spy missions to carry out. Any time somebody says they aren't allowed to talk about their time in Vietnam, feel free to be skeptical.

Other phonies that tighten my jaws are the ones who claim to be the sole survivor of their (squad, platoon, company, pick one) as the result of an enemy ambush. If as many units were wiped out except for one man as these "survivors" claim, there would not have been any troops left in Vietnam.

Myth Buster

I have heard Vietnam vets claim to have carried many different foreign made weapons on patrols. One story was that the M-16 wasn't reliable enough. Another was that if they carried AK-47s, and had to use them, they would sound like a gook unit and that would confuse the gooks. I have serious doubts that any conventional unit commander would allow that on any kind of routine basis. Special Operations units ... maybe, just maybe.

The first thing wrong with the idea is that unless everyone had the same weapon, regardless of origin, there would be a definite incompatibility of ammunition. M-16s will not fire the 7.62mm AK-47 round and contrary to popular belief, the American M-14, although it is also 7.62mm, will not fire the AK round and vice versa. The AK round is too short for an M-14 and the M-14 round is too long for an AK-47. If I have an AK, and you have an M-16, whoever runs out of ammo is in trouble because I can't help you and you can't help me.

That doesn't even take into account the myriad of French 8mm and Chinese 7mm and 9mm weapons that the Viet Cong carried. Some grunt units did have a few M-14s with them but that was for a specific purpose; usually as a counter-sniper weapon. On security patrols just outside the base at Quang Tri, we did carry one M-14. That's because the area was so open and flat that a long-range weapon might come in handy. The M-14 also chambers and fires the exact same round used in the M-60 machine gun. I have seen photos of troops with an assortment of weapons but they were always in a rear area, and posing for a picture doesn't make it so.

Myth Buster

American military dog tags have, for many years, had a small notch in one corner. Legend has it that when you get killed, one of the two dog tags that you wear is collected and turned over to Graves Registration. The other one is, get this, positioned in your mouth so that the notch fits between your two front teeth and then your jaw is kicked shut so the dog tag is jammed in place so that later on the authorities know which rotting carcass is which.

The notch is there so that when the dog tag is placed into the stamping machine it will rest against an alignment pin that keeps the tag straight while your name and other info is stamped into it. Can you even imagine having an open casket funeral with a chunk of metal protruding from between your broken teeth? Whoever dreamed that one up must still be laughing at the number of gullible idiots who truly believe that's what the notch is for.

Myth Buster

Hollywood would have us believe that war zones are crawling with beautiful, nubile nurses who bravely dodge shot and shell on the front lines. Then they either fall in love with the steel-jawed hero, or convince the wounded troops that war is "like, totally bad." I can only speak for myself here but after almost two weeks at the Naval Hospital in Da Nang when I contracted malaria, I saw exactly two female nurses. It was while I was on one of my feeble walks and they were coming down the sidewalk toward me. They were using the whole width of the sidewalk and as they got near it became clear that I would have to get out of their way. As they sailed by, I said, "Morning, ladies." They didn't even acknowledge that I had spoken.

And they were ugly, too!

Myth Buster

There has always been a lot of noise about drug use in Vietnam. I don't doubt that it was there. Drug use among the world's population is, and was, pandemic. That will probably never really change but I can testify as to drug use as it applied to my little world. The consensus was that Marines had too much discipline to use drugs, especially in the field where everyone's life depended on teamwork and looking after each other. To expect that to be 100 percent accurate, though, would be the limit of optimism.

We often heard rumors about this or that army unit being too buzzed to go to the field but it was always just that ... unsubstantiated gossip. Again ... not to say it never happened.

Personally, I know of exactly one instance of a Marine using drugs. We were hanging out in the team tent at Quang Tri one night and a member of my team (he had never been an exemplary Marine. Whined and cried a lot) strolled into the tent with a marijuana joint in his hand. He was grinning and carrying on about how good it was. It was the first time I ever smelled marijuana ... and I thought my cigars stunk! He came right over to me and held the joint out and said, "Try this, man." Before I could even react, two of my guys grabbed him and dragged him bodily out of the tent. They were out there for a few minutes and I could hear voices rising. I was about to go out when the two returned and stated, "We just told him if he used that shit again, we'd kill him," and they were serious. The guy did not return to the tent that night. He probably didn't want to be the recipient of a blanket party and to my knowledge, neither he nor anyone else got that stupid again.

Appendix C:
How We Lost the War

We lost the war in Vietnam, right? Not likely! The loss of over 58,000 Americans belies the fact that the U.S. military never lost a major battle in Vietnam. We were not driven out of the country by superior enemy forces. Our own government yanked us out. I will tell you who lost the war.

Lyndon Baines Johnson ... he tried to run a war from the White House while rarely listening to his military advisors. Then he bailed out when things got tough.

Robert S. McNamara ... in his 1995 book *In Retrospect,* he acknowledged not only that the war was "wrong, terribly wrong," but also that he had believed it was a mistake even while he was secretary of defense. Despite that, he devised a plan whereby a wall of bunkers and barricades was to be built from the seacoast to the Laotian border on the south side of the DMZ.

Even as the situation in South Vietnam improved, one of the war's architects had already lost faith. In the fall of 1966, Robert McNamara returned from a four-day trip to South Vietnam and quietly recommended that Johnson freeze troop levels and seek a negotiated solution. In essence, he told the President that the war was unwinnable. The symbol of McNamara's disillusionment was his further recommendation that the United States construct a security barrier south of the DMZ along the border with the North, from the South China Sea to the Laotian border. The project soon became known as McNamara's Wall.

Lieutenant General Phillip B. Davidson, General William Westmoreland's chief of intelligence, called the barrier "one of the most preposterous concepts of this singular war." It was conceived by Robert Fisher of the Harvard Law School, and pitched to John McNaughton, the assistant secretary of defense for International Security affairs, who then passed it on to the secretary. McNamara saw the barrier as a useful alternative to bombing and a way to shift the policy debate. But the idea ran into strong opposition. The military argued that a static barrier was too costly to construct and maintain, and would ultimately be ineffective. John Roche [special advisor to Johnson from 1966 to 1968] observed at a meeting on the barrier that unless it stretched all the way to the Indian Ocean it could easily be circumvented, and in any case the Ho Chi Minh Trail already went around the planned terminus at Khe Sanh. "If you cut this thing off at the Laotian border, it's futile," he said. Roche later noted, "That was the last 'barrier' meeting I was invited to."[1]

This would have cost billions and required probably the better part of a Marine division to build. Construction was actually begun in 1968 and was called Operation Dye Marker. It was a total joke and never got very far. Like the Siegfried Line, the Maginot Line, and the Atlantic Wall of World War I and World War II Europe, all the enemy had to do was walk around it. And they did!

Then we have McNamara's shameful brainchild, Project 100,000. By 1966, President Johnson was fearful that calling up the reserves or abolishing student deferments would further inflame war protesters and signal all-out (civil) war. And so, even after McNamara began privately declaring the war was unwinnable, the defense secretary devised Project 100,000. Under his direction, an alternative army was systematically recruited from the ranks of those who had previously been rejected for failing to meet the armed services' physical and mental requirements. Recruiters swept through urban ghettos and Southern rural back roads, even taking at least one youth with an I.Q. of 62. In all, 354,000 men were rolled up by Project 100,000. Touted as a Great Society program that would provide remedial education and an escape from poverty, the recruitment program offered a one-way ticket to Vietnam, where "the Moron Corps," as they were pathetically nicknamed by other soldiers, entered combat in disproportionate numbers. Although Johnson was a vociferous civil rights advocate, the program took a heavy toll on young blacks. A 1970 Defense Department study disclosed that 41 percent of Project 100,000 recruits were black, compared with 12 percent in the armed forces as a whole. What's more, 40 percent of Project 100,000 recruits were trained for combat, compared with 25 percent for the services generally.[i]

Walter Cronkite ... yes, Uncle Walter. "The most trusted man in America." His every word was considered gospel. In 1968, Cronkite journeyed to Vietnam to report on the aftermath of the Tet offensive. In a dramatic departure from the traditions of "objective" journalism, Cronkite concluded his reports with a personal commentary in which he voiced his strong belief that the war would end in stalemate. Cronkite's editorial would later be regarded as critical indices of public opinion of the Vietnam War.

After visiting Vietnam to report on the Tet offensive, Cronkite broke from his usual impartiality to editorialize that, from his perspective, the war seemed "unwinnable." President *Lyndon B. Johnson*, watching the telecast, reportedly turned to an aide and allegedly said, "If I've lost Cronkite, I've lost middle America."

Cronkite's "We Are Mired in Stalemate," broadcast of February 27, 1968.

Khe Sanh could well fall with a terrible loss in American lives, prestige and morale, and this is a tragedy of our stubbornness there; but the bastion no longer is a key to the rest of the northern regions [Expert military opinion?] and it is doubtful that the American forces can be defeated across the breadth of the DMZ with any substantial loss of ground. Another standoff.

On the political front, past performance gives no confidence that the Vietnamese government can cope with its problems, now compounded by the attack on the cities. It may not fall, it may hold on, but it probably won't show the dynamic qualities demanded of this young nation. Another standoff.

We have been too often disappointed by the optimism of the American leaders, both in Vietnam and Washington, to have faith any longer in the silver linings they find in the darkest clouds. They may be right, that Hanoi's winter-spring offensive has been forced by the Communist realization that they could not win the longer war of attrition, and that the Communists hope that any success in the offensive will improve their position for eventual negotiations. It would improve their position, and it would also require our realization, that we should have had all along, that any negotiations must be that — negotiations, not the dictation of peace terms. For it seems now more certain than ever that the bloody experience of Vietnam is to end in a stalemate. This summer's almost certain standoff will either end in real give-and-take negotiations or terrible escalation; and for every means we have to escalate, the enemy can match us, and that applies to invasion of the North, the use of nuclear weapons, or the mere commitment of one hundred, or two hundred, or three hundred thousand more American troops to the battle. And with each escalation, the world comes closer to the brink of cosmic disaster.

To say that we are closer to victory today is to believe, in the face of the evidence, the optimists who have been wrong in the past. To suggest we are on the edge of defeat is to yield to unreasonable pessimism. To say that we are mired in stalemate seems the only realistic, yet unsatisfactory, conclusion. On the off chance that military and political analysts are right, in the next few months we must test the enemy's intentions, in case this is indeed his last big gasp before negotiations. But it is increasingly clear to this reporter that the only rational way out then will be to negotiate, not as victors, but as an honorable people who lived up to their pledge to defend democracy, and did the best they could.

This is Walter Cronkite. Good night.

The American Media ... the Fourth Estate. This phrase was originally used as a synonym for newspapers. However, with the advent of radio, television, news magazines, etc., its meaning has been broadened to include all of what is known as the mass media.

Its coinage, with its present meaning, has been attributed to Edmund Burke (1729–1797), a British politician. It comes from a quote in Thomas Carlyle's book, *Heros and Hero Worship in History* (1841).

"Burke said that there were three Estates in Parliament, but in the Reporters Gallery yonder, there sat a Fourth Estate more important far than they all." The three estates refer to the British parliament, the Lords Temporal, the Lords Spiritual and the Commons. The Lords Temporal and the Lords Spiritual combined being the House of Lords, the upper House of parliament. And the Commons is the House of Commons, or the British lower House.

"In old days men had the rack. Now they have the press. That is an improvement certainly. But still it is very bad, and wrong, and demoralizing. Burke called journalism the Fourth Estate. That was true at the time, no doubt. But at the present moment it really is the only estate. It has eaten up the other three. The Lords Temporal say nothing, the Lords Spiritual have nothing to say, and the House of Commons has nothing to say and says it. We are dominated by Journalism."—*The Soul of Man,* Oscar Wilde.

"Seabees Build Three Schools for Vietnamese Kids"
"Combat Engineers Dig a New Well for a Nearby Village"

Did you ever see headlines like those? I doubt it. However, this kind of civic humanitarianism was taking place all over South Vietnam on an ongoing basis.

But:

"Marine Jets Strafe South Vietnamese Village.—Death and Destruction Result"

That was worth a two-inch high headline in the paper and at least three days of "in depth investigative reporting" by all the network news bureaus. Nationally known reporters would be flown to Vietnam. With the black smoke from an unseen burning six-holer in the background (smoke is smoke, right?), wearing a tailored safari jacket from LL Bean, a borrowed flak jacket and helmet tilted at just the correct "I'm a fearless journalist braving shot and shell on the front lines" angle (probably behind the officer's club at Da Nang air base), the dashing crusader for truth would look grimly into the camera. In a mellow baritone he intones, "Thundering Marine Corps fighter jets dropped tons of explosives on a friendly South Vietnamese village yesterday. Several deaths were recorded and considerable damage occurred! As responsible journalists, we will pursue the cause of this tragedy to the highest levels!" Today, only the place-names have changed.

What really happened in this fictional, but typical, situation was that the air strike was precisely coordinated to wipe out a nearby concentration of Viet Cong who had been terrorizing the villagers. In the end, three chickens were killed and a pigsty was blown down by the concussion. Several VC were also confirmed killed. Hypothetical? Yes, but sadly representative of the twist the media are capable of applying to any story they choose. Good news is dull and sells few newspapers.

The military is a choice target for these kinds of journalism because it rarely chooses to "fight back" knowing that the media has total control over any response they may make and will always have the last word. If all the public got from the media was half-truths and misinformation, who could blame them for their ignorance and, in many cases, outright hostility toward the military?

Hollywood ... I almost don't need to explain this one. Was an accurate, positive, morale-boosting movie ever made about Vietnam? Was a Vietnam veteran ever depicted as other than a psychotic sociopath? Not that I recall. Even as historically inaccurate as most of the World War II movies were, they were usually heroic and upbeat and we never lost. They often ended with the hero looking into the camera and encouraging the audience to buy war bonds.

Then there was Hanoi Jane Fonda. I don't think I need to say any more about that.

That's who lost the war in Vietnam. But that's just my opinion.

Maps

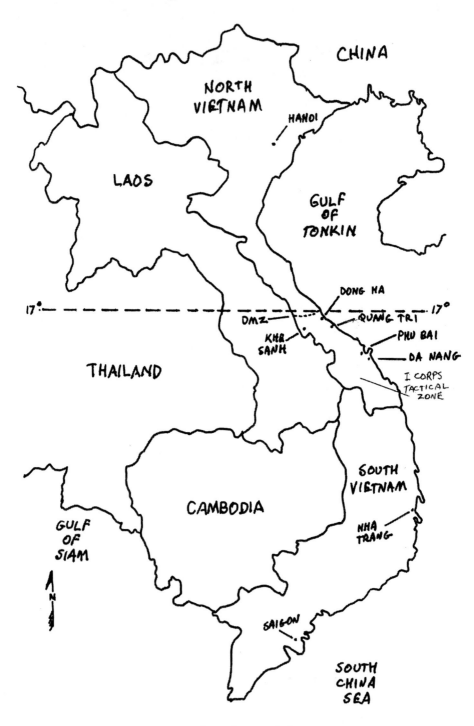

Southeast Asia

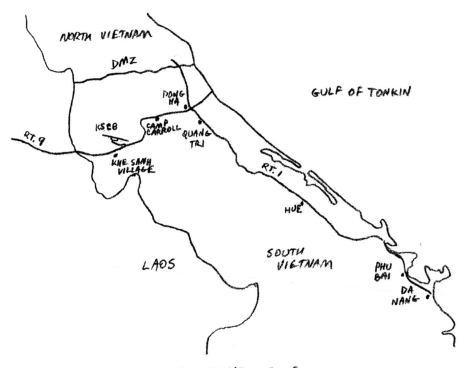

I CORPS TACTICAL ZONE

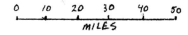

I Corps Tactical Zone

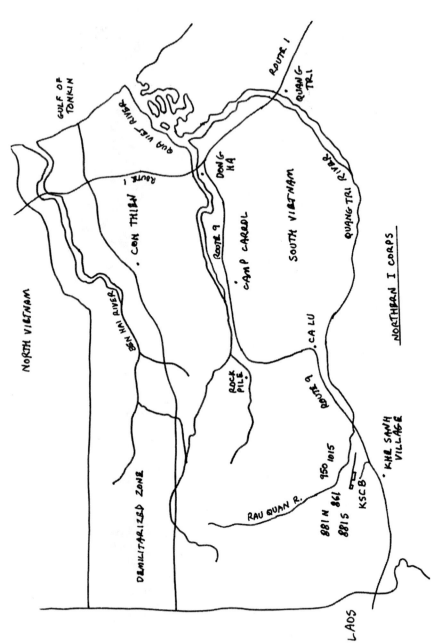

Northern I Corps

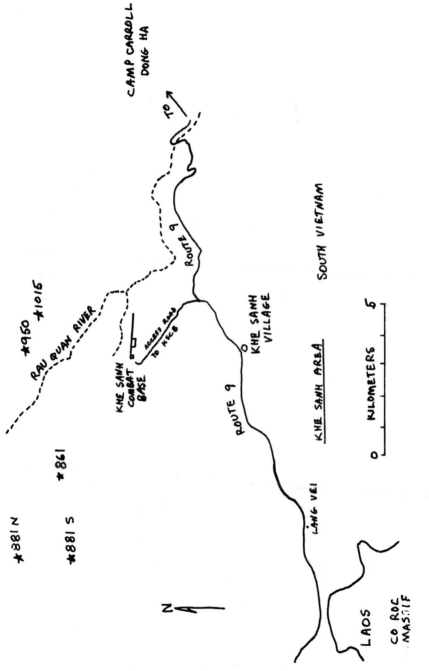

Khe Sanh Area

Glossary

APL   Assistant patrol leader.

Arty   The artillery guys. Gun bunnies. Canon Cockers.

ARVN Army of the Republic of Vietnam.

Automatic weapon   All M-16 rifles are capable of both single shot and full automatic fire. Three of the four members of the fire team keep their rifles on single shot but the automatic rifleman keeps his at full auto and uses it at the direction of the fire team leader.

BAS Battalion aid station

Bravo   The phonetic alphabet designation for the letter B. Alpha, Bravo, Charley, Delta, etc.

Bru or 'Yards   The Bru tribes belong to the Mon-Khmer language group of Montagnards who inhabit the mountain areas of Indochina. The Degar (referred to by French colonists as Montagnard) are the indigenous peoples of the Central Highlands of Vietnam. The term Montagnard means "mountain people" in French and is a carry-over from the French colonial period in Vietnam. Both peoples live in houses constructed of wood, bamboo, and thatch.

Bug juice   Insect repellant. It killed everything from mosquitoes to leeches. It also softened the rock hard sticks of camouflage paint (cammie stick). We also called the fruit flavored beverage we got in the mess tent Bug Juice for pretty much the same reason.

Butter bar   Marine second lieutenant or Navy ensign, from the gold color of their rank insignia. A pejorative term.

C-4   A plastique explosive in a 1-pound stick. It could be molded like clay and was much more powerful than the equivalent in TNT.

C.O.   Commanding officer.

C.O.C.   Combat Operations Center. The heart and brain of the regiment. All of the "S" shops are located there.

Cammie stick   This came in a metal tube that opened on either end. Inside was a stick of green paste that we used to camouflage any exposed flesh. The stick was light green on one end and dark green on the other and was usually hard as plaster.

CH-46 Sea Knight helicopter. A large double rotor chopper for carrying cargo or troops. As a troopship it could carry as many as 18 Marines and was a durable and reliable aircraft. They were affectionately known to aviators as "Phrogs." Some of those mechanical Vietnam vets are still on active duty.

CID Criminal Investigation Division. A unit of the Military Police charged with criminal investigations.

Claymore mine An anti-personnel mine consisting of a plastic body filled with C-4 and a couple hundred ball bearings. They were used for night defense and were horribly effective when set off by an electrical detonator attached to the mine by a wire.

Comm wire Communication wire that was strung between field telephones. Often more reliable than radios as long as they stayed intact.

Company Gunny Every company-sized unit has a billet for Company Gunnery Sergeant who is the ramrod and get-it-done guy. The rank of the company gunny is usually a gunnery sergeant, pay grade E7, but not always. "Gunny" is a casual term of respect for a gunnery sergeant but used only with the Gunny's permission.

Concertina wire Barbed wire that is manufactured in large coils about 30 inches in diameter. The coils are stretched out like a giant Slinky and secured by steel fence posts. Two or three layers of these are very difficult to get through.

Det cord Detonation cord — it looks like a white, plastic clothes line but was actually a C-4 rope which could be used by itself as an explosive or used to link several charges of C-4 together to detonate simultaneously.

Devil Dog In World War I, the Marines earned the nickname *Teufelhunden* from the Germans after the battle of Belleau Wood in 1918.

D.I. Drill instructor.

Ditty bag About the size of an overnight bag and serving the same purpose.

DMZ Demilitarized Zone.

Doc Absolutely every corpsman is given the nickname "Doc." It is a sign of greatest respect, but that respect must still be earned.

Dress blues Oddly enough most Marines are not issued dress blues unless they are in special, high profile units like recruiters, U.S. embassy guards, Sea Duty (which was eliminated in 1998 ... budget cuts!), and Headquarters Marine Corps personnel, to name a few.

Elephant grass The common name for a species of tropical grass that is anywhere from a foot to twelve, or more, feet tall. It grows as thick as the grass in your front yard. The base of each blade could be up to three inches across and the edges are serrated like a hack saw and can cut your skin just as effectively.

FAC Forward air controller. An aviation officer assigned to ground troops to call in air support.

FMF Fleet Marine Force. The ones you see charging onto some foreign beach.

FO Forward observer. An artillery officer assigned to ground troops to call in artillery.

G.I. can   Galvanized iron can. Garbage can.

Grunt   Mud Marine, ground pounder, infantry.

H&I   Harassment and interdiction fires. Randomly fired artillery rounds on locations that just might catch an NVA patrol off guard.

Harborsite   The place the team leader selects to spend the night on patrols.

Head   The head is the naval term for toilet. In the days of sail, the facilities were located out in front of the bow of the ship. Why in front and not behind? Sailing ships are pushed by the wind so the odor is pushed away downwind from the ship.

HN   The Navy rank of hospitalman, pay grade E3, equivalent to a lance corporal.

Hump   Walk, an extended hike, usually with a combat load.

ITR   Infantry Training Regiment. It is now called School of Infantry.

JP-4   Aviation fuel as used in turbine or jet engines.

Ka-bar   Combat knife. It is a fearsome Bowie type knife issued to Marines usually only in combat zones and was made for just one thing.

Khakis or tropicals   Both were tan colored uniforms. The khakis were starched cotton and everybody hated them. They were worn for guard duty or other on-base activities where the field uniform was inappropriate. The tropicals were a good grade of lightweight wool or gabardine and were the summer uniform for off-base liberty.

Klick   One klick is 1000 meters or 1 kilometer. Based on the 1000-meter grid squares on the maps.

KSCB   Khe Sanh Combat Base.

LAAW   Light anti-armor weapon. A one-shot, disposable, shoulder fired rocket to be used against vehicles or fortifications.

Leatherneck   A long-standing nickname for Marines that harks back from the days of the Revolutionary War up to the 1840s when the uniform included a wide leather collar, ostensibly to ward off sword blows.

Lister bag   A canvas bag holding 30 gallons of drinking water that hung from a tripod or tree limb. Around the base of it were four spigots. It was heavily chlorinated to kill bacteria. Have you ever drunk water from a swimming pool?

LZ or HLZ   Helicopter landing zone. A field position often designated with a name or number (LZ Lark, LZ Betty, LZ-3, or simply the LZ).

M-79 grenade launcher   A stubby, fat barreled, shoulder fired weapon that shoots a variety of 40mm (1½ inch diameter) grenades with extreme accuracy and effect.

Magazine, mags   Ammunition is loaded into a metal box-like affair, or magazine, that is then inserted into a rifle. The spring in the magazine pushes the 20 rounds (bullets) up into the rifle as you fire. When the mag is empty you remove it and put in another. A round is also any projectile fired out of a barrel (artillery, mortar, rifle).

MCAS   Marine Corps Air Station.

MCI   Marine Corps Institute. A correspondence course for almost every subject you can think of. It's provided to improve the military knowledge of Marines who are, of necessity, stationed all over the world. MCI courses are highly encouraged by unit commanders and are even factored into promotion considerations.

MCRD   Marine Corps Recruit Depot (Parris Island or San Diego).

Medevac number   The first letter of your last name followed by the last four digits of your serial number. This is radioed in so that if you are medevacked, the medical people at the BAS can identify you and get your medical records quickly. Mine was J2659.

MOS   Military occupational specialty. A number that identified your job area. For example 0311 is basic rifleman, 8651 was Recon Marine.

MP   Military Policeman.

MPC Military payment certificate, issued in lieu of American money.

NCO   Non-Commissioned officers. Corporals and sergeants.

NVA   North Vietnamese Army. Regular, professional soldiers and a very tough opponent.

Office pogue   Another less than complimentary term for "in the rear with the gear" types. The origin of the word is rather vague. See also "Remington Raider."

O.P.   Observation post. Any place where you can observe an area or an activity without being seen. Usually a hilltop but not always.

OpCon   Operational control. If a unit was temporarily assigned to support another unit, it comes under that unit's OpCon.

PFC   Private first class. One chevron on the sleeve. Only a private is of lower rank.

Piss tube   One does not use the head for standup business. For that purpose, near each head is a tube about 5 inches in diameter sunk into the ground at about a 45 degree angle. As the ground around it becomes saturated and soggy, the tube is relocated to another spot. The former location quickly dries up. Except in the monsoon. Then everything is soggy.

Pogey bait   Candy or other junk food usually bought from the geedunk, a snack bar on a ship, or any place that candy and pogey bait is sold. Pogey bait also came in the mail from home.

Poncho liner   A very lightweight camouflage quilt-like blanket that could be tied into the poncho to make a fair weather sleeping bag. We never used them as such but the liner was more than enough cover for sleeping in the summer.

Prep fire   Firing several artillery rounds at one or more of the LZs immediately prior to our landing on any one of them. It was safer but it sort of blew our cover.

PX   Post exchange.

R&R   Rest and recuperation.

Recon   Short for Reconnaissance.

REMF   Rear echelon mother figure (polite form).

Remington Raider   Clerk typist; see also "Office pogue"

Route step   Marching in formation but not in step. Usually over uneven ground.

SALUTE report A report on an enemy sighting that includes size (of the unit), activity, location, uniform (what they are wearing), time, and equipment.

School circle An informal circle, sitting or standing around a drill instructor or other instructor for receiving training or information.

782 gear So named for the form number used to record everything issued to an individual on a unit for unit basis. Except for uniforms issued, when you leave the unit, you turn that stuff back in.

Shelter halves Pup tents. Each Marine carries one half of a tent. At night, they pair up and button the halves together to make a very small tent. At least it's shelter.

Six holer An outhouse with seating for six.

Snuffies Privates or privates first class.

SOP Standing operating procedure.

Squids Ducks, anchor clankers, or swab jockeys, otherwise known as sailors.

SRB Service record book. Each Marine's official pedigree. A very important folder of documents.

Staff NCO Staff sergeants and above are SNCOs.

Starlight scope A night vision device. At that time they were large and awkward but they worked. We thought it was a technological marvel.

Stick An individual row or line of Marines lined up to embark or disembark a vehicle, aircraft, or ship.

Tail End Charlie The last person or element in a line or column.

TAOR Tactical area of responsibility.

TBS The Basic School. Officers' infantry training at Quantico, Virginia.

Trigger time Actual combat experience.

26th Marines Marine regiments are most commonly referred to in that manner. 1st Marines, 12th Marines, etc. When you say 21st Marines, it is automatically assumed you are referring to the 21st Marine Regiment.

Unit One Field medical kit that all corpsmen carry.

VC Viet Cong. Guerrilla fighters allied to the North.

Water Buffalo A 250-gallon water tank on wheels that contained potable water for washing, laundry, etc. It had spigots on the sides for filling water cans and was hauled away and refilled every couple of days.

Willie Peter From the phonetic alphabet for WP or white phosphorous. These grenades, in addition to the shrapnel, expelled burning WP that stuck to, and burned, anything it touched and was very dangerous. They are heavy and you never throw a WP uphill. WP was also an artillery round.

The Word Information supposedly received from a reliable source. Also, scoop, poop, skinny.

X.O. Executive officer and second in command of a unit.

Zoomies A not always complimentary term for Marines assigned to an aviation unit, or to all members of the Air Force. Wing wipers, wingers, airdales.

Chapter Notes

Introduction

1. These people were natives and were not ethnically Vietnamese. Montagnards or 'Yards (other tribes were the Bru and the Hmong) did not get along with Vietnamese but were very loyal to the Americans.

Chapter 2

1. Excerpt from author's letter home, April 24, 1967.
2. English translation of *Teufelhunden*. According to legend, this name was given to the Marines of World War I by the Germans at the battle for Belleau Wood.

Chapter 3

1. Excerpt from author's letter home, April 24, 1967.
2. I saw the same thing in 1991 when I got called up for Desert Storm. This time it was Jacksonville, N.C., outside Camp Lejeune, which is the home of the 2nd Marine Division.
3. I didn't think much of it until 22 years later. After retiring from the Jamestown Police Department in 1988, I, as a Marine Corps reservist then, went on two years of active duty as a recruiter in Jamestown. In June of 1989, I was ordered to Recruiters School at MCRD San Diego. Toward the end of that seven-week course, we were bused to El Toro to spend the night prior to doing a little OJT with some already qualified area recruiters. Guess what barracks they put us in? I was absolutely convinced that not a coat of paint had been applied since 1967. We even had to wire together some of the bunks with coat hanger wire to keep from falling out of them. Talk about déjà vu!
4. Excerpt from author's letter home, May 18, 1967.

Chapter 4

1. Excerpt from author's letter home, June 5, 1967.
2. Excerpt from author's letter home, June 5, 1967.
3. Excerpt from author's letter home, June 5, 1967.
4. Excerpt from author's letter home, June 19, 1967.

Chapter 8

1. A real joke. North Vietnam was a signer of the Geneva Convention of 1949 but did not abide by any of its rules. We still had to carry the cards, though, because we're the good guys.
2. Excerpt from author's letter home, June 27, 1967.

Chapter 10

1. Excerpt from author's letter home, July 6, 1967.
2. Our house in Jamestown was in a very ordinary neighborhood on a hill, but across the street, we overlooked the municipal golf course, baseball stadium, and a good part of the east side of town. Probably a few thousand acres.
3. Excerpt from author's letter home, July 6, 1967.
4. Excerpt from author's letter home, July 6, 1967.
5. Excerpt from author's letter home, July 6, 1967.
6. Excerpt from author's letter home, July 6, 1967.
7. Excerpt from author's letter home, July 6, 1967.

Chapter 11

1. Excerpt from author's letter home, July 12, 1967.

Chapter 13

1. Excerpt from author's letter home, July 19, 1967.
2. Excerpt from author's letter home, late July 1967.
3. Excerpt from author's letter home, late July 1967.

Chapter 14

1. A John Wayne can opener was the little mechanical marvel that was included in cases of C-rations.

Chapter 16

1. 26MAR 011212Z/Aug67, OPN ARDMORE SITREP #63 (Date/time group, Operation Ardmore Situation Report #63).

Chapter 17

1. Excerpt from author's letter home, August 26, 1967.
2. Diary entry for 20 August 1967 by Chaplain Ray W. Stubbe.
3. Comments by Capt. Williams (CO, B Co., 3rd Recon Bn.) to Chaplain Stubbe, 20 August 1967.

4. Comments of Capt. James L. Williams, USMC, Oral History Tape #1759.
5. Endnotes 2, 3, and 6 are excerpted from *Battalion of Kings* by Ray W. Stubbe, published by Khe Sanh Veterans, Inc., 2005.
6. Diary entry for 21 August 1967 by Chaplain Ray W. Stubbe.
7. Condensed from the Silver Star Medal file on 1/Lt. Albert Ritchie Pfeltz III.
8. Excerpt from author's letter home, early September 1967.
9. Excerpt from author's letter home, early September 1967.
10. Excerpt from author's letter home, early September 1967.

Chapter 18

1. Excerpt from author's letter home, mid September 1967.
2. Excerpt from author's letter home, October 29, 1967.

Chapter 19

1. Excerpt from author's letter home, November 20, 1967.

Chapter 23

1. International National Headquarters, Veterans of the Vietnam War, Inc., and The Veterans Coalition, 805 South Township Boulevard, Pittston, PA 18640-3327.
2. *Washington Monthly*, June 1995, by Myra MacPherson.
3. www.publichealth.va.gov/exposures/agentorange.

Chapter 24

1. 12 (date in March) 1520H (3:20 P.M. Hours) YD 162540 (map coordinates).
2. Declassified S-2 report of March 16, 1968.
3. Declassified S-2 report of March 16, 1968.
4. Declassified S-2 report of March 16, 1968.
5. Declassified S-2 report of March 16, 1968.
6. Declassified S-2 report of March 16, 1968.

Chapter 25

1. Excerpt from author's letter home, March 29, 1968.
2. Excerpt from author's letter home, early May 1968.

Chapter 28

1. Excerpt from author's letter home, July 30, 1968.
2. A cynical, sadistic nurse in the movie *One Flew Over the Cuckoo's Nest*.
3. Excerpt from author's letter home, July 30, 1968.
4. Excerpt from author's letter home, July 30, 1968.

Chapter 29

1. While writing this, in an effort to confirm what Moyer had told me then, I looked up the Command Chronology for 3rd Recon Battalion on the Internet for May 1968. I found a brief reference to that incident confirming the number killed and wounded, but when I pulled up the patrol reports, it, among many others, had the notation "Missing." In conversation with Christie in March 2011, he told me he had gotten a Vietnamese Cross of Gallantry w/bronze device. Not good enough, in my opinion.

2. From *Battalion of Kings* by Chaplain Ray Stubbe. Ref: CG3rd MarDiv 211330Z/May68 to SecNav, Report of death — Hostile (1068-68) in Library of Congress MIA microfilm, Reel #286, Folder #143.

Appendix C

1. From *This Time We Win: Revisiting the Tet Offensive* by James S. Robbins.
2. *Washington Monthly*, June 1995, by Myra MacPherson.

Index

Page numbers in **bold italics** indicate photographs.